Photographer's Guide to the Fujifilm X10 (Black and White Edition)

Photographer's Guide to the Fujifilm X10 (Black and White Edition)

Getting the Most from Fujifilm's Advanced Digital Camera

Copyright © 2012 by Alexander S. White. All rights reserved. No part of this publication may be reproduced, stored in a retrieval system or transmitted in any form or by any means, electronic, mechanical, photocopying, recording or otherwise, without the prior written permission of the copyright holder, except for brief quotations used in a review.

Published by
White Knight Press
9704 Old Club Trace
Henrico, Virginia 23238

ISBN: 978-1-937986-04-9

Printed in the United States of America

This book is dedicated to my wife, Clenise.

Contents

Acknowledgments	**12**
Introduction	**13**
Chapter 1: Preliminary Steps	**17**
Setting Up the Camera	17
Charging and Inserting the Battery	17
Inserting the Memory Card	20
Introduction to Main Controls	24
Top of Camera	25
Back of Camera	25
Front of Camera	26
Setting the Language, Date, and Time	26
Chapter 2: Basic Operations	**29**
Taking Pictures and Videos	29
Fully Automatic—EXR Auto Mode	29
Flash	33
Other Settings in EXR Auto Mode	35
Overview of Movie Recording	36
Viewing Pictures	40
Review While in Shooting Mode	40
Reviewing Images in Playback Mode	40
Playing Movies	41
Chapter 3: The Shooting Modes	**44**
Auto Mode	45
Recommended Settings	46
Shooting Menu	46
Setup Menu	47
Flash	49
Drive Mode	49
Self-timer	50
Focus Mode	50
EXR Mode	50
EXR Auto	52
Resolution Priority	54
High ISO and Low Noise	55
D-Range Priority	55
Program Mode	56
Shutter Priority Mode	58
Aperture Priority Mode	64
Manual Exposure Mode	69
Scene Position Mode	73
Natural & Flash	76
Natural Light	76
Portrait	77
Portrait Enhancer	77
Landscape	78
Sport	79
Night	79
Night (Tripod)	79

Fireworks	79
Sunset	80
Snow	80
Beach	81
Underwater	81
Party	81
Flower	82
Text	82
Advanced Mode	83
Panorama	84
Pro Focus	87
Pro Low-Light	89
The Custom Shooting Modes: C1 and C2	91
Chapter 4: The Shooting Menu	**96**
ISO	99
Image Size	103
Image Quality	108
Dynamic Range	110
Film Simulation	113
White Balance Shift	115
Color	115
Sharpness	115
Highlight Tone	116
Shadow Tone	117
Noise Reduction	117
Intelligent Digital Zoom	119
Advanced Anti Blur	121
Face Detection	124
AF Mode	125
Face Recognition	128
Flash	129
External Flash	130
Custom Set	131
Display Custom Setting	131
Chapter 5: Other Controls	**136**
Focus Switch	136
Manual Focus	137
Autofocus–Single Shot	139
Autofocus–Continuous	140
Lens Assembly	141
Autofocus Assist/Self-timer Lamp	143
Shutter Release Button	144
Exposure Compensation Dial	145
Function Button	147
Viewfinder Window	148
Diopter Adjustment Wheel	149
Playback Button	149
AE/Zoom-in Button	150
AF/Zoom-out Button	151
White Balance Button	152
Main Command Dial	159

AEL/AFL Button	160
Indicator Lamp	161
Sub-command Dial and Buttons	162
Sub-command Dial	162
Menu/OK Button	163
Direction Buttons	164
Up Button: Delete/Drive Mode	164
Still Image	167
Burst Shooting	167
Best Frame Capture	169
Exposure Bracketing	171
ISO Bracketing	173
Film Simulation Bracketing	173
Dynamic Range Bracketing	174
Right Button: Flash	174
Down Button: Self-timer	176
Left Button: Macro Focus	178
Display/Back Button	180
Display Button	180
Back Button	185
Silent Mode	185
Checking and Updating Firmware	185
RAW Button	186
Chapter 6: Playback and Printing	**190**
Normal Playback	190
Different Playback Screens	191
Histogram	191
Index View and Enlarging Images	193
Focus Point and Information Screens	197
Marking Favorites	198
RAW Conversion	199
Viewing Shots Taken in a Burst	200
Playback of Panoramas	203
Viewing Shots Taken with Face Detection	204
The Playback Menu	204
PhotoBook Assist	205
Image Search	208
By Date	209
By Face	211
By Favorites	212
By Scene	213
By Type of Data	213
By Upload Mark	214
Erase	215
Mark for Upload To	216
Slide Show	217
RAW Conversion	219
Red Eye Removal	222
Protect	223
Crop	224
Resize	225

Image Rotate	226
Copy	227
Voice Memo	228
Erase Face Recognition	229
Print Order	229
Display Aspect	231
Printing Images	231
Printing Directly from the Camera	232
Chapter 7: The Setup Menu	**234**
Date and Time	235
Time Difference	236
Language	237
Silent Mode	237
Reset	238
Format	239
Image Display	240
Frame Number	241
Operation Volume	241
Shutter Volume	242
Shutter Sound	243
Playback Volume	243
LCD Brightness	244
Auto Power Off	244
Quick Start Mode	245
Function Button	245
IS Mode	246
Red Eye Removal	247
AF Illuminator	248
AE/AF Lock Mode	248
AE/AF Lock Button	249
RAW	250
Focus Check	252
Focus Control Dial	252
Focus Scale Units	253
Framing Guideline	253
Color Space	255
Save Original Image	256
Autorotate Playback	256
Background Color	257
Guidance Display	257
Video System	258
Custom Reset	258
Power Management	259
Chapter 8: Movies	**260**
Movie-making Overview	260
Quick Guide to Recording a Movie Clip	261
Other Settings for Movies	262
Movie Mode	264
Face Detection	266
Autofocus Mode	266
White Balance	268

Exposure	269
Film Simulation	269
Zoom	270
Movie Playback	271
Taking Still Photos While Recording a Movie	272
Playing Movies on Portable Devices	274
Chapter 9: OTHER TOPICS	**275**
Macro (Closeup) Shooting	275
Using Flash	277
Flash Modes	277
Flash Exposure Compensation	281
Infrared Photography	282
Street Photography	285
Making 3D Images	288
Digiscoping and Astrophotography	289
Connecting to a Television Set	294
The "Orbs" Problem	296
APPENDIX A: Accessories	**298**
Cases	298
Batteries and Chargers	301
Add-on Filters and Lenses	301
External Flash Units	302
AC Adapter	306
Other Add-ons	308
APPENDIX B: Quick Tips	**311**
APPENDIX C: Resources for Further Information	**317**
Photography Books	317
Web Sites	317
Index	**321**

Acknowledgments

I have previously written eight books in the "Photographer's Guide" series about advanced compact digital cameras. It is always a challenge to pick the next camera to write about, because there are so many high-quality compact cameras being released in a steady stream. For this book, I chose the Fujifilm X10, a smaller and somewhat different sibling of the Fujifilm X100, which I wrote about in 2011.

As I did with the X100 and most other cameras I have written about, I turned to the excellent dpreview.com web site for assistance. In particular, I sought help from the many expert users of the X10 who participate in the "Fujifilm Talk" forum at dpreview.com. As was the case when I made similar calls for help in connection with earlier books, the response from forum members was extraordinarily helpful. I am particularly grateful to Al Alexander, David Anderson, Barry Bogart, Barry Geller, Paul Graber, Marco Güldner, Rob de Knegt, Paul Martin, D. Mores, Giorgio de Nola, Hans-Jürgen Reichelt, Enrico Rossi, Peter Rowe, David Shirley, David Tannahill, Arno Vosk, Andrew Walker, Andreas Wennlund, and Victor Zaveduk for their tremendous assistance in scouring a draft of the book for errors and points that needed further discussion. They made extremely valuable suggestions, which improved the book considerably. Any remaining errors or problems are solely my responsibility.

Finally, as with my earlier books, the greatest support in every possible way, from joining me on trips to take photographs for this book to editing and proofreading the final text, has come from my wife, Clenise.

Introduction

This book is a guide to getting excellent photographic results using the Fujifilm X10, an advanced compact digital camera introduced in late 2011 that has distinguished itself from the large number of other cameras available in the marketplace today. The X10 can be considered the "little brother" of the highly successful Fujifilm X100, a camera that attracted a great deal of attention upon its introduction in 2010, partly because of its alluring "retro" appearance and partly because of its sophisticated photographic features, its fixed prime lens, and its DSLR-sized APS-C sensor.

Although the sensor of the X10 is not as large as that of the X100, it is still larger than those of most "point-and-shoot" digital cameras. And the sensor of the X10 uses Fujifilm's EXR technology to emphasize resolution, low-light performance, or high dynamic range, depending on your needs and preferences.

In addition, the X10 has an excellent lens with a wide aperture of f/2.0 at its 28mm focal length, which shrinks only to f/2.8 at its 112mm telephoto end—much better than some other cameras in this class. Moreover, the X10 is equipped with many of the advanced image-processing attributes of the X100, including settings that let you adjust individually the color, sharpness, highlight tones, shadow tones, and noise reduction of each image. The camera also boasts dynamic range processing, RAW format for shooting "unprocessed" images, and a broad array of other useful features, including various drive modes for burst and bracket shooting; film-simulation options that let you vary the look and color density of your images with in-camera processing; a range of shutter speeds as fast as 1/4000 second and as long as 30 seconds; a built-in flash; a set of "scene" modes that let you instantly set the camera for sunsets, sports, fireworks, and other common subjects; as well as just about every other feature a photographer would ask for in a camera of this class.

Along with its sharp LCD display screen with 460,000 dots of resolution, the camera offers a bright optical viewfinder that zooms along with the view provided by the high-quality zoom lens. The camera is equipped with a hot shoe that accepts external flash units, and the X10, like the X100, has a shutter release button that is threaded to accept a traditional cable release, allowing you to trigger the shutter without jiggling the camera. The X10 also offers a reasonably good set of options for capturing full high-definition video clips, and it includes a limited capability for recording slow-motion video.

This discussion of the camera's attributes is, of course, not complete, but it serves to illustrate that the Fujifilm X10 is equipped with features that should be attractive to serious photographers—those who want numerous options for creative control of their images in a camera that is small enough and light enough to be carried around at all times, so they will be ready for action when a good picture-taking opportunity pops up. The X10 should be of particular interest to those photographers who have an interest in street photography and other forms of candid shooting, but it also is an excellent choice as an all-around photographic Jack of all trades.

Of course, as with all cameras, there are some trade-offs with the X10 that could be considered drawbacks, depending on your needs and preferences. The lens, while excellent in quality, is non-interchangeable, and, although it is a zoom lens, it has a limited range of 35mm equivalent optical focal lengths, from 28mm to 112mm. Although the X10 can shoot Full High-Definition video, that capability is limited in several ways, including restrictions on video length and the inability to make many adjustments to exposure. The camera also was the subject of a good deal of adverse publicity over its tendency to introduce excessively large white highlights, or "orbs," in certain images, though Fujifilm appears to have addressed that issue effectively as this book goes to print. Despite any faults it may possess, the X10 offers an excellent array of menu options and controls that will let you deal with a wide variety of subjects with ease; you will just have to figure out what settings to use to get optimal results for any given subject.

My goal with this guide is to provide a thorough introduction to the camera's features, explaining how they work and when you might want to use them. The book is aimed largely at beginning and intermediate photographers who are not satisfied with the technical documentation that comes with the camera and who need a more user-friendly explanation of the camera's many controls and menus. For those who are seeking more advanced information, I provide some discussion of topics that go beyond the basics, and I include in the appendices information that should help you uncover additional resources. I will also try to provide updates and other materials from time to time at whiteknightpress.com.

One note on the scope of this guide: I live in the United States, and I bought my camera in the U.S. market. I am not familiar with any variations (such as different battery chargers) for cameras sold in Europe, Asia, or elsewhere. The photographic functions are not different, though, so this guide should be useful to photographers in all locations, apart from that narrow range of issues. I have stated measurements of distance in both the Imperial and metric systems, for the benefit of readers in various countries around the world.

The photographs in this book that illustrate the capabilities of the X10 are ones that I took with that camera, using firmware version 1.02 for most images, and version 1.03 for some that were taken after that firmware upgrade was released on February 9, 2012. The photographs of the X10 and its accessories are images that I took using a Sony DSLR-A850 camera with a Sony f/2.8 50mm macro lens and a Sony f/2.8 SAM 28-75mm zoom lens. The screen images were captured with the EyeTV 250 Plus video capture device from Elgato Systems.

Please note that, in order to follow the discussions in this book so that the illustrations match the text, I am assuming that you have installed Firmware version 1.03, which changed some operations of the camera (notably the function of the RAW button on the camera's back). Also, unless stated otherwise, I am assuming that, when in Shooting mode, you have the camera set to show the Standard display screen, as opposed to one of the more detailed screens or the display-off setting. (To change the view on the display screen, press the Display/Back button on the right side of the camera's back until the Standard display appears.)

Finally, this is the black-and-white edition of the book. It has all of the same content as the original, full-color edition; the only difference is that the photographs in this edition have been converted to grayscale, so this edition can be provided at a lower cost. The text of this edition has not been altered in any way, and it still discusses the photographs as if they were in color. If any reader of this edition would like to see the photographs in color, just send an e-mail message to contact@whiteknightpress.com, and I will send you a complimentary copy of the book in the electronic version of your choice (PDF, ePub, or Kindle).

Chapter 1: Preliminary Steps

Setting Up the Camera

If you purchase the Fujifilm X10 brand new, besides the camera, the box should contain the battery, battery charger, lens cap, USB cable, neck strap, printed user's manual, CD with owner's manual and software, and a clip-attaching tool with clips for fastening the neck strap to the camera. There also should be a warranty card and one or two other items, such as an advertising sheet or safety notice.

It is generally a good idea to attach the neck strap to the camera right away, which requires that you use the clip-attaching tool to attach a metal clip to each of the metal eyelets at the sides of the camera; then thread the strap through those clips, using protective covers to insulate the camera body from the clips, as shown at pages 8-9 of the user's manual. You might want to consider alternatives, though, such as the SnapR strap and case combination, discussed in Appendix A. Also, if you should decide to purchase the official Fujifilm leather case, also discussed in Appendix A, that case comes with its own leather strap, which you can attach to the camera using the clips provided with the X10.

Charging and Inserting the Battery

The battery model for the X10 is the Fujifilm NP-50. The only way to charge the battery is with an external charger such as model BC-45W, which is the Fujifilm charger supplied with the camera. This charger is designed for two different models of battery, so you need to observe the label inside the charger and insert the X10's battery in the direction indicated by an arrow inside the charger for the NP-50.

If you are using the official Fujifilm battery, it has a black arrow pointing the correct direction in which to insert it into the charger. If you're using a replacement battery from another company, though, such arrows are likely to be missing. Personally, I prefer to look for the three gold-colored metal contacts that are spaced evenly apart on the battery and to insert the battery so those three contacts come into contact with the corresponding three metal prongs inside the charger; that way, you know you have the battery inserted correctly.

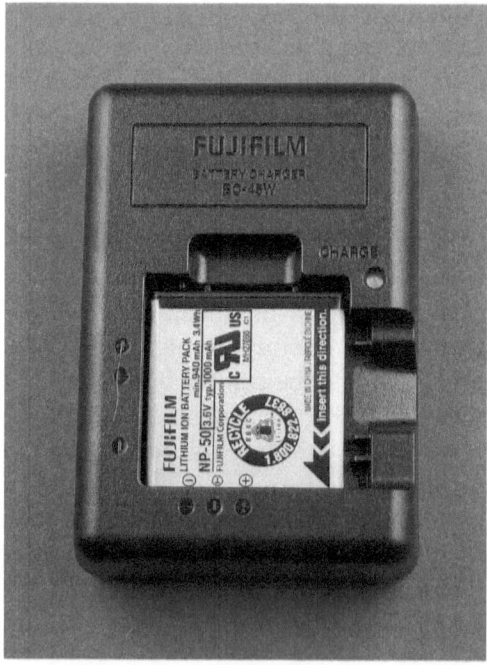

With the battery inserted in the charger, plug the charger's prongs (or power cord if your charger comes with one) into an electrical outlet. The light on the charger should be a solid yellow, to show that charging is taking place. A full charge of a depleted battery should take about 150 minutes, after which the charging light turns off to indicate that charging is complete.

Once you have a charged battery, hold the camera upside down and slide the latch on the battery compartment door towards the "Open" label; the door will pop open.

You need to be careful about inserting the battery, because it is possible to insert it incorrectly, although it will probably not click into place if inserted in the wrong direction. Make sure the three gold-colored contacts are facing down into the camera, and that they are next to the outer edge of the camera. You may have to nudge the yellowish-orange latch in the battery compartment to one side to let the battery slide past it. Once the battery is inserted, the latch should spring closed above the battery, holding it in place.

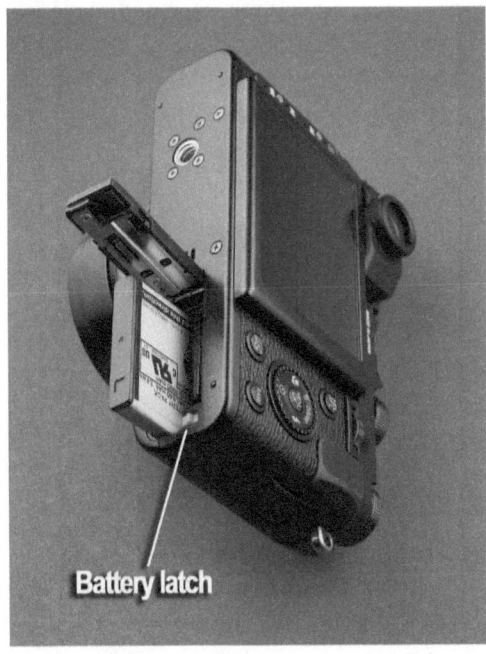

Close and latch the battery compartment door, and you're done. (Or, if you're also going to insert a memory card, leave the door open for the next step.)

Inserting the Memory Card

The X10 does not ship with any memory card included. With this camera, unlike some others, this is not a fatal omission, because the camera has some built-in memory that will let you take a few photographs even with no memory card inserted. The amount of built-in memory is not large—about 26 megabytes (MB)—which is pretty minuscule compared to the capacity of modern storage cards that can hold up to 128 gigabytes (GB), roughly 5,000 times greater capacity. But if you're in a situation where you need to take a picture and don't have an available card, 26 MB might be enough in some cases. The internal memory can hold about 35 still photos of the smallest size at Normal (lowest) quality, but only about 5 of the highest quality JPEG (non-RAW) images or one image shot in the RAW format, with proportional figures for intermediate levels of image size and quality. You can store about 12 seconds of the highest-quality video in the internal memory, or about 42 seconds of the lowest quality normal-speed video.

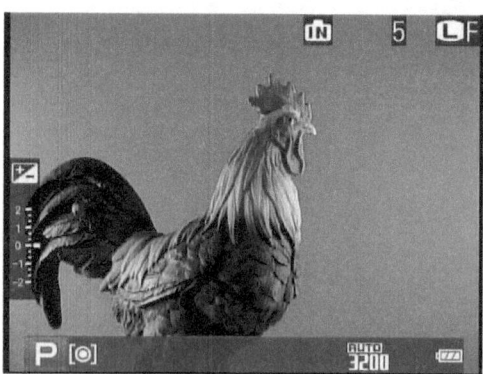

If you have no memory card inserted in the camera, the letters IN will display inside a white camera icon in the upper right half of the display (if one of the detailed display screens is selected), indicating that internal memory is being used.

If a memory card is inserted, the letters IN are not displayed, but you will usually notice a dramatic increase in the number in the upper right of the display, which represents the estimated number of remaining images that can be stored.

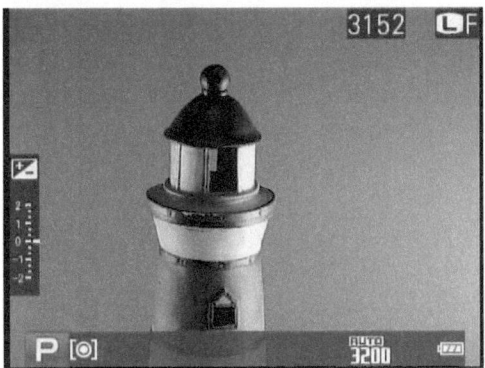

If you use up the internal memory, you will see a message saying that the internal memory is full, and your shooting will come to a halt unless you delete some images from the internal memory or insert an SD card that has some free space on it.

Because of its limited capacity, you don't want to rely on the built-in memory if you don't have to, so you need a memory card. The X10 uses SD cards, which are quite small, about the size of a large postage stamp. They come in several varieties.

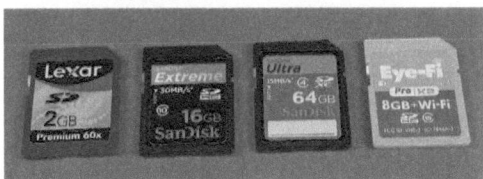

The standard card, called simply SD, comes in capacities from 8 MB to 2 GB. The next higher-capacity card, SDHC, comes in sizes from 4 GB to 32 GB. The newest, and highest-capacity card, SDXC (for extended capacity), comes in sizes of 48 GB, 64 GB, and up; this version of the card can theoretically have a capacity up to 2 terabytes (TB) (the same as 2,000 GB), and SDXC cards have faster transfer speeds than the smaller-capacity cards. Note that the X10 cannot use another type of memory card called a MultiMediaCard (MMC), even though those cards are the same size as SD cards.

Which card you should use depends on your needs. If you want to record a lot of high-definition (HD) video or many high-resolution stills, I recommend a 16 GB SDHC card, which has plenty of storage space. There are several variables to consider in computing how many images or videos you can store on a particular card, such as the aspect ratio you're using (4:3, 3:2, 16:9 or 1:1), image size, and quality. Here are some examples of what can be stored on a 16 GB card: It can hold about 650 photos shot in the RAW format, the largest size for stills; it can hold 3260 of the largest JPEG images at the highest quality; or it can hold more than 23,000 still images at the lower, Normal quality and the smallest file size. A 16GB card also can store about 150 minutes of the highest-quality HD video clips or about 232 minutes of the lowest-quality clips. (Each individual clip is limited in length, though, as discussed in Chapter 8.)

Of course, if you are going on a long trip and want to limit the number of memory cards to keep track of, you can opt for an SDXC card with huge capacity. As I write this, a card with a capacity of 128 GB is available. With that card, you could store more than 5,000 RAW images and even greater amounts for other formats. However, because of the capacity of such a card, it can take extra time for the camera to get ready to shoot after you turn it on with an SDXC card installed. Also, you take the risk of "putting all your eggs in one basket," and you could lose a great many images if you lose this card.

One other consideration is the speed of the card. If you plan to record video, you should get a card that is rated as Class 6 or higher for its speed. I hesitate to recommend any one card above others, because I have not tried them all, but I have had excellent results with a 16 GB SanDisk Extreme Pro SDHC UHS-1 card, which is rated as reading and writing at 45 MB/second, and is in UHS speed class 1. (UHS, not surprisingly, stands for ultra-high speed.) The extra speed can increase the efficiency of operations such as menu navigation.

If you have an older computer with a built-in card reader, or just an older external card reader, there is a chance it will not read the newer SDHC or SDXC cards. In that case, you would have to either get a new reader that will accept those cards, or transfer images from the X10 to your computer with the USB cable. If you have a fairly new computer and card reader, though, you should have no problem with the newer cards.

If you have access to a wireless (Wi-Fi) network where you use your camera, you may want to consider getting an Eye-Fi card. This special type of storage device looks very much like an ordinary SDHC card, but it includes a tiny transmitter that lets it connect to a wireless network and send your images to your computer over that network as soon as the images have been recorded by the camera.

I tested an 8 GB Eye-Fi card, the Pro X2 model, with the X10, and it worked well, after I upgraded the firmware of the card to version 5. Within seconds after I snapped a picture with this card in the camera, a thumbnail image appeared in the upper right corner of my computer's screen showing the progress of the upload. When all images were uploaded, they were found in the Pictures/Eye-Fi folder on my computer. The Pro X2 model can handle RAW files as well as the smaller JPEG files. (At this writing, that is the only variety of Eye-Fi card that can handle RAW files.) An Eye-Fi card is not a necessity, but I enjoy the convenience of having my images sent straight to my computer without having to put the card into a card reader or to connect the camera to the computer with a USB cable.

In summary, you have quite a few options for choosing a memory card. Personally, I like to use a high-speed 16 GB or sometimes a 32 GB SDHC card, just to have extra capacity and speed in case they are needed. I like the convenience of the Eye-Fi card also, but, unless you do a lot of photography within range of a wireless network so the images can be uploaded quickly, it may not be worth your while to get that type of card.

Whatever card you decide on, once you have selected it, open the same little door on the bottom of the camera that covers the battery compartment, and slide the card into the card slot until it catches, with the label facing the front of the camera.

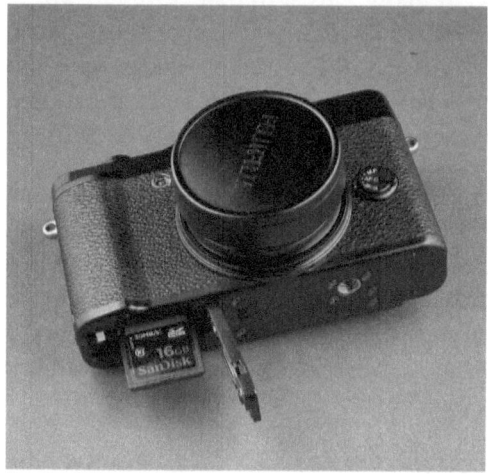

Once the card has been pushed down until it catches, close the compartment door and push the exterior sliding latch back to the locking position. To remove the card, you push down on it until it releases and springs up so you can grab it.

One note for when you're shooting continuous pictures: When the camera is writing images to the SD card, the indicator at the upper middle of the camera's back, below the hot shoe, glows orange or blinks orange and green. When that lamp is displaying either of these signals, it's important not to turn off the camera or interrupt its functioning, such as by taking out the battery or disconnecting an AC power adapter. You need to let the card complete its recording process in peace.

Introduction to Main Controls

Now it's time to discuss some of the basic options for setting up the camera using the menu system and controls. Before I start that discussion, I will introduce the main controls, so you'll have a better idea of which button or dial is which. I

CHAPTER 1: PRELIMINARY STEPS

won't discuss all of the controls here; they will all be covered in some detail in Chapter 5. For now, here is a series of images that show the major controls. As I discuss each one for the first time, I will describe its position and function; you may want to refer back to these images for a reminder about each control.

Top of Camera

On top of the camera are several important controls and dials, shown in the image here.

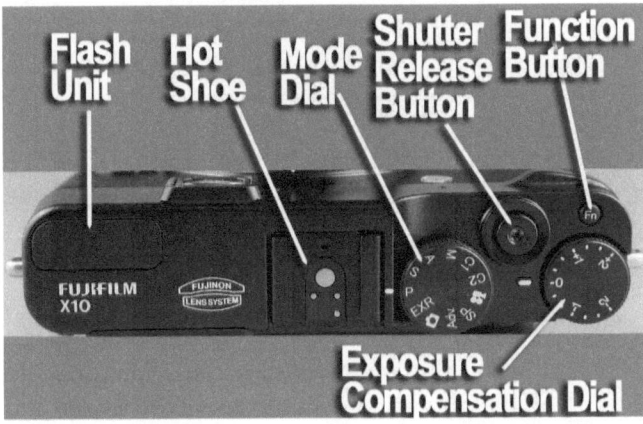

Back of Camera

There are numerous major controls on the camera's back, as seen in the image below.

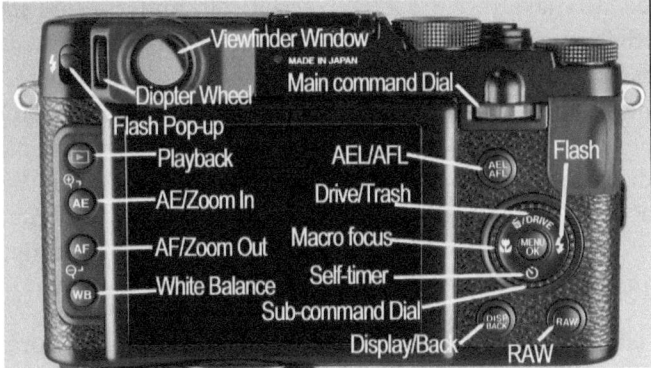

25

Front of Camera

On the front of the camera, the only control you can manipulate is the focus switch, which sits by itself on the right side of the X10 as you look at the front of the camera.

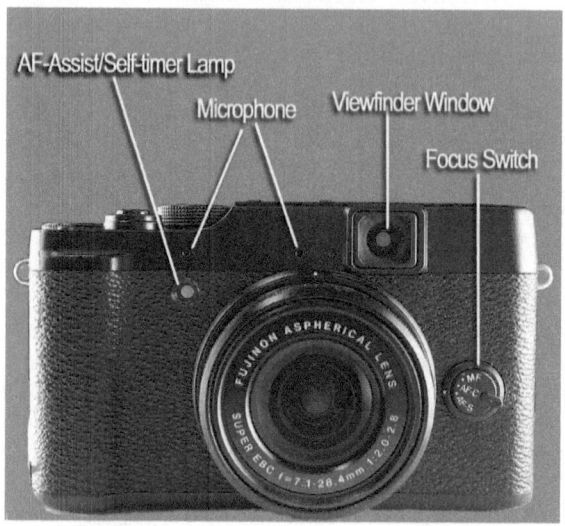

Finally, the lens barrel has two major functions. You turn it to power on and off the camera, and also to zoom the lens in and out. You can attach filters and other accessories to the front of the lens using a lens adapter, as discussed in Appendix A.

Setting the Language, Date, and Time

You need to make sure the X10's internal date and time are set correctly before you start taking pictures, because the camera records that information (sometimes known as "metadata," meaning data beyond the information in the picture itself) invisibly with each image, and displays it later if you want. Someday you may be very glad to have the date (and even the time of day) correctly recorded with your archives of digital images. If you purchase the camera brand new, it will prompt you to set the date and time when you first power it on.

If you later need to set the time and date, here is the procedure.

Turn the camera's power on by grasping the lens barrel and twisting it to the left (if the camera is facing you) until the lens is zoomed at least to the 28mm mark. Then press the Menu button in the center of the circular pad on the camera's back to display the Menu screen. Press the left side of the ridged black wheel inside the circular area, which is known as the sub-command dial. That spot on the left side is marked with a flower icon. When you press on that spot, the small triangular selection markers will move out of the menu screen to the left side of the display, highlighting one of the icons—a camera for the Shooting menu or a wrench for the Setup menu. Press on the down button of the sub-command dial, labeled with a timer icon, once or more until the wrench icon is highlighted. Then press on the right side of the sub-command dial, marked with a lightning bolt, to move the selection markers back into the menu list. Move the black selection rectangle up and down through the menu items by pressing the up/down buttons on the sub-command dial or by turning the sub-command dial, until the Date/Time item is highlighted.

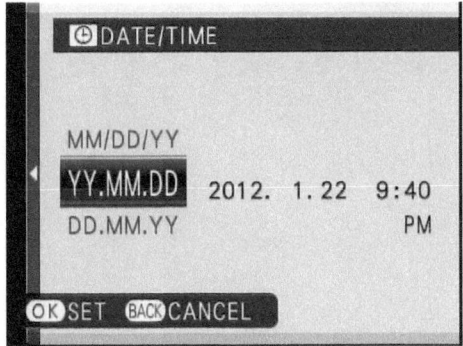

Then, press the center button in the sub-command dial, marked Menu/OK (the same as the Menu button), to activate the date and time settings. Move left and right through the date, year, and time settings using the left/right buttons of the sub-command dial, and change the settings with the up/down buttons, or by turning the sub-command dial. When everything is set correctly, press the center MENU/OK button to confirm, and press the Display/Back button, to the lower left of the sub-command dial, to exit the menu system.

If you need to change the language that the camera uses for the menus and other messages, navigate on the Setup menu to the line that says Lang. for Language, and press the OK button or the right direction button (right edge of sub-command dial) to move to the list of available languages.

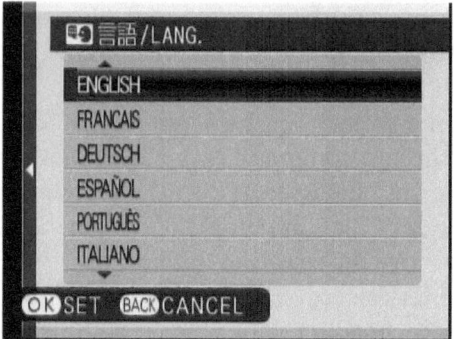

Then navigate with the up and down direction buttons (the top and bottom edges of the sub-command dial) to the language of your choice, and press the OK button to select it. Finally, press the Display/Back button, or press the shutter button halfway down, to exit from the menu system.

Chapter 2: Basic Operations

Taking Pictures and Videos

Now that the X10 has the correct time and date set and has a fully charged battery inserted along with a memory card, let's explore some scenarios for basic picture-taking. For now, I won't get into discussions of what the various options are and why you might choose one over another. I'll just lay out a reasonable set of steps that will get you and your camera into action and will deposit a decent image or video on your memory card.

Fully Automatic—EXR Auto Mode

Although the X10 is equipped with an impressive set of features for advanced photographers, it also comes with not just one, but two fully automatic settings for those who want to spin the mode dial to one of these positions and start taking high-quality pictures without having to deal with a lot of complex settings. One of these settings, called simply Auto, sets the camera to use standard settings to achieve good results in situations with good, even lighting.

The other automatic setting, called EXR Auto, accomplishes the same thing, but also takes advantage of the camera's special EXR sensor to get the best possible results in a wider range of shooting conditions, including those marked by low light or high contrast. In my opinion, it is generally worthwhile to take advantage of the EXR features, and I recommend using the EXR Auto mode for general photography. In Chapter 3, I discuss these and other shooting modes, along with the considerations that go into choosing a mode. For now, though, I will describe the use of the EXR Auto mode for getting started taking still images with the camera.

So, if you have just set up the camera, or you have not yet had a chance to study its features and want to start capturing still images, here are some basic steps you can follow to get your first pictures taken:

1. Remove the lens cap from the lens and put it in your pocket or some other safe place where it won't get lost; unfortunately, Fujifilm does not provide a way to attach it to the camera by a string or other mechanism. (See Appendix A for ways to address this problem.)

2. Turn on the power by grasping the camera's body in one hand and turning the lens barrel left (as you face the camera) with the other hand, so the lens extends outward from the camera and one of the numbers on the lens lines up with the white line on the camera's body. The LCD screen will illuminate to show that the camera has turned on.

3. Find the mode dial on top of the camera to the right of the flash shoe, and turn that dial until the letters EXR are lined up next to the white dot on the right side of the flash shoe.

4. You should now see the EXR Auto icon on a red background at the lower left of the LCD display, indicating that the camera has been set to the EXR Auto shooting mode.

If you don't see any red icon there, press the Display/Back button, at the lower left of the right side of the camera's back, repeatedly until you see the word Standard appear. You will then be viewing the Standard information display, which includes the icon for the current shooting mode—in this case, the EXR Auto icon.

CHAPTER 2: BASIC OPERATIONS

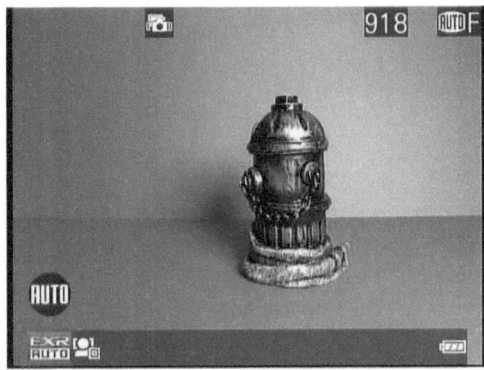

5. If you see a red icon, but with the letters HR, SN, or DR instead of EXR Auto, press the Menu button in the center of the sub-command dial on the back of the camera to enter the Shooting menu. Press the up and down direction buttons (top and bottom edges of the sub-command dial), or turn the sub-command dial itself, to navigate to the menu entry for EXR Mode, at the top of the list of menu items. Select that item with the OK button or the right direction button, then, on the next screen, use the up and down direction buttons or the sub-command dial to highlight the EXR Auto setting, and press OK. Press the Display/Back button to exit the menu system.

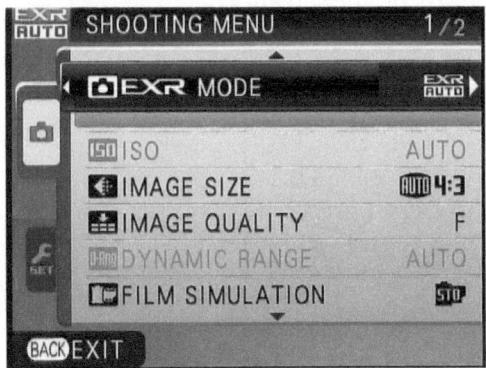

6. Use the same procedure as in step 5 to enter the Shooting menu, then navigate to the Image Size setting, select it, and choose Auto 4:3, meaning the camera will automatically set the image size, with an aspect ratio of 4:3.

31

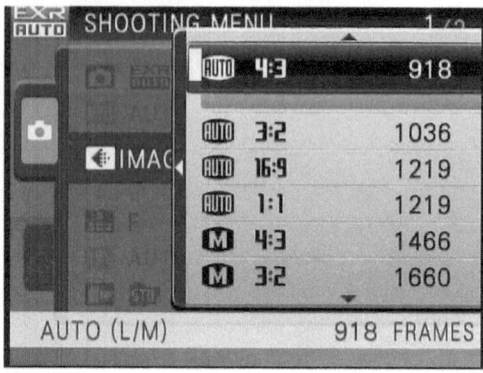

Press the Display/Back button, at the lower left of the control area on the right of the camera's back, to exit from the menu screen back to the live shooting screen.

7. If you are indoors or otherwise in conditions that might call for the use of flash, slide down the flash pop-up switch marked with a lightning bolt, which is at the far left edge of the top of the camera's back, to pop up the built-in flash unit. Then press the other button marked with a flash symbol, which is also the right edge of the sub-command dial. Quickly press this button again or turn the sub-command dial, until the Auto Flash setting appears on the screen.

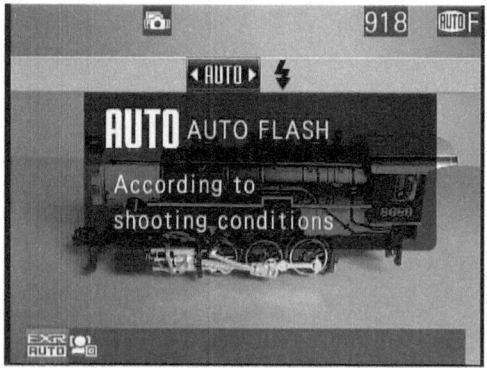

There should not be any lightning bolt on the screen; the lack of a lightning bolt means the camera is set to Auto Flash mode.

CHAPTER 2: BASIC OPERATIONS

8. Aim the camera toward the subject and look at the LCD screen (or into the viewfinder window if you prefer) to compose the image as you want it. Once the picture is set up to your satisfaction, push the shutter button halfway down. You should hear a little beep and see a small green cross appear on the screen, indicating that the picture will be in focus.

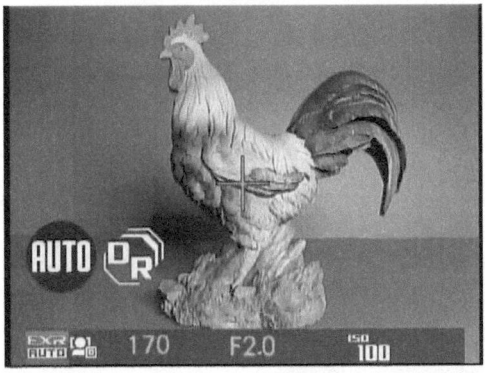

If the cross is red, that means the camera is having difficulty achieving focus. In that case, try moving the camera to a different angle or distance from the subject before pressing the shutter button halfway down again.

9. Grasp the lens and turn the lens manually to zoom, if needed, until you have composed the shot as you want it. (There is no electronic switch with which to control the zoom.)

10. Push the shutter button fully down to take the picture.

Flash

Now I'll go into a bit more detail about using the X10's built-in flash unit, because that is something you may need to use on a regular basis. In Chapter 5, I'll discuss the use of the Flash button, in Chapter 9 I'll discuss other options for using the flash, such as controlling its output and preventing "red-eye," and in Appendix A, I'll discuss using other flash units.

The built-in flash on the X10 is not especially powerful, but it can provide enough illumination to let you take pictures in

33

dark areas and to brighten up subjects that would otherwise be lost in shadows, even outdoors on a sunny day. As with several features of the X10, the use of the flash is not as obvious or automatic as similar features on less advanced cameras. But, once you have used the flash once or twice, the procedure should seem quite simple.

I have already discussed how to turn on the flash unit and set it to the Auto Flash mode. If, instead of Auto Flash, you choose Forced Flash, you will see the lightning bolt icon on the screen at all times, and the flash will fire regardless of whether the camera's exposure system believes flash is needed.

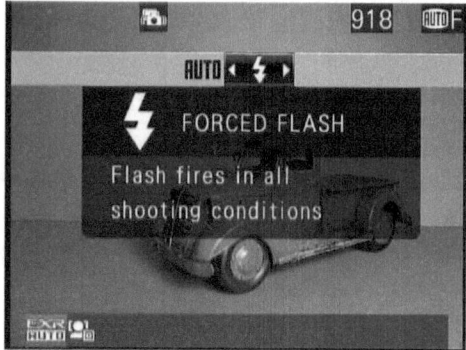

This setting, sometimes called Fill Flash, can be of use in some outdoor settings, such as when you need to reduce the shadows on your subject's face. The portrait below was taken with Forced Flash to reduce shadows.

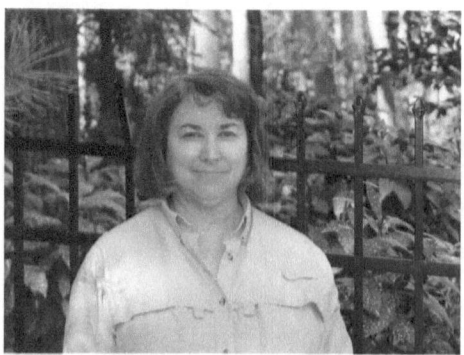

Here is one important point to note about the use of flash with the X10: The flash cannot fire if you do not pop it up manually using the flash pop-up switch. (That switch is at the far upper left of the camera's back; it is different from the Flash button that is also the right direction button on the sub-command dial.) With some other cameras, the built-in flash can pop up by itself, but that is not the case with the X10; you have complete control over whether the flash is available. If you do not first pop up the flash unit, then pressing the Flash button on the sub-command dial will have no effect at all.

The fact that the flash must be popped up manually provides one distinct advantage: You can be certain that the flash will not fire when you don't want it to. That is, if you are in a museum or at a religious ceremony, for example, you can just leave the flash unit tucked down inside the camera, and you can rest assured that it will not embarrass you by firing when you thought you had it turned off.

One more note on the use of flash: If you turn on Silent Mode using the Setup menu or by holding down the Display/Back button on the right side of the camera's back, the camera suppresses all of its operational sounds, and the flash is deactivated and cannot be turned on. In this situation, if you try to select a flash mode the camera will display a message telling you to turn off Silent Mode, which you can quickly do by pressing and holding the Display/Back button. The flash also cannot be activated if any of the continuous-shooting options have been turned on using the Drive mode button. Those shooting options are discussed in Chapter 5.

Other Settings in EXR Auto Mode

With some other compact cameras, when you have set the shooting mode to its most automatic setting, there are very few other settings that are available for you to make. With the X10, which is intended for use by more demanding photographers, even in EXR Auto mode there are several settings that you can adjust. For now, I will provide a list of the settings that can be made in this mode, along with my recommendations for the settings to use. In later chapters I will discuss each of these options in more detail, so that you can decide for yourself what settings to make.

In this chapter, I won't go into detail about how to make each of these settings; I will just provide the name of the feature, where to find it, and the recommended setting. For more details about items on the Shooting menu, see Chapter 4; for details about using the physical controls, see Chapter 5. Note that you will see some settings on the menu, such as ISO, Dynamic Range, and AF Mode, that are legible but are "grayed-out," which means they are not available for adjustment in this shooting mode; you can ignore them for now.

Recommended Settings for EXR Auto Mode	
Image Size	Auto 4:3
Image Quality	Fine
Film Simulation	Provia (Standard)
Intelligent Digital Zoom	Off
Advanced Anti Blur	On
Face Recognition	Off
Drive Mode	Still Image
Flash	Auto (if used)
Self-timer	Off

Overview of Movie Recording

Next, let's take a look at recording a short movie sequence with the X10. Later, in Chapter 8, I'll discuss other options for video recording, but for now, I'll stick to the basics.

Once the camera is turned on, turn the mode dial on the top of the camera to select the movie camera icon, for Movie mode.

Then, press the Menu button to get access to the Shooting menu. There is only one screen with four items on that menu, because there are few options available in Movie mode. On the top line of the Shooting menu, with Movie Mode highlighted, press the right direction button to go to the sub-menu with the six choices for the "mode" or format of movie recording. For now, be sure the top option, Full HD 1920, is highlighted; that format provides the highest quality for your videos.

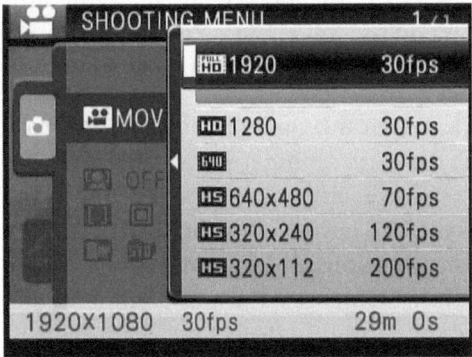

Next, press the left button to go back to the main Shooting menu screen, and proceed down the list to the next option, Face Detection. If you will be shooting video that includes human faces, it is a good idea to turn this option on by selecting On from the sub-menu. With this setting activated, the camera will attempt to detect faces and will set its focus and exposure for any faces it finds.

If you are not shooting video of people or don't care about using Face Detection, navigate down to the next item on the Shooting menu, AF Mode, and select either Center or Continuous. (If you are using Face Detection, AF Mode is not available for selection in Movie mode, so you can skip this step.)

With AF Mode set to Center, the camera will focus just once, on the center of the image; with Continuous, the autofocus mechanism will keep adjusting focus as the subject inside the focus frame moves closer to or farther from the camera. Choose Center if you are filming a scene that will have a steady focus range, such as a graduation speaker or a concert where the performer stays in one place; choose Continuous for sports or other active events with constant motion. With Continuous, the battery will drain more quickly than with Center, and the camera may pick up the sounds of the autofocus adjustments, so choose Continuous only if you really need to track moving subjects.

Finally, go to the last choice on the Shooting menu, Film Simulation; leave this setting on the top choice, Provia. I'll discuss the Film Simulation settings in some detail in Chapter 4.

Now, you should check two of the camera's physical controls. First, take a look at the exposure compensation dial at the far right of the top of the camera, and make sure it is set to the zero point. Then, press the WB button at the bottom of the line of controls at the left of the camera's back. Make sure White Balance is set to Auto; if it isn't, rotate the sub-command dial or use the up and down direction buttons to move it back to that setting, and exit from the White Balance menu by pressing the Display/Back button.

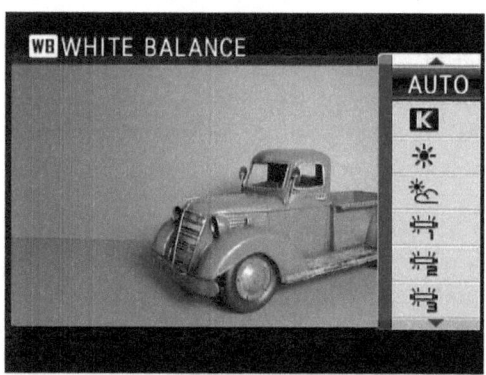

That is really all the preparation you need at this point. Now compose the shot the way you want it, and when you're ready, press the shutter button. You don't need to hold the button down; just press it once and release it. The reddish indicator light on the camera's back, just below the flash shoe, will glow during the recording, and the screen will display a flashing red icon on the display, next to a countdown of the minutes and seconds remaining for the recording.

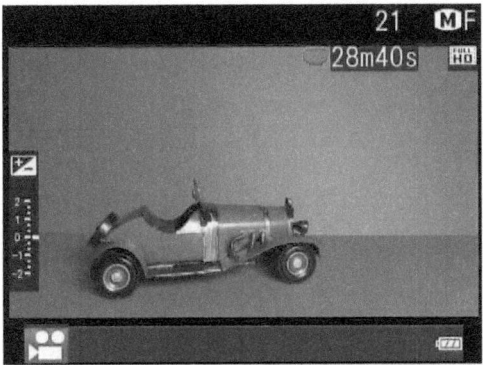

The camera will keep shooting until it reaches a recording limit, or until you press the shutter button again to stop the recording. Don't be concerned about the level of the sound that is being recorded, because you have no control over the audio volume while recording.

The camera will automatically adjust exposure as lighting conditions change. You can zoom the lens in and out as needed, but you should do so sparingly if at all, to avoid distracting the audience and to avoid putting the sounds of zooming the lens on the sound track.

One other point that's not specific to the X10: Unless you have a good reason to do otherwise, hold the camera as steady as possible (using a tripod if possible), and don't move the camera except in very smooth, slow motions, such as a pan (side-to-side motion) to take in a wide scene gradually. Video from a jerkily moving camera can be very disconcerting to the viewer.

Those are the basics for recording video clips with the X10. I'll discuss the movie options in more detail in Chapter 8.

Viewing Pictures

Before I delve into more advanced settings for taking still pictures and movies, as well as other matters of interest, I will discuss the basics of viewing your images in the camera.

Review While in Shooting Mode

Every time you take a still picture, the image will show up on the LCD for a short time, if you have the Setup menu's Image Display option set to turn on this function. I'll discuss the details of that setting in Chapter 7. By default, your image will stay on the screen for 1.5 seconds after you take a new picture. If you prefer, you can set that display to last for three seconds, to last until you press the OK button, or to be off altogether.

Reviewing Images in Playback Mode

If you are viewing images that were taken previously, you enter playback mode by pressing the Playback button, marked with a small green triangle, to the left of the LCD. You can scroll through the recorded images using the left and right direction buttons or by turning the sub-command dial. If you hold down the left or right button, the pictures will scroll rapidly.

You can enlarge any image by pressing the AE/Zoom-in button to the left of the LCD. Repeated presses bring greater zoom levels. You can scroll around in an enlarged image using all four direction buttons. You can zoom back out using the AF/Zoom-out button. You also can zoom in quickly on the focus point by pressing in on the center of the main command dial and zoom out again using the Display/Back button.

If you have used the continuous-shooting features of the camera, you will see some images that display a small inset image in the lower right, and that initially display a down-pointing triangle along with the message, PLAY CONTINUOUS SHOTS. (If you don't see these indications, press the Display/Back button repeatedly until the standard (Information On) display screen appears on the LCD.) In that case, you can press the down direction button to "open" a series of continuous shots, and then use the left and right buttons to move among the various individual shots in the series.

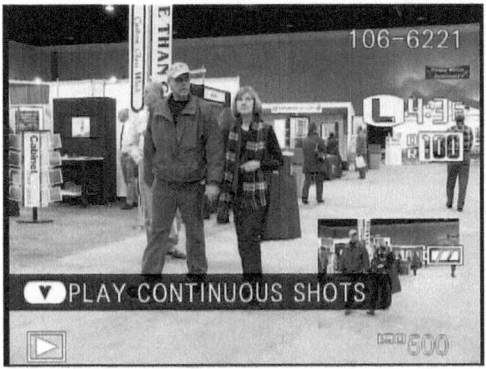

To go back to the main screen so you can see other images and series of images, press the Display button. If you want to view only the first image in each series, just continue to scroll through the images normally without "opening" the sequence of continuous shots with the down button. I'll discuss playback options in more detail in Chapter 6.

Playing Movies

To play back motion pictures, move through the recorded images by the methods described above until you find an image that is bordered by vertical columns of gray rounded rectangles, which represent the sprocket holes of movie film.

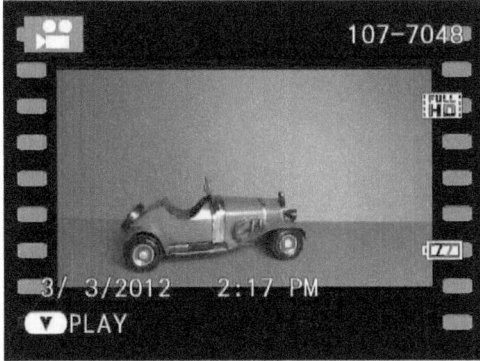

With the still frame from the motion picture displayed on the camera's display, press the down button and the movie will start playing on the LCD.

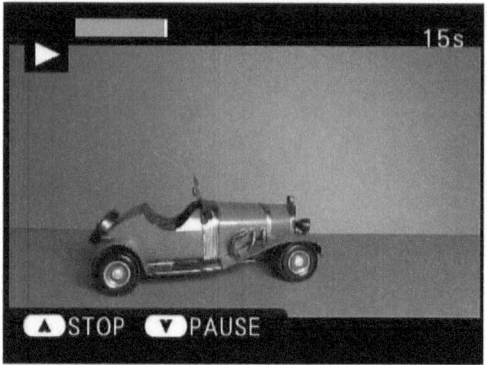

At the top of the display there will be a gray bar that moves across the screen to show the progress of the playback. You can pause and resume playback using the down button and stop playback completely with the up button. While the movie is paused, you can move through it one frame at a time using the left and right buttons. While it is playing, you can fast-forward at increasing speeds by pressing the right button repeatedly, and you can rewind in the same way using the left button.

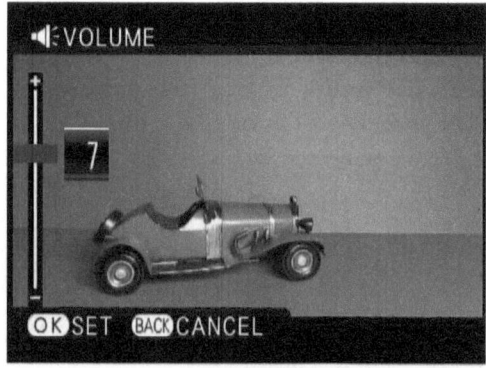

To adjust the volume of the sound, press the OK button in the center of the sub-command dial, and then increase or decrease volume using the up and down buttons or by turning the sub-command dial right or left.

If you want to play the movies on a computer or edit them with video-editing software, they will import nicely into software such as iMovie for the Macintosh, or any other program for Mac or Windows that can deal with video files with the extension .mov. This is the extension for Apple Computer's QuickTime video playback software; a basic version of QuickTime can be downloaded from Apple's web site. For some Windows-based video-editing software, you may need to convert the X10's movie files to the .avi format before importing them into the software. You can do so with a program such as mp4cam2avi, which is easily found through an internet search.

I will discuss more of your options for shooting and playing movies in Chapter 8.

Chapter 3: The Shooting Modes

Up until now I have discussed the basics of how to set up the camera for quick shots, relying heavily on the EXR Auto shooting mode, which lets you take pictures whose settings are controlled largely by the camera's automation. As with others of the more sophisticated digital cameras, though, with the X10 there is a wide range of options available for setting the camera, particularly for recording still images. One of the main goals of this book is to explain those options clearly and concisely. To do this, I need to turn my attention to several areas, including shooting modes, menu options, and the functions of the camera's physical controls. In this chapter, I will discuss the shooting modes and how to take advantage of the particular strengths of each one.

Whenever you set out to record still images, you need to use the mode dial on top of the camera to select one of the numerous available shooting modes: Auto, EXR, Program, Shutter Priority, Aperture Priority, Manual exposure, Custom 1, Custom 2, Scene Position, or Advanced. (The Movie mode is not ordinarily used for taking still images, although you can do so; I will discuss that mode in Chapter 8.) So far, we have worked only with the EXR Auto mode, because it is probably the best one to start with when you want to take pictures with the X10 without too much difficulty. Now it is time to discuss each of the camera's shooting modes in some detail.

To follow this discussion so that the LCD screen appears as it is described in the text, you should press the Display/Back button, at the lower left on the right side of the camera's back, as many times as necessary to bring up the Standard display screen, which is labeled "STANDARD" at the very bottom center of the screen.

Auto Mode

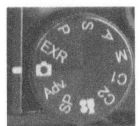

On many other cameras, the shooting mode called Auto or something similar is the most automatic mode available. With the X10, the most automatic mode is EXR Auto, in which the camera makes most of the decisions for you and uses the special features of its EXR sensor. However, the X10 has another mode called simply Auto, in which the camera makes many decisions but still gives you considerable latitude for making various settings yourself.

The existence of two "Auto" modes on the same camera is somewhat unusual, and it may well lead you to wonder which mode to choose, especially when just starting out with the camera. I will give you my thoughts on this question, though you may have a different approach, based on your own particular background and needs.

In my opinion, the answer to the question of which "Auto" mode to choose comes down to how much control you want to cede to the camera. In EXR Auto mode, the camera leaves only a few Shooting menu choices up to you, in whole or in part: Image Size, Image Quality, Film Simulation, Intelligent Digital Zoom, Advanced Anti Blur, and Face Recognition. Matters of focus, exposure, ISO, and white balance are left entirely up to the camera's programming. You also have some control over continuous shooting options and you can use the self-timer.

In the regular Auto mode, you have more options for making settings on the Shooting menu, including ISO, more flexibility in setting Image Size, and Face Detection. Perhaps most importantly, you can choose the camera's overall focus mode by using the focus switch on the front of the camera, including manual focus, and you can select an autofocus mode (Area or Tracking) with the AF Mode option on the Shooting menu.

So, if you want a large degree of automation but would like to have some flexibility in making settings involving features such as ISO and focus, the normal Auto shooting mode may be the best choice to make.

To set this mode, turn the mode dial on top of the camera so that the white camera-shaped icon is next to the white indicator mark to the right of the flash shoe. You will now see the white camera icon against a red background at the bottom left of the display, to indicate that Auto mode is selected.

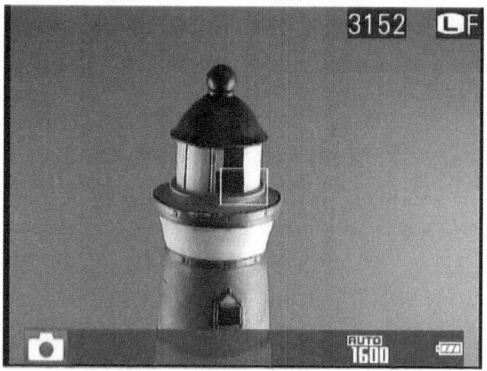

Recommended Settings

Next, I will give you my recommendations for the settings to use with Auto mode; I will discuss those settings in more detail in later chapters that cover the Shooting menu, physical controls, and the Setup menu.

Shooting Menu

I discussed the procedure for making settings on the Shooting menu in Chapter 2. As a reminder, enter the menu system by pressing the Menu/OK button in the center of the sub-command dial, then scroll through the menu items and screens by turning that dial or by pressing the up and down direction buttons, which are the upper and lower edges of the dial. Once you have reached the item to set, such as ISO, press the Menu/OK button or the right direction button to go to the sub-menu. Then, scroll through that list as before. Once you have highlighted the value you want (such as AUTO (800) for ISO, for example), you can press the Menu/OK button to confirm its selection, and then press the Display/Back button to exit back to the previous screen.

With that introduction, here are my recommendations for the settings that are available on the Shooting menu for AUTO mode:

Shooting Menu Settings for Auto Mode	
ISO	Auto (800)
Image Size	L 4:3
Image Quality	Fine
Film Simulation	Provia (Standard)
Intelligent Digital Zoom	Off
Face Detection	On, if subjects are people
AF Mode	Area
Face Recognition	Off
Display Custom Setting	All Items Checked

Setup Menu

Next, there are numerous items on the Setup menu that can be adjusted in Auto mode, although some of these items are not ongoing settings like those on the Shooting menu. For example, some of the items on this menu are commands, such as Format, that can be used as needed, but that do not affect the images you take. In the listing below, I will include only those settings that will have an immediate impact on how the camera operates as you take pictures.

To get access to the Setup menu, press the Menu/OK button, then press the left direction button (left edge of the sub-command dial in the center of the control area on the right side of the camera's back) to highlight the camera icon to the left of the menu screen. Then press the down button to highlight the wrench icon at the bottom left of the screen; the wrench represents the Setup menu. Now, press the right button to move the highlight back into the list of menu items; you will now be navigating in the various screens of the Setup menu.

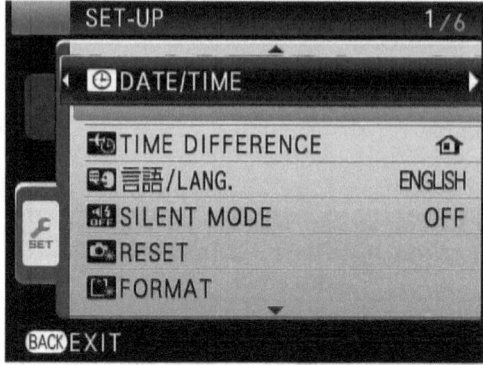

The following table gives my recommended settings. Of course, you may want to change some or many of these. I have not included items such as Date & Time or Language, whose settings are obvious.

Setup Menu Settings for Auto Mode	
Silent Mode	Off (unless needed)
Image Display	1.5 Second
Frame No.	Continuous
Shutter Volume	Medium
Shutter Sound	Personal Preference
Playback Volume	Personal Preference
LCD Brightness	0
Auto Power Off	2 Minutes
Quick Start Mode	Off
Fn Button	ISO
RAW Button	RAW
IS Mode	Continuous + Motion
Red Eye Removal	Off
AF Illuminator	On
AE/AF-Lock Mode	P (On When Pressing)

Setup Menu Settings for Auto Mode	
AE/AF-Lock Button	AE-L
RAW	Off
Focus Check	On
Focus Control Dial	CW
Framing Guideline	Grid 9
Color Space	sRGB
Save Original Image	Off for all selections
Autorotate Playback	On
Background Color	Black
Guidance Display	On
Video System	NTSC (if in US)
Power Management	Power Save

There are still a few more settings you can make when the camera is in Auto mode. These are all controlled by the camera's physical buttons and dials, as follows:

Flash

If the built-in flash unit is popped up with the flash pop-up switch, you can then press the Flash button, which is the right direction button on the sub-command dial, to choose between Auto Flash and Forced Flash. For most purposes, I recommend Auto Flash when you are using the Auto shooting mode.

Drive Mode

If you press the top direction button on the sub-command dial, marked Drive, you will see a short menu with options for shooting rapid bursts of images. I recommend leaving this setting at its top option, called Still Image, in which the camera takes a single shot when you press the shutter button down.

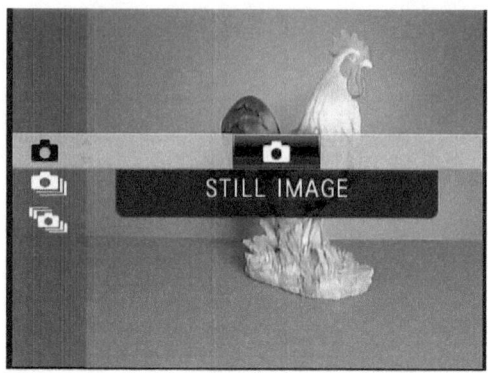

Self-timer

You can set the self-timer with the bottom direction button. For now, leave it in its Off position.

Focus Mode

The rotating switch on the front of the camera chooses among three methods of focusing. For now, leave it set to AF-S, for autofocus-single.

Those are all the settings that you can make in Auto mode. Note that two of the camera's controls—the exposure compensation dial at the right of the top of the camera and the WB button, which controls white balance, do not have any effect in Auto mode. If you operate them, nothing will happen.

EXR Mode

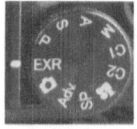

The next shooting mode on the mode dial is the EXR mode, which I discussed in Chapter 2 because one of its settings, EXR Auto, is the recommended setting for those who are new to this camera or to digital photography.

EXR is a special mode designed to let you take advantage of the

CHAPTER 3: THE SHOOTING MODES

unusual features of the Fujifilm X10's EXR CMOS image sensor. Most digital cameras today use a sensor that is designated as CCD, for charge-coupled device, or CMOS, for complementary metal oxide semi-conductor. The EXR designation is a proprietary technology of Fujifilm cameras. In essence, what EXR does is allow the sensor to change the configuration of the individual light-gathering sites on the sensor.

The sensor of the X10 camera has 12 million such sites, corresponding to the pixels of resolution that are available to create images; thus, the X10 is designated as a 12 megapixel (MP) camera. However, with the EXR technology, the sensor's behavior can be changed to emphasize one of three attributes: resolution, light-gathering, or dynamic range. In other words, either the camera, through its automatic circuitry, or you, the user, can decide whether to set up the EXR features of the sensor to emphasize one or the other of these values.

In practical terms, what this means is that, if there is plenty of light for a scene, the camera can emphasize resolution and use all 12 million of its pixels individually to make a high-resolution image. However, if the lighting is dim, the EXR technology lets the camera combine the pixels into groups of two pixels, each such pair having greater light-gathering abilities than any individual pixel. In that way, the camera can take clear images in low light, but, because the pixels are doubled up, there are only 6 million pairs of pixels available to create the image. Therefore, although the images may be quite clear and low in visual noise, they cannot exceed 6 MP of resolution.

Finally, if the lighting conditions are high in contrast, such as when part of the scene is in bright sunlight and part in dark shade, the EXR feature can cause one-half of the pixels to maintain high sensitivity to light, thereby pulling details out of shadow areas, and the other half of the pixels to use reduced light sensitivity, thereby avoiding blown-out, overexposed highlights in the bright areas.

In effect, the EXR shooting mode gives you a "switch" with

which to select among these three modes of operation, or to let the camera do so automatically. In order to use these settings, first you turn the mode dial to the EXR position. Then, you press the Menu/OK button to bring up the Shooting menu. In EXR mode, the top item on the Shooting menu is EXR Mode. Press the right direction button to move to the sub-menu, where you can select from the four available settings: EXR Auto; Resolution Priority; High ISO & Low Noise; and Dynamic Range Priority. I will describe these all in turn.

EXR Auto

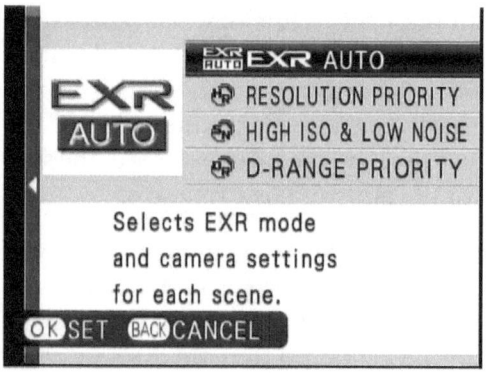

I discussed the EXR Auto mode in Chapter 2, because this is probably the best mode to use when you are just starting out with this camera, particularly if you are new to digital photography. If you select EXR Auto, the camera will take care of most settings for you, including focus. In fact, you cannot choose manual focus in this mode, even though it is controlled by a physical switch. You also cannot use the Custom display screen with features such as the histogram; that screen is unavailable in EXR Auto mode, though it is available in the other EXR shooting modes.

Also, you are letting the camera choose which of the three EXR settings to use: high resolution, low light, or high contrast. You will see the EXR Auto icon on a red background in the lower left corner of the LCD screen. To the right of that icon will be an icon representing a human head inside brackets and a

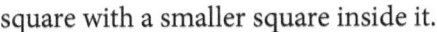

square with a smaller square inside it.

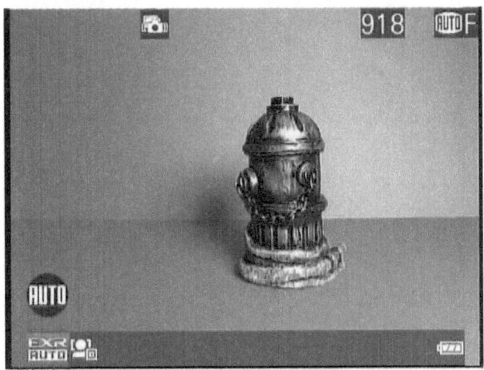

That icon means the camera is using its Face Detection feature, and is searching for and focusing on any human faces that it finds. If it finds one or more faces, it will place a green frame on the one nearest the center of the image, and white frames on others. Because of the constant searching for and focusing on faces, the battery will be drained more heavily than usual.

In addition, the camera will attempt to determine the general type of scene it is faced with, from a wide range of possibilities as set forth at page 28 of the X10 Owner's Manual. Those scene types include Landscape, Night, Macro, Beach, Sunset, and several others. The camera will also attempt to determine the main subject as being either a portrait, a moving object, a portrait with motion, or a non-portrait.

When you press the shutter button halfway to evaluate focus and exposure, the camera also evaluates the scene, the subject, and decides on the appropriate EXR mode—high resolution, low light, or high contrast. The camera will display corresponding icons in the lower left corner of the screen, just above the icon for the shooting mode. For example, in the image on the next page, in which the camera was aimed at a small toy knight on horseback at close range, the camera displayed the flower icon, indicating that the camera considers this to be a macro (close-up) shot.

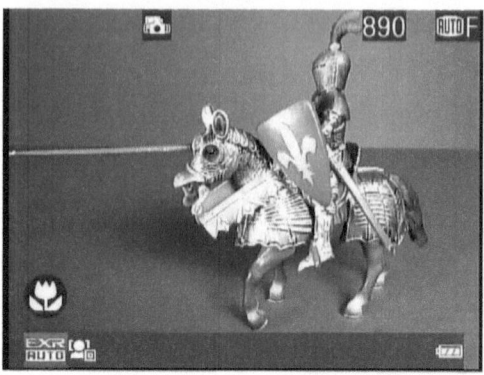

As I discussed earlier, the EXR Auto shooting mode is essentially a somewhat more-automatic alternative to the standard Auto shooting mode. In addition, it gives you the advantage of using the camera's EXR technology in difficult lighting conditions. If you feel as if you are in a situation in which the lighting is excessively dim or high in contrast, you might want to select this mode and let the camera do its best to help improve the situation with its EXR technology.

On the other hand, if you are certain that you need to take advantage of one or the other of the EXR system's features, you can take a more assertive approach and set the EXR mode manually. To do this, go into the Shooting menu while in EXR mode, and choose the top menu item, EXR Mode. Then scroll down to select one of the three choices other than EXR Auto. Those three choices are Resolution Priority, High ISO & Low Noise, and D-Range Priority. All three are described next.

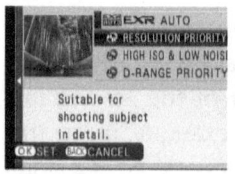 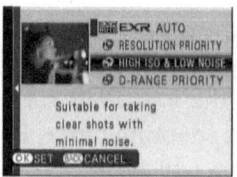 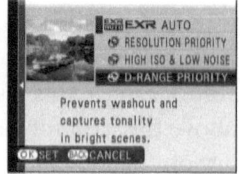

Resolution Priority

With this selection, the X10's sensor uses all of its pixels individually, to achieve the highest resolution possible. (Of course, if you select an image size that is not of the maximum size, the camera will use the smaller image size that you have selected.) You may want to select the Resolution Priority mode if you will need to make large prints from your images, or if you believe you may have to crop the image down to use a small part of it. The camera will display the HR icon in the lower left of the screen, to indicate High Resolution.

High ISO and Low Noise

This next selection is the one to use when you are faced with a low-light scene, such as a dimly-lit room or an outdoor area at twilight. This setting forces the EXR sensor to combine its pixels so they will gather light more efficiently, and consequently reduces the available number of pixels to 6 million rather than 12 million. This reduction will be reflected in the image size, which will change automatically to M, for Medium, if it had been set at L, for Large. The camera will display the SN icon, which represents the High ISO and Low Noise setting.

D-Range Priority

Finally, if you are faced with a scene that is partly in bright light and partly in shadow, you can force the sensor to emphasize dynamic range processing, which should even out the contrast to some extent. One important feature of this shooting mode is that it is the only mode in which you are able to set the camera's Dynamic Range setting, on the Shooting menu, to its highest values of DR800 and DR1600. In other modes, the maximum value for Dynamic Range is DR400. The camera will display the DR icon to indicate this setting.

In my experience it is not that big an advantage to make the Dynamic Range setting manually; if the dynamic range of a scene is an issue, I usually find it preferable just to use the EXR Auto shooting mode and let the camera determine the optimum setting for the Dynamic Range feature.

In summary, I suggest that you look upon EXR mode as a special group of settings for two particular types of scene—those with low light and those with high contrast. For other situations, I prefer to use Program mode and make various individual settings on the Shooting menu. But it is very nice to have the EXR mode settings available, because they allow you to quickly alter the behavior of the sensor to improve the quality of certain types of image.

Program Mode

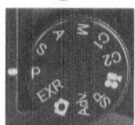

Choose the Program shooting mode by turning the mode dial to line up the P with the indicator mark. In this mode, the camera still uses its automation to select what it judges to be the best combination of shutter speed and aperture, but it also lets you adjust most of the settings available on the Shooting menu and through the camera's controls. This is the mode to use when you want to rely on the camera's judgment about exposure, but still retain the ability to override that judgment to some extent, and to tweak many other settings to achieve the appearance you want for your images.

I will discuss all of the Shooting menu settings in Chapter 4, and settings set with physical controls, including exposure compensation, in Chapter 5. There is one other setting that you can adjust in Program mode, Program Shift, which I will discuss here.

Program Shift is a feature that lets you alter the pair of values the camera selects in Program mode for shutter speed and aperture. For example, if the camera selects 1/160 second at f/2.0, the Program Shift feature will find equivalent combinations that result in the same exposure, such as 1/125 second at f/2.2, 1/100 second at f/2.5, or, as shown in the screen shot on the next page, 1/80 second at 2.8.

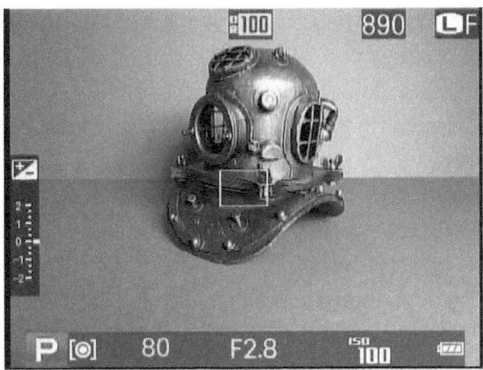

To use this option, when the camera is in Program mode, aim at your subject and let the camera's metering system evaluate the exposure. The selected shutter speed and f-stop (aperture setting) will appear to the right of the P for Program mode. Then, just turn either the sub-command dial or the main command dial right or left to find an equivalent set of shutter speed and aperture values. (If manual focus is in use, only the main command dial can be used for Program Shift.) When the camera is using one of these equivalent pairs of settings rather than the originally chosen setting, it displays those settings in yellow, as shown in the example here; the original settings selected by the camera will appear in white if you turn the control dial back to that point. If you want to cancel Program Shift without taking a picture, you can pop up the flash, which will turn off this feature, and then retract the flash again.

In some cases Program Shift is not available, and turning the sub-command or the main command dial will not change the camera's settings of aperture and shutter speed. Those cases are when the flash is turned on, when the Dynamic Range option on the Shooting menu is set to Auto, or when the ISO option on the Shooting menu is set to any of its Auto settings.

Why would you use the Program Shift option? Does it make sense to let the camera make its best calculation of the proper exposure and then alter the settings? Well, yes, it may, in some cases. For example, you may want to see what the "proper" exposure is, and then decide if you can use a somewhat wider aperture to achieve a blurred background, or a somewhat faster shutter speed to stop the action or prevent blur from camera motion. And, when you're experimenting with the camera to see what it is capable of, it can be very helpful to try various combinations of aperture and shutter speed to find out which combination gives you the best results in different situations. With a digital camera, there's no added cost for trying these different approaches, and Program Shift is one good way to experiment.

One way to look at Program mode is that it greatly expands the choices available through the Shooting menu. You will be able to make choices involving autofocus mode, picture quality, ISO sensitivity, film simulation, dynamic range, metering method, and others. I won't discuss all of those choices here; if you want to explore that topic, go to the discussion of the Shooting menu in Chapter 4 and check out all of the different selections that are available to you.

There is one limitation of Program mode that is worth remembering: With this mode, the slowest shutter speed that the camera will select is ¼ second. In some other modes, the camera can use shutter speeds as slow as 30 seconds. In Program mode, though, even if the lighting conditions would call for a speed of, say, 2 seconds, the camera will not set it. In that case, you could just switch to one of the other modes, such as Shutter Priority, Aperture Priority, or Manual exposure, and make the appropriate settings.

If the camera cannot achieve a proper exposure at any settings because the light is too bright or too dim, the shutter speed and aperture figures will display in red.

Shutter Priority Mode

In Shutter Priority mode, you choose whatever shutter speed you want, and the camera will set the aperture in order to

CHAPTER 3: THE SHOOTING MODES

achieve a proper exposure of the image. In this mode, you can set the shutter to be open for a variety of intervals ranging from 30 full seconds to 1/4000 of a second in some circumstances. If you are photographing fast action, such as a baseball swing or a hurdles event at a track meet and you want to stop the action with a minimum of blur, you will want to select a fast shutter speed, such as 1/1000 of a second. In other cases, for creative purposes, you may want to select a slow shutter speed to achieve a certain effect, such as leaving the shutter open to capture a trail of automobiles' taillights at night.

Controlling shutter speed is a powerful tool for creative photography. Here are some examples, using a working model of a Ferris Wheel that has white lights arranged on the rim of the wheel. All shots were taken indoors under artificial light.

For the first exposure, below, I used a shutter speed of 1/100 second, which was sufficient to stop the relatively slow motion of the wheel. In this image, the wheel is basically frozen in place; you can see details on the wheel and its structure.

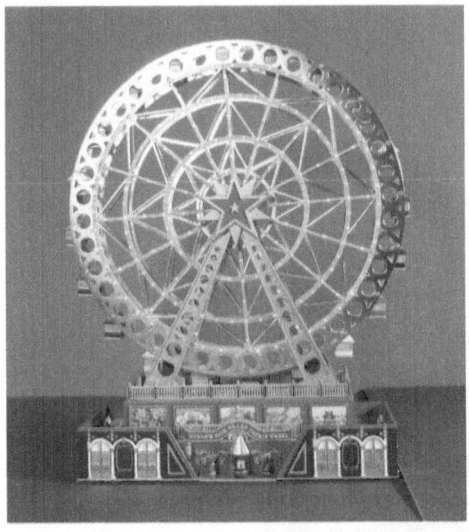

For the second exposure, shown next, I used a shutter speed of 1/10 second, considerably slower than with the first image, but still fast enough to make the wheel look as if it's stopped.

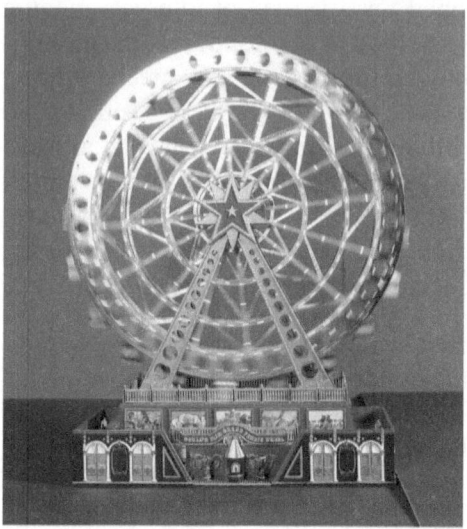

For the next photo, I used a shutter speed of 1/4 second. With this fairly slow shutter speed, the wheel is definitely blurred because of the motion that takes place during the exposure.

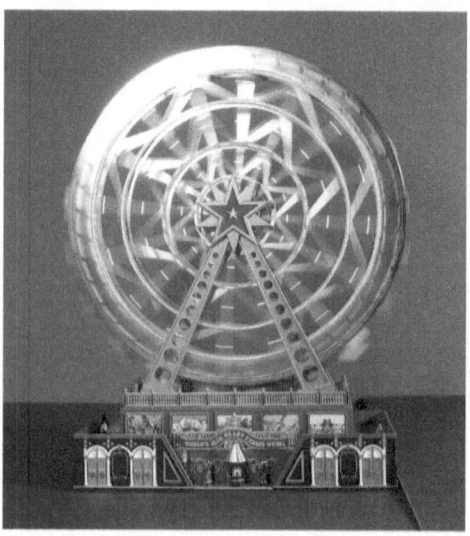

Finally, for the last shot, I use a shutter speed of one full second and turned out the lights in the room to allow the lights on the wheel to trace a complete set of circles. This approach resulted in solid trails of light traced by the wheel's bulbs as the wheel spun around in the dark room.

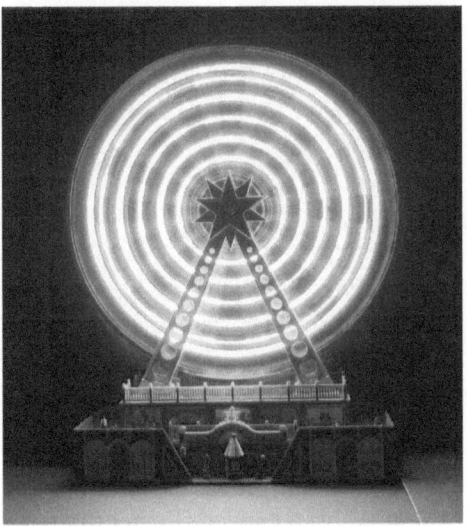

Using this very slow shutter speed essentially transformed the subject of the picture into a different object.

You select Shutter Priority mode by turning the mode dial to line up the letter S with the indicator mark. Then you select the shutter speed by turning either the main command dial or the sub-command dial. (If you are using manual focus, shutter speed is adjusted by the main command dial and manual focus is adjusted by the sub-command dial.) The LCD will display the selected shutter speed at the bottom left of the screen, immediately to the right of the S indicating Shutter Priority mode and the small white icon that indicates the metering mode. (The metering mode is discussed in Chapter 5.)

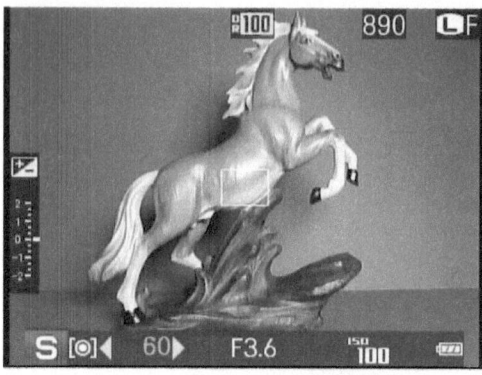

As you point the camera at scenes with varying lighting, the camera will select and display the appropriate aperture (such as f/3.6 in this example, displayed as F3.6 on the screen) to achieve a proper exposure.

Also, although the camera's overall range of shutter speeds is 1/4000 second to 30 seconds, not all these speeds are available in every situation. For example, shutter speeds longer than one second are not available when ISO is 2000 or higher, shutter speeds longer than two seconds are not available with ISO settings of 1000 or higher, and shutter speeds longer than four seconds are not available with ISO settings of 500 or higher.

After you have selected a shutter speed and pushed the shutter button halfway down, you need to watch the aperture number (F-number) on the display. If that number turns red, that means that proper exposure at the selected shutter speed is not possible at any available aperture, according to the camera's calculations. For example, if you set the shutter speed to 2 seconds in a well-lighted room, the shutter speed number may turn red, indicating that proper exposure is not possible. One good thing in this situation is that the camera will still let you take the picture, despite having changed the color of the number to warn you. The camera is saying, in effect, "Look, you may not want to do this, but that's your business. If you want an overly bright picture for some reason, help yourself." (Note: This situation is less likely to take place when you're in Aperture Priority mode, because in that mode, there is a wide range of shutter speeds for the camera to choose from—a range from 30 seconds to 1/4000 second in some situations, depending on certain factors, as discussed later in this chapter.)

Some other notes on the shutter speed numbers: When you are setting the shutter speed, the values will appear in different colors. A blue number means the speed is set appropriately. A red number means that the displayed value is not available in this particular situation because of the restrictions on certain settings that are programmed into the camera.

When setting the shutter speed, note that the faster values can be tricky to read, because only the denominators of the fractions are shown. For example, 1/500 second is shown as 500 and ½ second is shown as 2. The longer times may be easier to read; the camera displays them using quotation marks. So, for example, 2 seconds is displayed as 2", and 1.3 second is displayed as 1.3." In addition, any shutter speed of one second or longer is displayed in yellow, as an added reminder that this is a speed that may require the use of a tripod.

Also, three of the camera's shutter speeds are displayed as decimal numbers, such as 1.3. I would have trouble understanding that number without doing some arithmetic, so here is a brief chart that converts these few values into terms that may be easier to comprehend:

Shutter Speed Equivalents	
2.5	1/2.5 = 0.4 = 2/5 second
1.6	1/1.6 = 0.625 = 5/8 second
1.3	1/1.3 = 0.77 = 10/13 second (approx. 0.8 sec)

Aperture Priority Mode

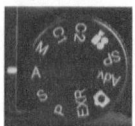

Aperture Priority mode is the inverse of Shutter Priority. You set this mode by turning the mode dial to the A position. Before discussing details of the settings for this mode, let's talk about what aperture is and why you would want to control it. The camera's aperture is a measure of the current width of its opening that lets in light to create the image. The aperture's width is measured numerically in f-stops. For the X10, the range of f-stops is from f/2.0 (wide open) to f/11.0 (most narrow). The amount of light that is let into the camera to create an image on the camera's sensor is controlled by the combination of aperture (how wide open the lens is) and shutter speed (how long the shutter remains open to let in the light).

For some purposes, you may want to control the aperture but still let the camera choose the corresponding shutter speed. Here are a couple of examples involving depth of field. Depth of field is a measure of how well a camera is able to keep multiple objects or subjects in focus at different distances from the lens. For example, say you have three of your friends lined up so you can see all of them, but they are standing at different distances—five, seven, and nine feet (1.5, 2.1, and 2.7 meters) from the camera. If the camera's depth of field is quite shallow at a particular focal length, such as five feet (1.5 meters), then, in this case, if you focus on the friend at that distance, the other two will be out of focus and blurry. But if the camera's depth of field when focused at five feet is deep, then it may be possible for all three friends to be in sharp focus in your photograph, even if the focus is set for the friend at five feet.

What does all of that have to do with aperture? One of the rules of photographic optics is that the wider open the camera's aperture is, the smaller its depth of field is at a given focal length. So in our example above, if you have the camera's aperture set to its widest opening, f/2.0, the depth of field will be relatively shallow, and it will be possible to keep fewer items in focus at varying distances from the camera. If the aperture is set to the narrowest opening, f/11.0, the depth of field will be considerably greater, and it will be possible to have more items in focus at varying distances.

The following images show the effects of aperture settings on depth of field, using three figurines and a poster with large print, so you can see the effects of the settings by how sharply focused the letters are. In these photos, for all of which I focused on the peacock, the peacock was 8.5 inches (21.5 cm) from the lens; the eagle in flight was at 55 inches (140 cm); the perched eagle was at 99 inches (2.5 m); and the poster was 10 feet 5 inches (3.18 m) from the lens.

For the first image below, the X10's aperture was set at f/2.2, almost the widest possible. With this setting, much of the image is out of focus, because the depth of field at this aperture was quite shallow. (I needed to zoom the lens in slightly in order to compose the shot properly, so I could not use f/2.0, which is available only at the full wide-angle position of the lens.)

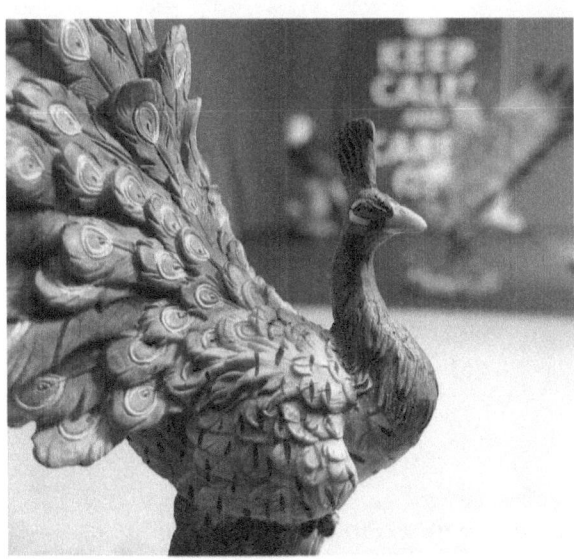

The second image, below, was taken with the aperture set to f/5.6, resulting in a considerably deeper depth of field, and consequently more of the image is in focus.

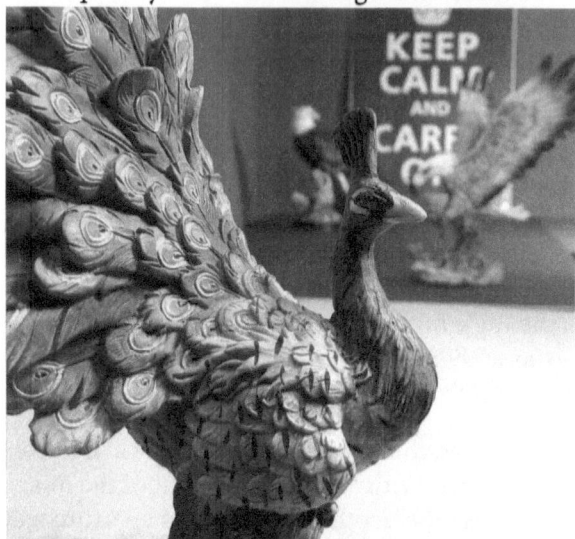

The third image, below, was taken with the aperture set to f/11.0, the most narrow aperture available with the X10.

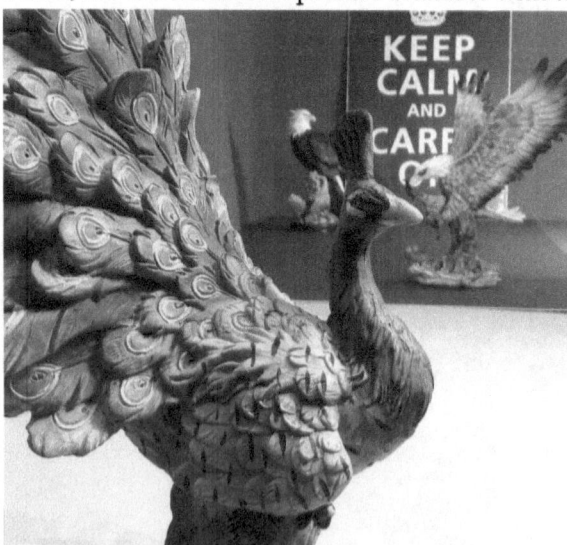

As you should be able to see, in the final image the depth of field is considerably greater than with either of the first two shots, and the image is quite sharp from the peacock all the way back to the sign.

These photos should illustrate fairly clearly the advantage of "stopping down" to a narrow aperture such as f/8 or f/11 when you want to enjoy a broad depth of field and keep as many subjects as possible in sharp focus.

In practical terms, if you want to have the sharpest picture possible, especially with subjects at varying distances from the lens that you want to be in clear focus, then you may want to control the aperture, and make sure it is set to one of the higher numbers (narrowest openings) possible. (However, if you choose the most narrow aperture, f/11.0 with the X10 camera, you do run some risk of an image that is blurred from the diffraction effect of a very narrow aperture.)

On the other hand, there are occasions when photographers prize a shallow depth of field. This situation arises often in the case of outdoor portraits. For example, you may want to take a photo of a person standing outdoors with a background of trees and bushes, but there are other, more distracting objects, such as a swing set or a tool shed, also in the background. If you can achieve a narrow depth of field, you can have the person's face in sharp focus, but leave the background quite blurry and indistinct. This effect is sometimes called "bokeh," a Japanese term describing an aesthetically pleasing blurriness of the background. You have undoubtedly seen images using this effect. In this situation, the blurriness of the background can be a great asset, reducing the distraction factor of unwanted objects and highlighting the sharply focused portrait of your subject. In the example shown on the next page, the X10 was set to a wide aperture of f/2.8, using a shutter speed of 1/40 second. The ISO setting was 800, under artificial lighting. With this wide aperture, the depth of field was shallow, so the small figurines are in sharp focus, while the busy background is blurred so as not to distract from the main subject.

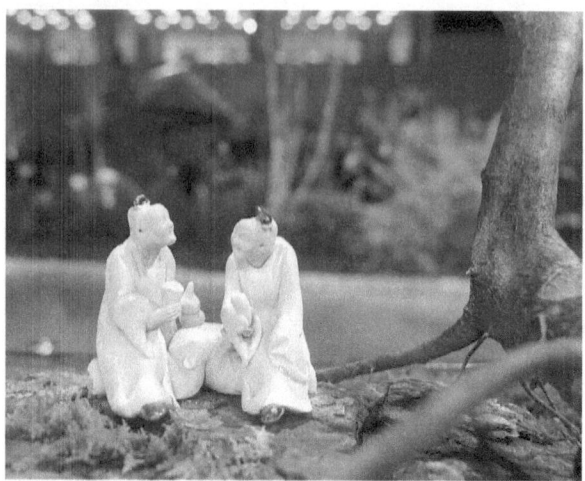

Here is how to make settings in this mode. Once you have moved the shutter speed dial on top of the camera to the A setting, the next step is quite simple. Aim the camera at your subject, and use either the main command dial or the sub-command dial to change the aperture. (If manual focus is in use, you will need to use the main command dial to change the aperture.) The number of the f-stop will appear at the bottom center of the display. The shutter speed chosen by the camera will show up also, to the left of the aperture.

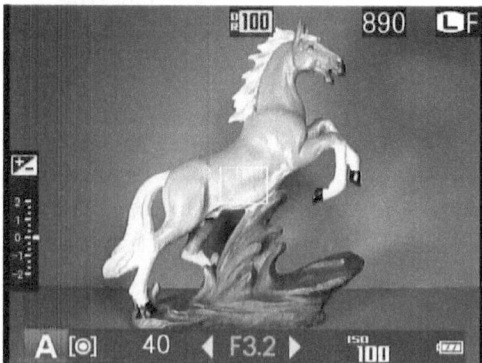

As with shutter speed, the aperture numbers, such as F3.2 in the example shown here, will appear in blue if they are appropriately set. If proper exposure cannot be achieved using the aperture you have set, because of underexposure or overexposure, the shutter speed number will display in red.

There are limitations on the settings that are available in Aperture Priority mode. For example, at f/2.0, the camera will not select a shutter speed faster than 1/1000, and to set the shutter speed at 1/4000, the aperture must be set at f/8 or f/11. The complete set of restrictions is shown in the following table:

Shutter Speed Range Restrictions	
1/4000 to 30 sec	Available at f/8 and f/11
1/2500 to 30 sec	Available at f/5.6 and smaller
1/2000 to 30 sec	Available at f/4 and smaller
1/1250 to 30 sec	Available at f/2.8 and smaller
1/1000 to 30 sec	Available at all apertures

Note: You cannot set the narrowest aperture, f/11, unless the camera is in Aperture Priority or Manual exposure mode. In all other modes, the smallest aperture available is f/9.0.

Manual Exposure Mode

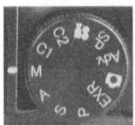

Next, the X10 has a fully manual shooting mode, which is a necessity for photographers who want to choose the best settings for any given lighting situation. This is not a mode you would use for taking snapshots at a party or when you are photographing quickly-unfolding events that won't be repeated. However, I have found myself using Manual mode more and more in certain situations. For example, I like to use Manual mode when I'm shooting indoors with artificial lighting with no time constraints. In this way, I can vary shutter speed, aperture, or both, to take shots with different levels of exposure, and choose the best one later, when editing them on my computer. Also, in unusual lighting situations, such as taking long time exposures after sunset, Manual mode lets you experiment until you find the effect you are looking for.

One situation in which I find Manual mode very helpful is in creating HDR (High Dynamic Range) images by merging multiple shots with different levels of brightness to create an image with a range of brightness values much greater than normal. When you create HDR images in software such as Photoshop, you need to take several shots of the same scene at different exposure levels, and then combine them in the software so the final image provides clear detail in both the shadowed and bright areas of the scene. One way some photographers create these images is by using autoexposure bracketing, which is a feature available with the X10, as discussed in Chapter 5.

In my experience, though, a better way to create the component images for HDR done with software is to take multiple shots at different exposure levels using Manual exposure mode. In this way, you can, for example, set the camera on a tripod with the aperture set to, say, f/5.6, and then take shots at shutter speeds of, say, 1/500, 1/250, 1/125, 1/60, 1/30, 1/15, and 1/8 second. If the metered exposure is at 1/60, half of the other shots will be underexposed and half overexposed. When all of these shots are combined in the HDR software, the resulting composite image should have the characteristic super-realistic look of HDR images. (There is an example of this type of HDR image in Chapter 4, in connection with the discussion of the X10's Dynamic Range settings.)

There are other times when Manual exposure mode can be of great use, including when you are looking for creative effects with underexposure or overexposure and you want to take several shots to decide which look is the best one. You also may want to use manual exposure in tricky lighting situations, when you're not sure the camera's metering system is giving the best possible exposure reading for the results you seek.

The technique for using Manual exposure mode is not too different from using Aperture Priority and Shutter Priority modes. To control exposure manually, turn the mode dial on top of the camera so the letter M is next to the white indicator line. To adjust shutter speed and aperture, you use the main command dial and the sub-command dial. There are some variations in how these controls work, though, depending on the focus mode, as discussed below.

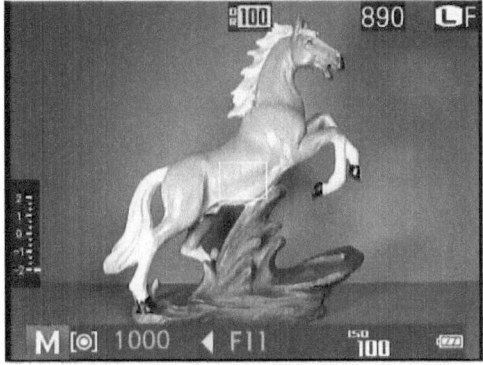

When the focus mode is set to autofocus with the rotating switch on the front of the camera, you can use either the main command dial or the sub-command dial to adjust either shutter speed or aperture. To switch the functions of the dials between those values, you press in on the center of the main command dial; it acts as a button, and switches the roles of the two dials between shutter speed and aperture. When this switching takes place, the camera displays a pair of yellow triangles around the value that is active.

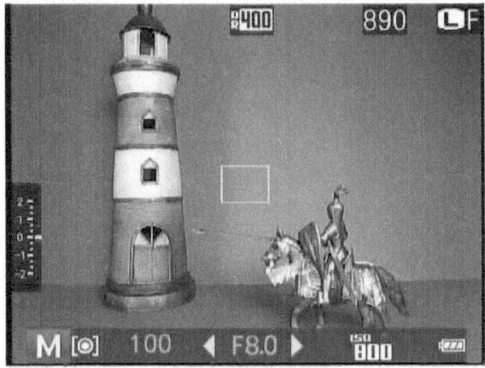

For example, in the image on the previous page, the triangles on either side of the F8.0 indicate that the main command dial is currently controlling aperture, which means the sub-command dial is controlling shutter speed. To make the main command dial control shutter speed instead, press in on the center of that dial, and the triangles will move to surround the shutter speed number. Note that, in the above image, there are two yellow triangles surrounding the aperture number; that means you can adjust that value either up or down. If there is only one yellow triangle, as in the previous image, that means you can adjust the value only in the direction of that triangle. In other words, the value is already set at its maximum or minimum possible level, given the current conditions.

When the camera is set to manual focus mode, the system works somewhat differently. In that case, the sub-command dial is always used to adjust focus, so it is not available to adjust aperture or shutter speed. Therefore, the main command dial will control either shutter speed or aperture; you can switch these functions by pressing in on the center of the main command dial. The value (shutter speed or aperture) that is marked by yellow triangles will be the value that is controlled by the main command dial; the value that is not inside the triangles will not be controlled by either dial, unless you switch the function of the dial by pressing in on it.

As with the other shooting modes, you will see a large letter, in this case M for Manual, at the lower left of the display. To the right of that letter will be the icon showing what metering mode is selected, and, to the right of that icon, the value for the shutter speed, and further to the right, in the center of the display, will be the aperture setting.

With Manual mode, there will be one added feature in the display—a vertical scale at the far left of the screen with values from -2 to +2 and a small white line that can move up and down at the right side of the scale. As you adjust the values for aperture and shutter speed, watch that small white line. As you continue to adjust either aperture or shutter speed, the small white line will move either upward or downward along the scale. If it moves upward, above the zero point, that means the current settings would result in an image that is overexposed, according to the metering system. If the line moves below the zero point, the resulting image would be too dark. If you want to select values that agree with the metering system, just adjust aperture, shutter speed, or both, until the white line is lined up with the zero point in the middle of the vertical scale.

Of course, you don't have to set the white line at the zero point; the line exists only to give you an idea of how the camera would meter the scene. You very well may want parts of the scene (or the whole image) to be darker or lighter than the metering would indicate to be "correct." With Manual exposure mode, the settings for aperture and shutter speed are independent of each other. When you change one, the other one stays unchanged until you change it manually. The camera is leaving the creative decision about exposure entirely up to you, even if the resulting photograph would be washed out by excessive exposure or underexposed to the point of near-blackness.

It's also worth noting that, in Manual mode, the camera's exposure compensation dial has no effect. You can turn it to a positive or negative value, but that value will not alter the exposure while the camera is set to Manual exposure mode.

Finally, as with other shooting modes, the camera's programming imposes restrictions on the combinations of shutter speed and aperture that you can set.

Scene Position Mode

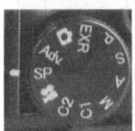

The next shooting mode to be discussed is Scene Position, which you select by turning the mode dial to the SP setting.

With this mode, the X10 gives you the choice of numerous specialized settings that are designed for use in particular situations. These scene types are rather different from the other shooting modes we have discussed. These settings do not have a single defining feature, such as permitting control over one or more aspects of exposure. Instead, when you select SP mode and then choose a particular scene type within that mode, you are in effect telling the camera what type of environment the picture is being taken in, and what type of image you are looking for, and you are letting the camera make a group of decisions as to what settings to use to produce that result.

Some photographers may not like scene modes because they take some creative decisions away from you and limit your options in some ways. For example, you will find that your options for setting the ISO, controlling the flash, and choosing Film Simulation settings are restricted with many of the SP types. In most cases, you cannot use macro focusing, you cannot use bracketing for any of the modes, and you can't choose your autofocus mode or your metering mode or set the white balance for any of the SP selections. You cannot shoot RAW images with any of the scene types. You can, however, use exposure compensation with all selections other than Fireworks. (For a chart of the restrictions in various shooting modes, see pages 126-129 of the X10 Owner's Manual.)

Despite the limitations, though, I have found the various SP settings to be quite useful in certain situations. Remember that you don't have to use the various settings only for their labeled purposes; you may find that some of them offer particular photographic approaches that are well-suited for some shooting scenarios that you are regularly faced with. For example, you may find the Sport setting works well for shots of children at play, or that the Sunset setting, which emphasizes red hues, is great for images in a particular garden that is rich with reddish plants and flowers.

When you first turn the mode dial to SP, if the camera is still

CHAPTER 3: THE SHOOTING MODES

using its default settings, the Portrait choice within the SP mode will be selected. Assuming you have the display set to Standard mode (press the Display button one or more times to activate it if necessary), you will see an icon of a person's head on a red background at the lower left of the LCD display.

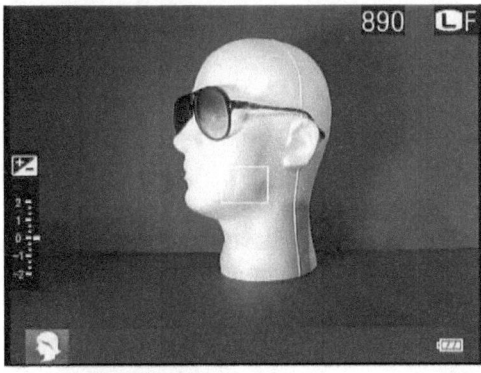

To change to one of the 15 other varieties of SP settings, press the Menu button to enter the menu system, and highlight the first item at the top of the first menu screen, which will be Scene Position when the camera is in SP mode. Press the right button to move to the sub-menu that lists the 16 different choices: Natural & Flash, Natural Light, Portrait, Portrait Enhancer, Landscape, Sport, Night, Night (Tripod), Fireworks, Sunset, Snow, Beach, Underwater, Party, Flower, and Text.

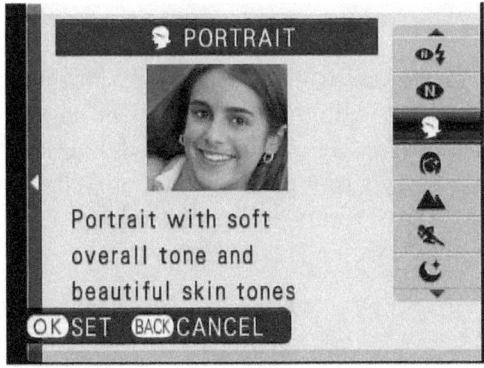

Following are some details about each of the 16 scene types.

75

Natural & Flash

This first setting on the Scene Position menu is a good one to use if you are undecided as to whether it would be helpful to use flash for a particular shot. In Natural & Flash mode, the camera takes two shots in rapid succession, the first one without flash and the second one with the flash forced on. It is actually quite a useful mode, because sometimes you may believe that Fill Flash would be helpful, but you may not be certain, and you may be taking a shot that cannot easily be repeated, such as a portrait of a group of restless kids who have assembled briefly and will disperse very soon.

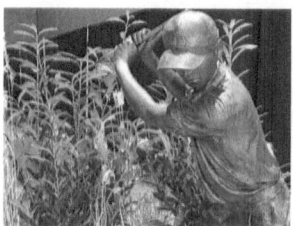 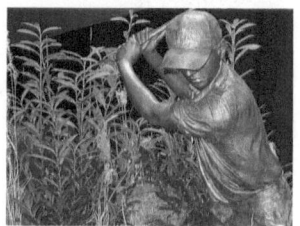

As you can see from the examples above, the appearances of the shots can differ considerably; even though both are reasonably well exposed, there is a distinctly different "look" from the natural-light shot on the left to the one taken with flash. The camera allows the use of macro focusing in this mode, although you cannot use such focusing in most other SP modes.

Natural Light

This scene type is similar to the no-flash aspect of Natural & Flash, but it is described by Fujifilm as intended for shooting under "low-light conditions." I have found that the camera tends to boost the ISO in this mode, to produce a well-exposed image without having to resort to excessively long shutter speeds or the use of flash, which is disabled.

CHAPTER 3: THE SHOOTING MODES

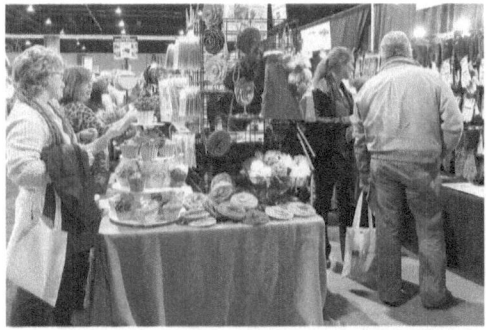

In this mode, unlike any of the other 15 choices for Scene Position, you can use Super Macro focusing and Macro focusing. In a few others, you can use Macro, but none permit Super Macro except for Natural Light.

Portrait

This mode is for taking portraits of individuals. You have the ability to take continuous shots, though not at the highest speeds. This system makes sense, because, although it is useful to take multiple shots in portrait sessions in order to catch fleeting expressions, there is no need for the super-high-speed shooting that you might need to capture sporting events.

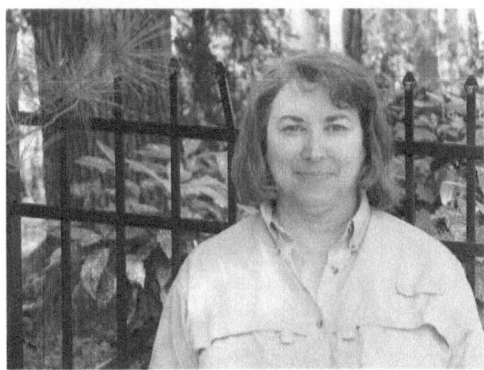

Portrait Enhancer

In this mode, also intended for portraits, the camera attempts to impart a smoother appearance to the skin of the subject.

77

Here, again, you can use slower-speed burst shooting. You cannot, however, use manual focus with this setting; this is the only Scene Position setting that does not permit the use of manual focus.

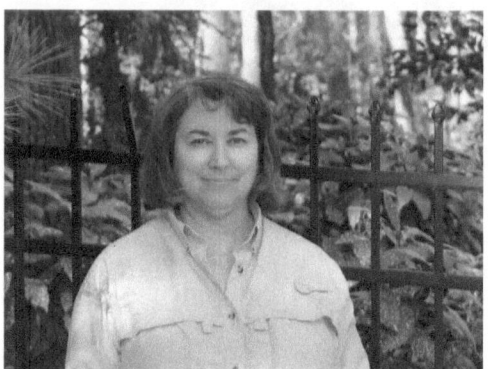

Landscape

The Landscape option is one I have used quite a bit for shots of scenery, like the one below of woods near a river bank.

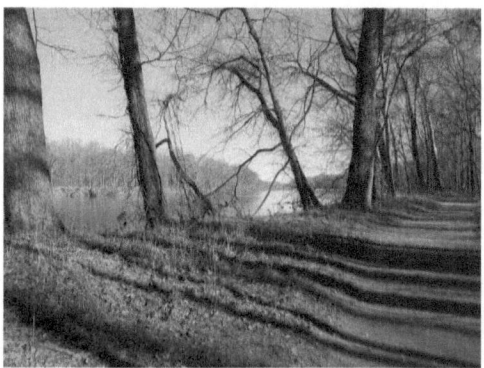

With this option, the X10 disables all use of flash, but, oddly enough, it allows you to set all speeds of burst shooting, including the most rapid shots. It sets white balance for daylight, and you cannot change that setting, so you probably will not want to use this setting under artificial lighting.

Sport

With the Sport setting, the camera boosts the ISO to a relatively high level, such as 1600, so it can use a rapid shutter speed to stop action. The camera enables the use of all speeds of continuous shooting, so you can choose to fire off a rapid burst to capture fast-moving events.

Night

The Night variety of Scene Position is one of the X10's multiple tools for shooting images in low-light conditions. With this option, the camera sets itself up for making a reasonably clear exposure without a tripod in dim lighting. However, although this mode is intended to capture the scene with ambient light, the X10 will still permit you to turn on the flash, but only in Slow Synchro mode. (I'll discuss Slow Synchro in Chapter 9; essentially, in that mode, the camera uses a slow shutter speed to capture the background with ambient light.) In Night mode, the camera selects a relatively high ISO value in order to expose the scene sufficiently without using a shutter speed so slow as to lead to blurring from camera motion.

Night (Tripod)

With this mode, the camera is programmed to use a lower ISO value, such as ISO 100, and a slow shutter speed, in order to create an image with optimum quality. The idea, of course, is that the camera is on a tripod, and the slow shutter speed therefore will not result in blur from camera motion during the long exposure. As with the previous setting, you can use the flash, but in Slow Sync mode only.

Fireworks

With the Fireworks option, the camera sets a shutter speed of two full seconds so it can capture the full range of a burst of fireworks. It uses a low ISO in order to maximize the quality of the image. Of course, you should place the camera on a tripod, unless you would like to have an image with streaks of light resulting from camera motion during the exposure.

Sunset

With the Sunset option, the camera adjusts its color settings to emphasize the reddish tones of sunrise and sunset images.

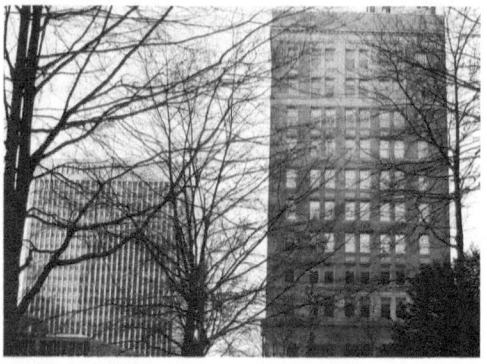

Of course, you are not limited to using this setting at sunrise and sunset; you can use it for any situation in which you would like to place emphasis on that range of colors. The example shown here was taken in the early morning, when the sun was casting some reddish rays toward the building.

Snow

The Snow setting is designed to let you get natural-looking images against a bright backdrop of white snow. The camera adjusts its color settings to counteract the bluish color temperature of a snowy atmosphere. It also lets you set the flash to Auto Flash or Forced Flash, which you may want to do if you are taking a picture of a person; you may need a fill-flash in order to overcome the contrast caused by the camera's exposure for the snow.

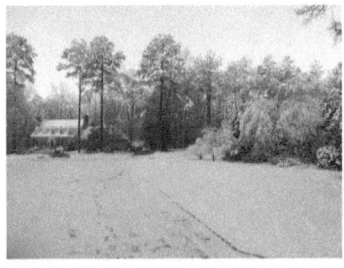 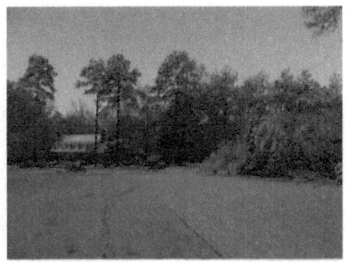

I took the shots above to illustrate how the camera processes the same scene using the Snow and Sunset settings. For the image on the left, taken with the Snow setting, the camera boosted the exposure enough to compensate for the brightness that would otherwise cause the camera to reduce exposure. For the shot on the right, taken with the Sunset setting, the camera did not boost the exposure, but changed the color balance somewhat to emphasize the reddish hues of the sunlight.

Beach

With the Beach setting, the camera again uses a Daylight white balance setting and gives you the option of using the flash in order to compensate for the brightness of the scene, which otherwise might put a human subject into shadow.

Underwater

This setting is intended for use when the camera is in a protective housing and shooting underwater. The camera sets its color balance to counteract the bluish light that prevails underwater. You can use the flash if you want to.

Party

With this setting, the camera is likely to use a high ISO on the assumption that the lighting is dim. The flash mode will be set to Auto, and you do not have the option to turn it off (unless you decline to pop up the flash unit). So, if the camera decides flash is needed, it will fire, with Red Eye Removal activated.

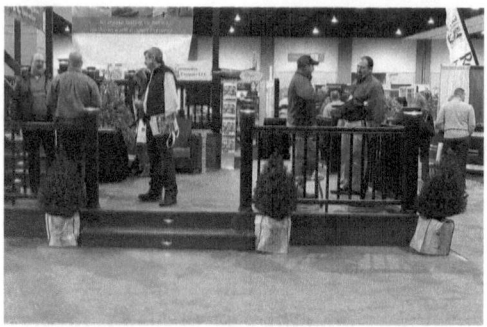

In the example shown here, the camera used a relatively high ISO of 800 and was able to expose the image at f/2.0 for 1/160 second. The camera did not use flash, because the available lighting was relatively bright.

Flower

The Flower option is set up for taking close-up shots of colorful flowers and plants. The camera sets its focus to macro and alters its color processing to increase the vividness of the colors. In addition, it disables the flash.

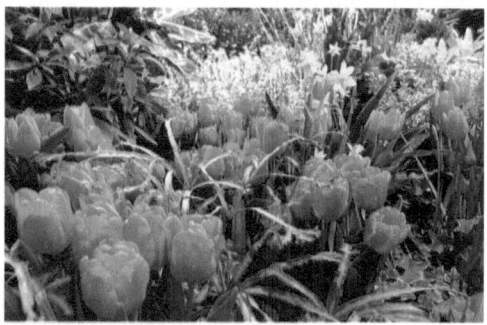

The example shown here illustrates how the camera boosts the vividness of the flowers' colors.

Text

The final choice for Scene Position settings, Text, is intended for when you are using your X10 more as a portable copy machine than for photography. The camera uses a relatively high

ISO setting, if called for, so you can use a fast shutter speed to avoid blur. It turns on macro focus and allows you to turn on the flash if you believe it is needed. It sets the Sharpness value to Hard in order to achieve crisp, clear rendering of text.

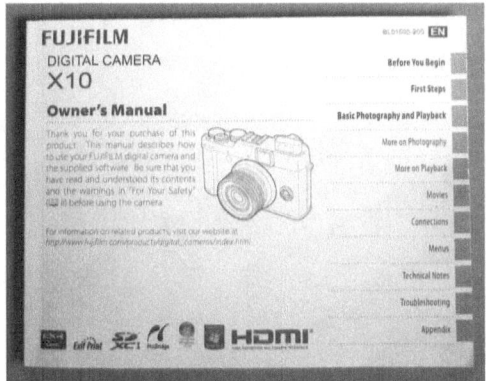

In this example, I used the Text setting to capture an image of the cover of the X10 Owner's Manual under artificial lighting. You can easily use the Text setting to make quick copies of receipts, notes, recipes, or other items, without having to find a photocopy machine

Advanced Mode

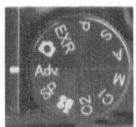

Next to SP on the mode dial is the mode labeled Adv., for Advanced. The word "advanced" in this situation refers more to the camera's functioning than to the experience level of the photographer. In other words, this mode allows you to accomplish some advanced results without necessarily having a lot of background in photography. The mode includes specialized settings for three particular types of photography: panoramas, shots with purposely blurred backgrounds, and shots taken in dim lighting.

When you turn the mode dial to the Advanced setting, the

menu system changes so that the first item at the top of the Shooting menu is now called Adv. Mode. When you press the right direction button to move to the sub-menu, you are presented with three options—Motion Panorama, Pro Focus, and Pro Low-Light. I will discuss each of these below.

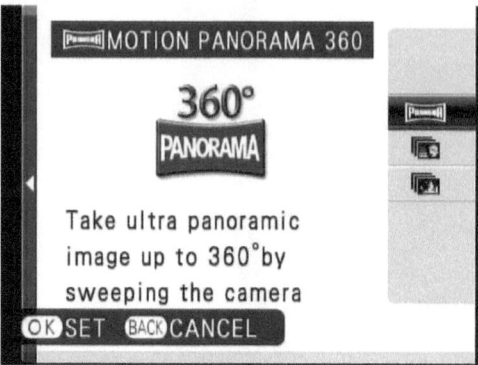

Panorama

To select Panorama, highlight the top choice on the sub-menu, press the OK button, then press the Back button or press the shutter button halfway to exit back to the shooting screen.

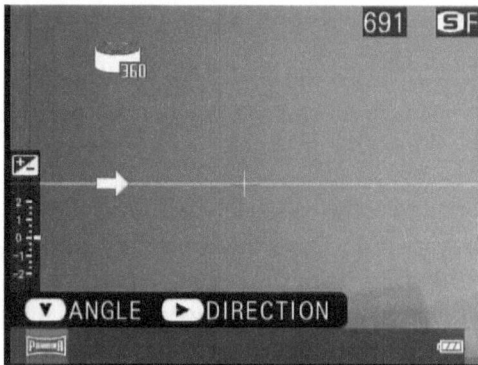

Now you will see prompts on the screen indicating that you can press the down direction button to select the angle or the right button to select the direction. If you press the down button, you are taken to a screen letting you choose the angle in degrees: 120, 180, 360 normal, or 360 seamless. If you choose

360 seamless, the camera will record the panorama in a loop that will play back in a way that makes it appear to have no starting or ending point.

Once you have chosen the desired angle, you can, if you wish, press the right button to select the direction in which you will move the camera—left to right, bottom to top, top to bottom, or right to left. If you don't make a selection, the camera will use whatever choice was previously selected.

After both the angle and direction have been set, aim at the first part of your panoramic scene and keep the camera as level and steady as possible. You will get the best results using a tripod with a smoothly-panning head (or a tilting one, for vertical panoramas). If you don't have a tripod available or prefer not to use one, you might try wrapping the camera's strap around your neck and holding the camera out from your body with the strap tight to stabilize it. However, with the X10 I have had good results hand-holding the camera and keeping it as steady as possible while panning slowly from left to right.

When you are ready, press and release the shutter button, and move the camera slowly through the full extent of your chosen angle in the direction you chose. When you have moved it completely through that angle, the camera will stop shooting. The exposure is set with the first frame, and it will not vary through the rest of the shots the camera takes to create the panorama. If you can see ahead of time that you want to expose the panorama for lighting conditions that will be in the middle or later part of the shot, you can aim at that part of the scene and press the shutter button down halfway to lock exposure before starting to shoot the panorama.

If you press the shutter release button all the way down while the panorama is in progress, the shooting will stop.

On the next page, I am including two sample panoramas. The outdoor one was taken with the camera on a tripod; for the indoor one, the camera was handheld.

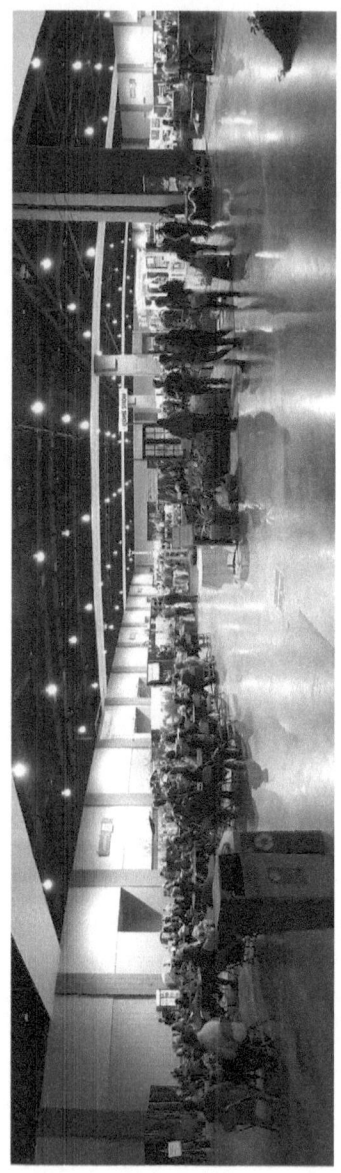
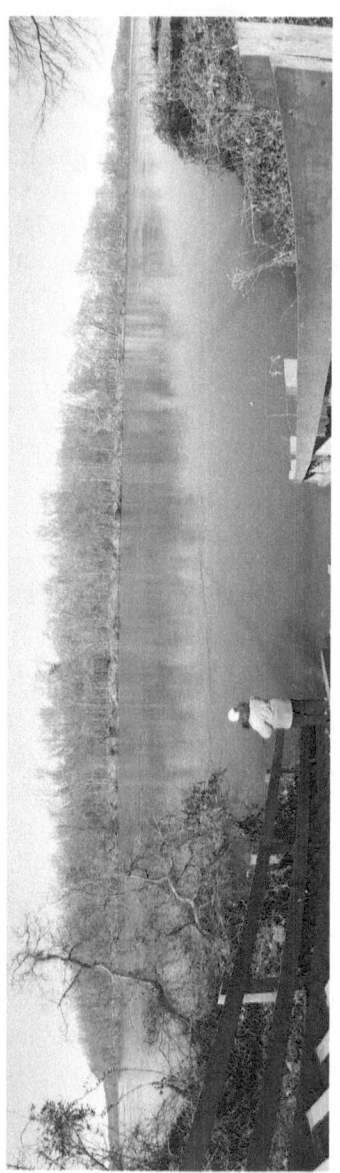

Here is a tip for getting the maximum resolution for your panoramas. With the X10, the resolution for each type of panorama is greater for vertical panoramas than for horizontal ones. For example, if you are shooting a 120-degree panorama in the horizontal mode, the resolution is 3840 tall x 1080 pixels wide. However, if you shoot a 120-degree panorama in the vertical mode, the resolution is 3840 tall x 1624 wide.

So, if you want to shoot a horizontal panorama with the maximum resolution, just set the camera to shoot a vertical panorama, but hold the camera sideways, with the left or right side in the air, and pan it around horizontally.

Pro Focus

The next selection for Advanced Mode on the Shooting menu is the Pro Focus mode.

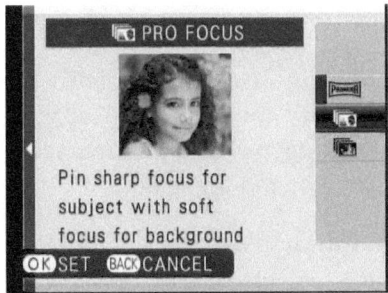

This feature simulates the blurred background or "bokeh" that is more readily produced by DSLRs and other cameras with larger sensors. As I discussed in connection with Aperture Priority mode, bokeh ordinarily is produced when you take a picture at a wide-open aperture such as f/2.0. The effect is particularly distinctive when the lens is zoomed in, the foreground subject (which is to be sharply focused) is fairly close to the lens, and the background (which is to be blurred) is separated from the main subject by a fair distance.

With a camera such as the X10, which does not have as large a sensor as a DSLR, it is somewhat difficult to create the blurred-background effect. The Pro Focus mode gives you another way to achieve this sort of effect, through a different approach.

With the Pro Focus mode, the camera takes a rapid burst of shots, either two or three, with different focus points. In other words, it takes one shot with normal focus and then at least one other with the background purposely de-focused. The camera then combines the multiple shots internally to produce a composite image with a background that is more blurry than would be possible using the wide-aperture effect alone.

After selecting Pro Focus from the Advanced Mode sub-menu, press the Back button to return to the live image. You then can turn the main command dial or the sub-command dial to select the intensity of the effect, from level 1 through 3. The camera will then display a number on the screen showing how many images will be taken to achieve the effect; that number may be the same as the intensity level, or it may be different.

To use this mode, the subject to be in focus must be fairly far in front of the background; if they are not sufficiently separated, the camera will give you a warning message, Cannot create effect! In that case, rearrange the shot and try again.

I have found this effect to be most useful when using the lens at its wider-angle settings. When the lens is more zoomed in, it is fairly easy to achieve this effect just by using a wide aperture. But when you use Pro Focus, even at the widest angle of 28mm, the effect is quite dramatic, as shown below.

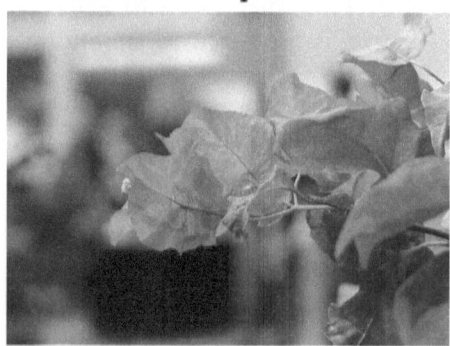

This shooting mode, like other special modes, comes with several limitations, most notably that the composite images produced will be no larger than Medium in size, and, of course, cannot be RAW. If you would like to save the unprocessed images that are used to create the composite image, you can do so if you turn on the Save Org Image option on the Setup menu, as discussed in Chapter 7.

Pro Low-Light

The third and final choice on the Advanced Mode sub-menu is the Pro Low-Light mode.

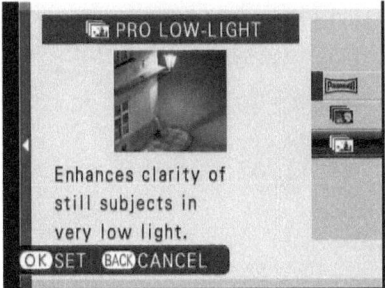

As I noted earlier, the X10 gives you several tools for taking usable images in dim light, including the Night and Night (Tripod) choices in Scene Position mode. You also can use settings in the EXR shooting mode, including the Advanced Anti Blur setting in EXR Auto mode and the High ISO & Low Noise sub-mode of EXR mode. Of course, you also have the option of using Program mode or another standard shooting mode and selecting a high ISO setting, up to the elevated level of 12800 ISO. With that sort of setting, however, comes the inevitable visual "noise," or graininess that can mar the image.

Pro Low-Light mode is designed to give you the benefits of a high ISO setting without so much of the bothersome noise. With this setting, when you press the shutter button the camera rapidly takes four shots at high ISO settings (if called for by the lighting conditions) and then quickly combines them internally into a composite image. If all goes as planned, the final result will be well exposed and will not exhibit as much noise as a single shot would at that ISO level, because the camera is able to combine the pixels from the four images in such a way as to smooth out the grain and reduce the noise.

The Pro Low-Light mode is useful when you need to shoot in a dimly lighted area with no flash or other artificial lighting, and no tripod. (If you put the camera on a tripod, you could lower the ISO and use a long shutter speed, thereby reducing the risk of noise in the image.) When handholding the camera in this mode, you need to hold the camera quite still so it can shoot several images that are able to be combined into a composite. For the example below, I handheld the camera for a shot with dim lighting, and the result was quite acceptable.

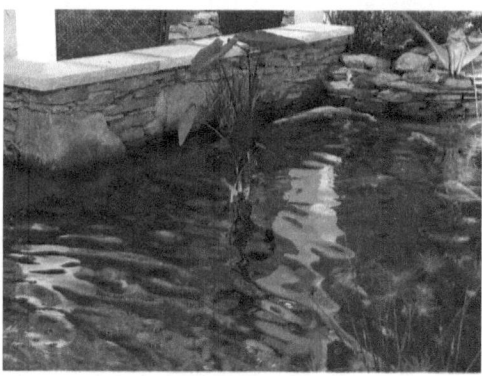

This mode has limitations similar to those for Pro Focus mode, including the use of images no larger than Medium size. And, as with the previous mode, you can save the component images using the Save Org Image selection on the Setup menu.

Finally, it's worth noting that the Pro Low-Light setting is actually the functional equivalent of the Advanced Anti Blur option, which can be used only in the EXR Auto shooting mode. However, if you turn on Advanced Anti Blur, the camera will decide whether or not to use it. If you want to make sure the camera uses this sort of multiple-shot processing in low-light conditions, you should use the Pro Low-Light setting.

The Custom Shooting Modes: C1 and C2

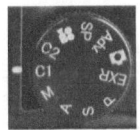

The final two shooting modes are labeled C1 and C2 on the mode dial. When you turn the mode dial to one of these two settings, you are not selecting a shooting mode that has its own set of characteristics, like the modes discussed above. Instead, these two modes are really like two blank slates, or like empty bins into which you can store a set of your favorite settings from the four standard shooting modes: Program, Aperture Priority, Shutter Priority, and Manual, as well as most EXR modes, along with certain menu settings.

Each of these two slots gives you the ability to set up several parameters on the Shooting menu for a particular type of shooting session and then save them to this spot on the mode dial for instant recall by turning the dial to that position.

In other words, using the two Custom shooting mode slots, you can store your two favorite combinations of settings, and, with a quick turn of the mode dial, you can recall either one of those two sets at any time.

This system is convenient because it lets you quickly set up the camera for a particular type of shooting without having to go into several menu items individually to change their settings.

Here is how this option works. First, using the mode dial, select one of the shooting modes whose settings can be stored in the C1 or C2 slot: Program, Aperture Priority, Shutter Priority, Manual, EXR-Resolution Priority, EXR-High ISO & Low Noise, or EXR-D-Range Priority. (You cannot store values for EXR Auto or for any modes other than those listed here.)

Next, go into the Shooting menu and set the following items as you want them: ISO, Image Size, Image Quality, Dynamic Range, Film Simulation, WB Shift, Color, Sharpness, Highlight Tone, Shadow Tone, Noise Reduction, Intelligent Digital Zoom, Face Detection, Face Recognition, AF Mode, Flash, and External Flash. (All of these settings are discussed in Chapter 4.)

Then, on the Setup menu, adjust the settings for AF Illuminator and RAW as you like.

Finally, using the camera's physical controls, as discussed in Chapters 2 and 5, select your desired values for metering, White Balance, Drive mode (burst or bracketing), Macro focus, Flash mode, Program Shift, shutter speed, aperture, and monitor display options as set by the Display/Back button.

Because of the wide range of options that can be stored to the C1 and C2 slots, this feature is quite powerful. It is probably best illustrated with a specific example. Let's say you have a hobby, or a business, involving miniature figures, and you periodically need to photograph a new figure using a certain group of settings. Rather than laboriously entering all of those settings into the camera every time you have a new photo session, you can store those settings to one of the Custom slots and recall them instantly whenever you need to.

For example, let's say the settings you use for the images of the miniatures are the following:

Sample Settings for Custom Shooting Mode	
Shooting Mode	Aperture Priority
ISO	200
Image Size	L 4:3
Image Quality	Fine
Dynamic Range	100%
Film Simulation	Velvia
WB Shift	Neutral
Color	Medium-High
Sharpness	Medium-Hard

Sample Settings for Custom Shooting Mode

Highlight Tone	Medium-Soft
Shadow Tone	Standard
Noise Reduction	Low
Intelligent Digital Zoom	Off
Face Detection	Off
Face Recognition	Off
AF Mode	Area
Flash	0
External Flash	Off
AF Illuminator	Off
RAW	Off
Metering	Spot
White Balance	K at 2700 Kelvins
Drive Mode	Still Image
Macro Focus	Super Macro
Program Shift	Not Used
Shutter Speed	(Not Applicable in A Mode)
Aperture	f/2.0
Monitor Display Option	Custom

When all settings are made and the camera is aimed at your figure, your screen should like something like the image below.

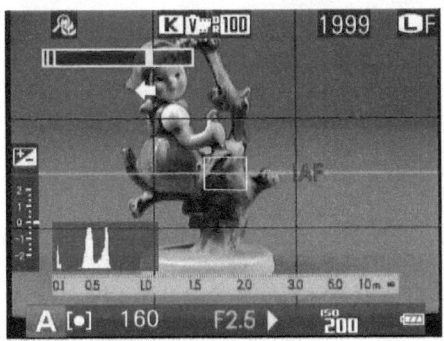

If you zoom in somewhat, as shown here, the aperture will

change to a slightly more narrow one, here f/2.5, because the widest aperture available varies as the lens is zoomed in to longer focal lengths. The resulting photograph should like the image shown below.

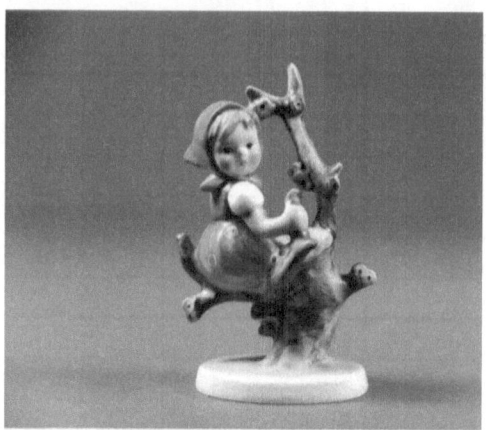

To lock in all of these settings, on the Shooting menu go to the Custom Set item, which is the next-to-last item on the menu, press the right direction button to go to the next screen, and highlight C1 (or C2), then press the right button again, and, on the final screen, highlight OK and press the Menu/OK button.

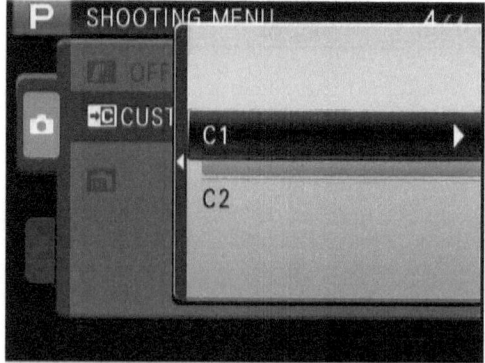

Your settings are now saved to the C1 slot on the mode dial. To test this system, you might try setting the camera to a very different group of settings, such as, say, Manual exposure, ISO 6400, Image Size Small, Film Simulation Black and White, and any others you like. Then, just turn the mode dial back to C1 and watch the previous settings pop right back into place.

Also, of course, don't forget that you can change any settings you have made, even after switching to a custom group of settings using the C1 or C2 slot. For example, if you use the group of settings included in the table discussed earlier, with Film Simulation set to Velvia, you can switch that setting to, say, Black & White - Red Filter, to take a few shots. Of course, the settings that are saved to the C1 or C2 slot will not change unless you take the further step of choosing the Custom Set option on the Shooting menu and saving the current settings to one of those slots.

As you can see, the Custom modes provide you with a powerful ability to store one or two sets of preferred settings. It's a good idea to experiment with this tool and fine-tune its use until you have the two "perfect" groups of settings stored in your C1 and C2 slots. Personally, I like to store a group of settings for street photography (as discussed in Chapter 9); I haven't yet found a need for a second slot, but I am glad to have the option available when the need arises.

Chapter 4: The Shooting Menu

Much of the power of the X10 lies in the many options included in the Shooting menu, which provides the user with considerable control over the appearance of the images and how they are captured. With the X10, perhaps more than with most compact cameras, it is important to become familiar with the items on the Shooting menu, because some of the camera's more basic options, such as ISO, image size, image quality, and autofocus mode are accessible only in that way, unless you program the Fn button or the RAW button (discussed in Chapter 5) to summon one of those items.

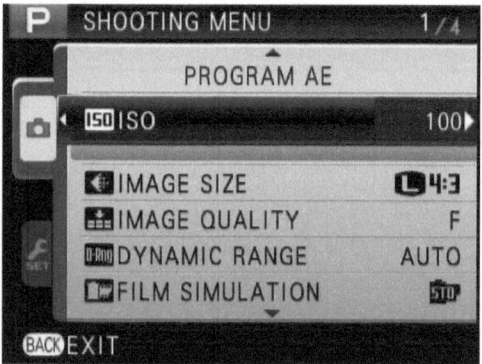

The Shooting menu on the X10 is quite easy to use once you have played around with it a bit. To get access to this menu, press the Menu/OK button in the center of the sub-command dial on the back of the camera, and the first of the menu's four screens will appear on the display. (I'm assuming the camera

CHAPTER 4: THE SHOOTING MENU

is in Program mode; in some other shooting modes there are fewer than four menu screens.)

To navigate through the items on the menu screens, turn the sub-command dial or use the up and down direction buttons to move the selection bar from one item to the next. The menu will automatically advance to the next screen as you scroll down from the last item on a screen. You can wrap around from the bottom of the last screen to the top of the first screen, and from the top of the first screen to the bottom of the last screen. So, for example, if the selection bar is on the Flash item on the third screen and you want to move to the Image Quality item on the first screen, the quickest way to do so is to scroll down through the last two screens, and then wrap around back to the Image Quality item on the first screen.

In some situations, the available menu options will change depending on the camera's current settings. For example, in Movie mode the Shooting menu options are very limited, because very few options are available for setting when movies are being shot. Also, if you are shooting panoramas in the Advanced shooting mode, certain items, such as ISO and Image Size, will appear "grayed out" on the menu screens, so you can still read them but cannot select them, because they are incompatible with the current setting, as shown below.

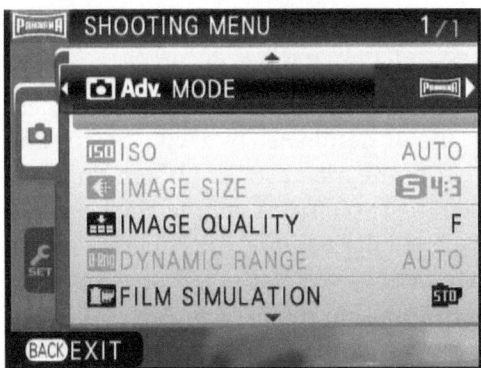

When you have highlighted a menu item you want to adjust, press either the right direction button or the Menu/OK button (in the center of the sub-command dial) to move to the screen with choices for the setting. For example, once you have highlighted the ISO menu item, press the Menu/OK button or the right direction button and you will see a sub-menu screen with the available choices. Use the up and down buttons or turn the sub-command dial to highlight the selection you want, and then press either the left direction button or the Menu/OK button to confirm the selection.

Once you are done making your selection for a menu item, press the Display/Back button at the bottom left of the control area on the right of the camera's back to exit the menu system. Or, if you prefer, you can press the shutter button down halfway to return to the shooting screen.

Now I will discuss all of the options that are available through the Shooting menu. For the following discussion, I'm assuming you have the camera set to Program mode, rather than Movie mode or one of the other shooting mode options. In Program mode, you have access to most of the options that are available on the Shooting menu. Of course, there are some options on the Shooting menu screens that appear only when the camera is set to other modes, such as EXR, Advanced, or Scene Position. Those menu options were discussed in connection with the discussions of those shooting modes in Chapter 3.

One final note before discussing the Shooting menu options: In the menu system, when the camera is in shooting mode, besides the Shooting menu, which is marked by a red camera icon, there is the Setup menu, designated by a wrench icon and the word SET, at the left of the menu screen. When the camera is in playback mode the two choices are the Playback and Setup menus. For now, I will discuss only the Shooting menu, designated by a capital letter at the upper left of the screen, standing for the current shooting mode: P, S, A, or M, or an appropriate label or icon when the camera is set to another shooting mode, such as EXR, Advanced, or Scene Position.

On the Shooting menu, you'll see a fairly long list of options.

Each option (such as ISO) occupies one line, with its name on the left and its current setting (such as 800) on the right.

In Program mode, you should have access to every basic option on the Shooting menu, unless an incompatible setting has been made. If you have trouble getting to some menu options and can't figure out what setting is causing the problem, you can go the Setup menu (marked at the left by the wrench icon) and scroll down to the Reset option, the fifth option on the first screen of the menu. Using that operation will reset all of the camera's basic shooting functions to their default values. In this way, you will undo whatever setting is causing a conflict with the setting you are trying to make.

Starting at the top line of the Shooting menu, I will discuss below each option on the menu's four screens.

ISO

The initials ISO stand for International Standards Organization. This standard formerly was called ASA, for American Standards Association. The ISO acronym reflects the more international nature of the modern photographic industry.

The original use of the ISO/ASA standard was to designate the "speed," or light sensitivity, of film. For example, a "slow" film might be rated ISO 64, or even ISO 25, meaning it takes a considerable amount of light to create a usable image on the film. Slow films yield higher-quality, less-grainy images than faster films. There are "fast" films available, some black-and-white and some color, with ISO ratings of 400 or even higher, that are designed to yield usable images in lower light. Such films often can be used indoors without flash, for example.

With digital technology, the industry has retained the ISO concept, but it applies not just to film, but to the light sensitivity of the camera's sensor, because there is no film involved in a digital camera. The ISO ratings for digital cameras are essentially equivalent to the ISO ratings for films. So if your camera is set to its minimum level, ISO 100, there will have to be a fair amount of light to expose the image properly, but if the camera is set to the maximum of ISO 12800, a reasonably good (but "noisier" or "fuzzier") image can be made in very low light.

Generally speaking, you should shoot with the camera set to the lowest ISO possible that will allow the image to be exposed properly. (One exception is if you want, for creative purposes, the grainy look that comes from shooting at a high ISO value.) For example, if you are shooting indoors in low light, you may need to set the ISO to a high value (say, ISO 800) so you can expose the image with a reasonably fast shutter speed. Otherwise, if the camera uses a slow shutter speed, the resulting image would likely be blurry and possibly unusable.

To summarize: Shoot with low ISO settings when possible; shoot with high ISO settings when necessary to allow a fast shutter speed to stop action and avoid blurriness, or when desired to achieve a creative effective with graininess.

Although very high ISO settings on other cameras can result in images that are badly degraded with noise and artifacts, even the highest settings on the X10 yield very usable results.

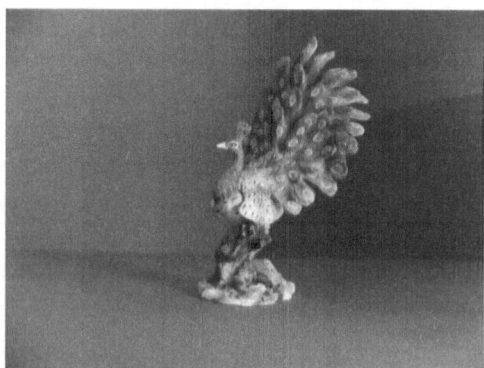

For example, the above shot of a peacock figurine was taken at night in a room in which the only light came from a hallway through a half-closed door. The image was shot at ISO 12800 with a shutter speed of 1/10 second at f/2.5. For comparison, I

CHAPTER 4: THE SHOOTING MENU

turned on the lights in the room and took another shot of the peacock, shown below, with the camera set to ISO 200, using an exposure of 1/8 second at f/2.5. There is a clearly noticeable difference in quality between the two images, but the high-ISO image at least presents a recognizable picture of the peacock.

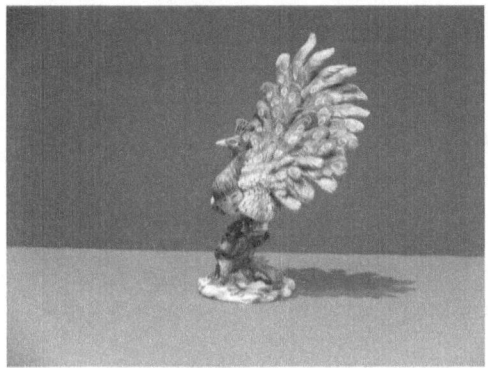

With that background, here is how to set ISO on this camera. Press the Menu/OK button and move to the ISO line, then press the right direction button to get to the screen that lets you select a value as low as 100 or as high as 12800, although not all of those settings are available in all situations. For example, when you have set the camera to take RAW images, the ISO can be set only in a range from 100 to 3200.

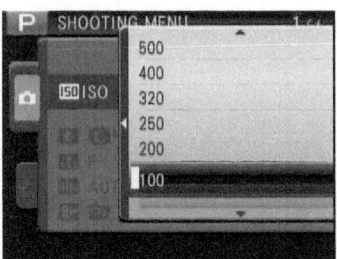 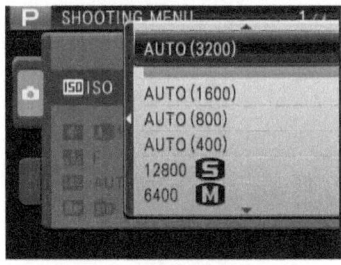

Note that the ISO settings from 4000 to 6400 have the M icon next to them, and the 12800 setting has the S icon next to it. (Not all settings are shown above.) Those icons stand for the maximum image size available with a given ISO value. This situation is related to the functioning of the X10's EXR sensor, which, as discussed in Chapter 3, can be set to emphasize reso-

101

lution, low-light ability, or dynamic range, but not all at once. If you select the higher ISO values, the sensor has to switch the use of its pixels to emphasize low-light ability, and cannot produce the higher resolutions of the larger image sizes.

You also have the option to select one of several options for Auto ISO. These settings are indicated on the Shooting menu as Auto (400) or Auto (3200), for example. If you select one of these options, the camera will automatically choose an ISO value from 100 up to the value listed in parentheses. In several of the more automatic shooting modes, namely, EXR Auto, Advanced, and Scene Position, the camera selects an ISO setting called Auto and chooses the ISO value with no input from the user. You cannot select the Auto ISO setting yourself; it is set automatically in those shooting modes.

You don't necessarily have to use the Shooting menu to set the ISO level. You can assign the ISO setting to the Function button (marked Fn) on top of the camera, to the right of the shutter release button. As discussed in Chapter 5, ISO is the default setting for that button, though there are numerous other items that can be assigned to that button instead. If ISO is assigned to the Function button, you can press the button at any time to call up the ISO menu. And, with the upgrade to firmware version 1.03, you can use the RAW button in a similar way.

With the X10, the Auto ISO settings with upper limits are available even when in Manual exposure mode. With some cameras, when you are using Manual mode you cannot use an automatic ISO setting; you have to select a numerical value for ISO. That approach seems logical, because the word "manual" implies that you are making all of the choices yourself. If you use one of the Auto ISO settings, though, you are letting the camera take over some of the decision-making for your shooting session. It will try to center the exposure meter by raising or lowering the ISO if it can do so. Of course, you can set the upper limit for the Auto ISO setting to a low value such as 400, in which case the camera will not have much leeway to alter the ISO setting. And, of course, you are free to set a specific (non-Auto) ISO value yourself, which will restore your Manual exposure mode to truly manual operation. My preference is to set the ISO to a specific value when I'm using the Manual shooting mode.

Image Size

The next option on the menu, Image Size, works along with Image Quality, the option below it, to determine the overall resolution and quality of your images. This option will be grayed out and unavailable for selection in some situations—such as when you have turned on the RAW option on the Setup menu or have the camera in Advanced shooting mode. (If the camera is in Movie mode, this and many other menu options will not appear at all.) If you are using the RAW option on the Setup menu, the images will all be at the maximum image size of Large, in the 4:3 aspect ratio. However, if you turn on the RAW+JPEG option on the Setup menu, you will find that you can set the Image Size to Medium or Small. If you set the Image Size to M or S with RAW+JPEG turned on, and the ISO value is at least twice the Dynamic Range setting, you will find that the camera produces RAW files that are about 10 MB in size, or about half the size of normal RAW files. This somewhat odd situation is a function of the camera's EXR sensor, which doubles up the pixels on the sensor when the image size is Medium or Small.

With the X10, Image Size has two components, which can be selected separately on some other cameras: resolution and aspect ratio. On the X10, these two components are not named, but their numerical values are listed on the Image Size menu.

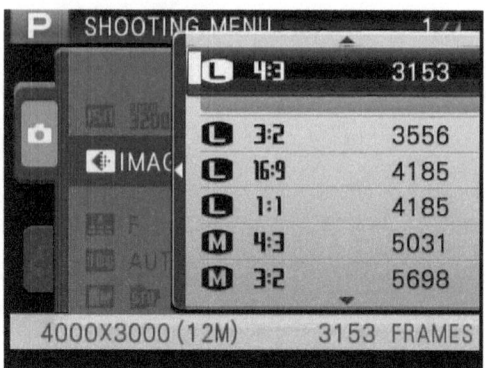

The resolution of the image is the number of pixels it has, given in a formula that contains the horizontal pixel count followed by the vertical pixel count. Therefore, the largest Image Size setting available on the X10 is 4000 x 3000, meaning the image has 4000 pixels horizontally and 3000 vertically. When you multiply these two numbers together, the result is 12 million pixels, also written as 12 megapixels, or 12M. So, you will see the figures 4000 x 3000 and 12M at the bottom of the menu screen when you select this largest value for Image Size.

Note: When you select Image Size on the menu and move to the screen to choose an image size, the number on the menu line is not related to the size of the image; rather, it is the number of images that can be taken with that setting. This can be confusing at times. For example, right now I have a 32 GB SDHC card in my camera. On the Image Size menu, to the right of the top entry is the number 3153, which looks as if it might be the horizontal or vertical pixel count, but it really means I can take 3153 images with current settings. The image size for each setting is shown at the bottom left of the menu screen. In this case, the size is shown as 4000 x 3000 (12M).

The sizes available on the X10 become smaller after the 12M size, at 11M, 9M, 6M, 5M, 4M, 3M, and 2M. You can also see the aspect ratio for each of these settings by examining the Image Size setting. For example, the 4000 x 3000 setting yields an image that is 4 units wide and 3 units tall, for a 4:3 aspect ratio. Three of the Image Size settings are in that ratio, a standard one for digital images, being the same shape as an older (VGA) computer screen or standard TV screen. Other settings are in the 3:2 aspect ratio, the same shape as standard photographic prints in the United States, which are 6 by 4 inches (15 by 10 cm). The 16:9 aspect ratio, often known as "widescreen," conforms to the shape of high-definition (HD) TV displays. Finally, the 1:1 aspect ratio, of course, is square.

To illustrate, I took several images of the same scene, with the only change between shots being the image size and aspect ratio. The first shot, below, was taken with the 4:3 aspect ratio, using all of the sensor's 12 million pixels.

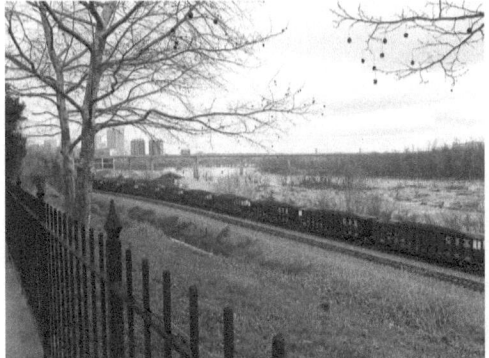

The next shot, below, was taken with the 3:2 aspect ratio, which yields a pixel count of 4000 x 2664, or 11 megapixels.

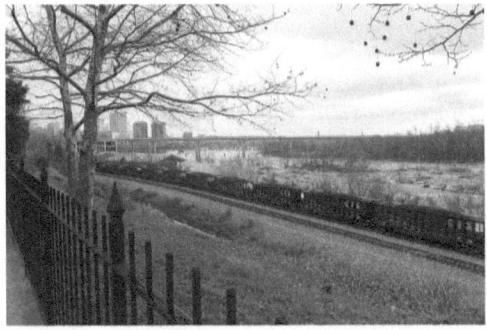

Then, as shown on the next page, I shot the scene using the widescreen aspect ratio of 16:9, with a pixel count of 4000 x

2248 or 9 megapixels.

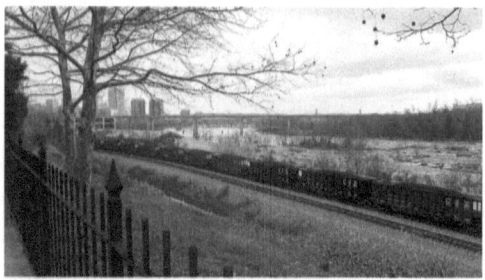

Finally, I shot the scene with the square aspect ratio of 1:1, which gives a pixel count of 2992 x 2992, also 9 megapixels.

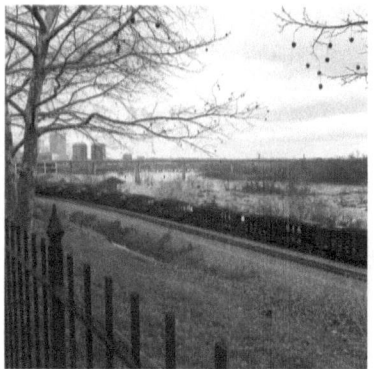

So, with Image Size, you have two choices to make. First, you can choose your images' resolution, or number of pixels (MP). The larger the number of pixels, the larger you can make clear-looking enlargements on paper, and the more options you have for cropping the image to highlight particular details. Second, you have the option of selecting an aspect ratio of 4:3, 3:2, 16:9, or 1:1. Of course, you can always just decide to shoot with the maximum image size of 4000 x 3000 and then crop the image later using software; in that way, you can create any aspect ratio you want, including 16:9, 3:2, 1:1, or any other. But, if you know you will soon be displaying your images on an HDTV set, for example, you can select an image size with the 16:9 widescreen aspect ratio, and the desired result will come straight out of the camera. If you do so, you will have the advantage of seeing on the LCD display the shape of the final image, so you can compose the shot with that shape in mind. (If you're using the optical viewfinder, there is no such guidance available; you will have to imagine how the scene will appear in its final aspect ratio.)

Finally, there is another important point to note about the Image Size setting. Because of the special features of the X10's EXR sensor, the Image Size setting has a particular effect on the way the camera processes your photographs. As I discussed in connection with the EXR shooting mode in Chapter 3, this sensor can be configured to emphasize either resolution, high ISO/low noise, or Dynamic Range, but it cannot provide maximum performance for all of these values at the same time. This situation arises because of the nature of the sensor, which has a special arrangement of its photosites, or individual locations that accept light from the lens.

In the standard, resolution-oriented mode, the camera uses all 12 million of its pixels individually, devoting them all to resolution. Therefore, in that mode, the maximum image size is 12 MP. In the other two modes, however, the X10 reconfigures the EXR sensor to use the pixels in matched pairs. In those modes, each pair of pixels is devoted to improving the processing of the camera for either low light or high dynamic range. Therefore, the end result is that only one pixel of resolution is produced by each pair of pixels, and the maximum image size available is 6 MP.

What this means in practical terms is that, if you set the Image Size to be Medium (6 MP) or less, the camera can use the EXR sensor to emphasize its low-light performance or its high dynamic range performance. In particular, when Image Size is set to those lower values, you will be able to set ISO to higher values on the Shooting menu. (Actually, even if the Image Size is set to Large, you will see the higher ISO values on the Shooting menu, but they will be accompanied by an M or S, indicating that the camera will automatically change the Image Size to Medium or Small if you select an ISO setting at that range.)

With Dynamic Range, the effect of the Image Size setting is not as obvious. No matter whether the Image Size is set to L, M, or S, you will see the same possible settings for Dynamic Range on the Shooting menu: Auto, 100%, 200%, and 400%. However, even though the level of Dynamic Range is the same whether the sensor is in EXR mode or not, the camera achieves its Dynamic Range enhancement differently depending on whether the sensor is using its EXR functionality.

In other words, if Image Size is Large, the camera uses a method of Dynamic Range enhancement that does not involve use of the EXR technology. In that mode, the Dynamic Range setting is limited by the ISO setting. Specifically, if you set Dynamic Range to 400%, then the ISO must be set to at least 400. If you set the ISO to a lower value than 400, the camera will automatically change the Dynamic Range to a lower value.

However, if you set the Image Size to Medium or Small, then the camera is able to devote at least half of its sensor's capacity to Dynamic Range processing, in the EXR mode. In that case, if you set Dynamic Range to 400%, then you will see that you are able to set ISO to any value you want, including 100, because the camera is now using the EXR technology to achieve Dynamic Range expansion, and it is not depending on the use of a relatively high ISO to achieve that result.

The discussion above was fairly involved, so let me sum it up in a nutshell: If Image Size is set to Large, the camera cannot use the special features of the EXR sensor; it must use all 12 million pixels for resolution. If Image Size is set to Medium or Small, then the EXR technology is available, and the camera can process images with low noise in low light or enhance the dynamic range using the special features of the EXR sensor.

Image Quality

As noted above, the Image Quality setting is closely related to Image Size. The Image Quality option lets you select how much "compression," if any, the camera applies. That is, with some settings, the camera "compresses" the data by squeezing out a certain amount of information, preserving enough to recreate the image, but trimming it down so the file does not take up too much storage space. When image files are compressed in this way, they are known as JPEG files. Therefore, as with Image Size, if you select the RAW format for your images on the Setup menu, the Image Quality item on the Shooting menu will be grayed out and unavailable, and the RAW indicator will appear on the menu to remind you why you cannot set this value. However, if you select RAW+JPEG on the Setup menu, you will be able to set the image quality for the JPEG images that will be produced along with each RAW image.

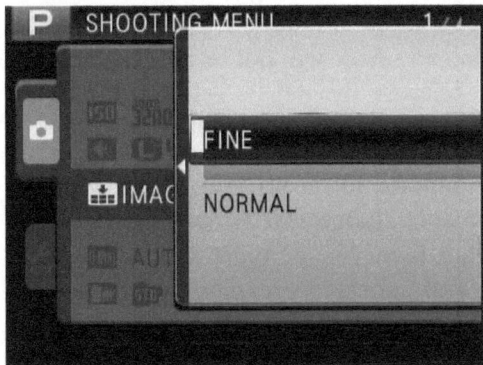

Assuming you are shooting JPEG images (that is, RAW is not turned on in the Setup menu), the two available options for image quality on the X10 are Fine and Normal. The only differences between images shot with these two settings are that Fine images take up more space on your memory card than Normal ones and have higher quality, because they are not as heavily compressed. Both of these formats yield digital files that are considerably smaller than RAW files.

For example, I just took a group of sample images of similar subjects at different sizes and qualities, all with the 4:3 aspect ratio. The RAW file was about 19 megabytes in size; the Large file with Fine quality was 4.3 MB; the Large file with Normal quality was 2.7 MB; the Small file with Fine quality was 1.4 MB; and the Small file with Normal quality was 0.83 MB. So, as you can see, there is a very substantial difference in size among the sizes and qualities of files especially between RAW and JPEG (non-RAW) files. (Note, though, that some RAW files produced by the X10 are only about half the normal size.) If storage space on your memory card or computer is at a premium, using Normal quality is an option, but ordinarily there is no purpose served by using this lesser quality.

Dynamic Range

This next option lets you choose how much dynamic range processing the X10 applies to your images. Dynamic range is the range between the brightest and darkest parts of an image. If the range is too great, an image will not be able to show the details in both parts, because the details will get lost in the shadows or be blown out by excessively bright highlights.

To deal with such situations, in recent years photographers have used High Dynamic Range (HDR) processing. With HDR, the photographer takes two or more shots of a scene, some underexposed and others overexposed, then merges them using Photoshop or special HDR software to blend the best-exposed parts from all of the images. The result is a composite HDR image with clear details in all areas of the image.

Because of the popularity of HDR, many camera makers have incorporated some degree of dynamic range processing into their cameras in an attempt to help the cameras even out areas of excessive brightness and darkness to preserve details. With the Fujifilm X10, this feature takes the form of the Dynamic Range option on the Shooting menu, although it also is present in the EXR shooting mode, as discussed in Chapter 3.

There are four possible settings from the menu screen in the standard (non-EXR) shooting modes: Auto, 100%, 200%, and 400%. If you want the minimal degree of processing, choose

100%. The Auto setting is available with Program, Aperture Priority, and Shutter Priority shooting modes; it is not available with Manual exposure. When you choose Auto, the camera's metering system evaluates the scene and determines what level to use—either 100%, 200%, or 400%. The higher values are appropriate for use with scenes that exhibit increasingly stark contrast between light and dark, such as scenes that are partly in shadow and partly in bright sunlight. In just one mode—EXR-Dynamic Range Priority—Dynamic Range can also be set to two higher values, of 800% and 1600%.

To experiment with the Dynamic Range setting, I took a series of shots of a clock in bright sunlight and a vase in fairly deep shadow. The first two images, taken in Manual exposure mode, are included to illustrate the strong contrast between the amounts of light falling on the two objects.

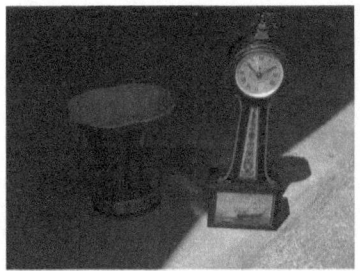 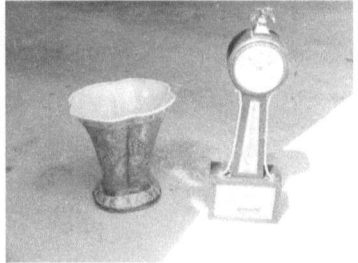

In the next shot, below, I used Program mode with Dynamic Range set to 100% to see how the X10 would handle this situation. The vase is hidden in shade and the clock is overexposed.

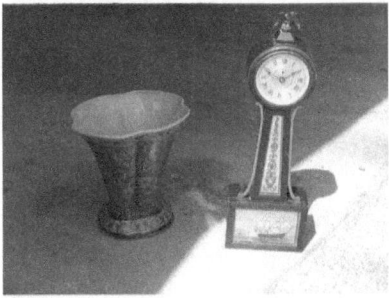

Next, I set the camera to EXR mode, and selected Dynamic

111

Range Priority for the sub-mode. The shot below was taken with Dynamic Range set to 400%. There appears to be a bit more detail visible on the clock.

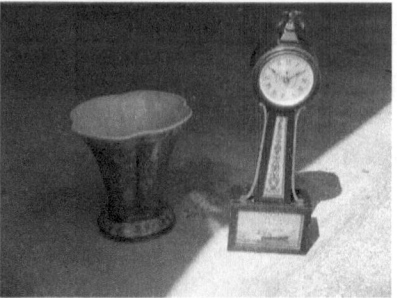

For the next shot, with Dynamic Range at 800%, the camera evened out the highlights and shadows to some extent.

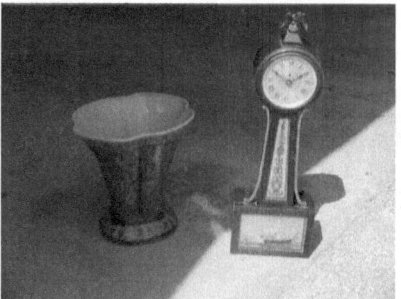

The image below has Dynamic Range at its maximum, 1600%.

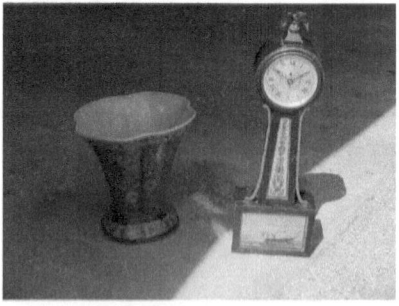

Finally, for comparison, I also took several shots of the same scene in Manual exposure mode using a wide range of exposure levels. I merged those images together in a program called Photomatix Pro, available at hdrsoft.com. In my opinion, the HDR image done in software, shown on the next page, does a better job of evening out the dynamic range of the scene than the internal Dynamic Range processing of the X10.

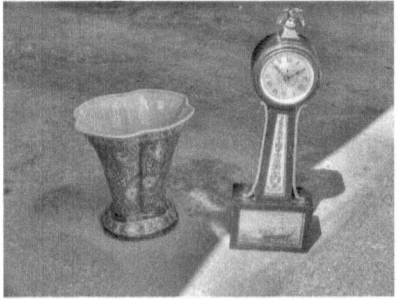

However, the X10's Dynamic Range option can be of use when you need to take pictures in conditions involving extremes of contrast. In my experience, the best approach in this sort of situation is to use the EXR shooting mode's option for Dynamic Range Priority, and then set Dynamic Range to Auto on the Shooting menu. In this way, the camera will use the special capabilities of the EXR sensor and will determine the optimum setting to even out the contrasting parts of the scene.

If you have time, though, the best option may be to take multiple shots using autoexposure bracketing (discussed in Chapter 5) or in Manual exposure mode, and then combine them in HDR software like Photoshop or Photomatix to produce a composite image that evens out the lighting as well as possible.

Film Simulation

With the Film Simulation menu option, Fujifilm lets you produce images with appearances modeled after various types of film, including three well-known Fuji slide films: Provia, Velvia, and Astia. Provia is a normal-contrast color film that yields images with moderate levels of color saturation, or intensity. Velvia, on the other hand, produces high-contrast images with extra levels of color saturation. Finally, Astia is designed to give you images with accurate color and a softer, lower-contrast appearance than either of the other two. The X10 also offers five other non-color film emulations: monochrome, monochrome

113

with yellow, red, or green filter, and sepia.

To select an option, just highlight it on the screen and press the OK button. The examples shown below illustrate the looks that can be achieved with these settings. The differences are fairly subtle, but still noticeable. For example, the Black & White with the green filter setting darkens reds quite noticeably, while the setting with the red filter lightens reds.

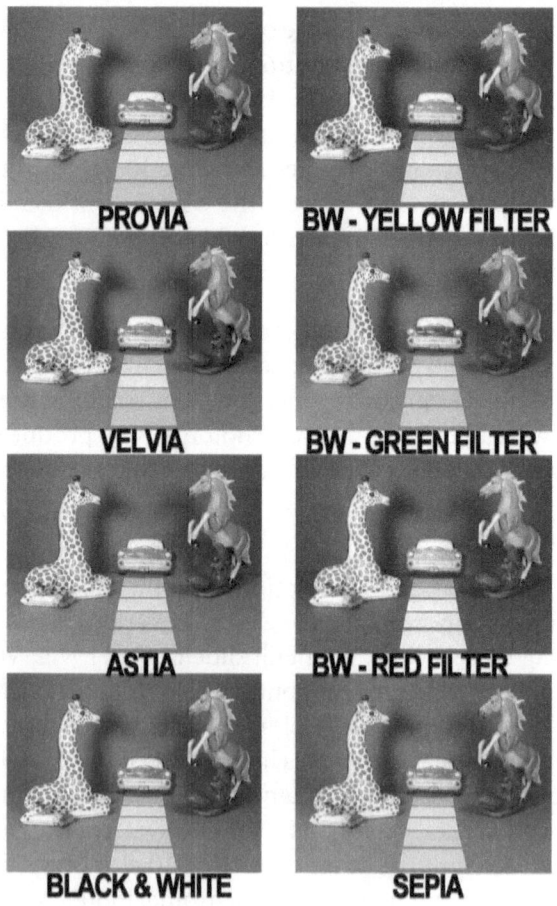

Fujifilm X10 Film Simulation Settings

White Balance Shift

I will briefly mention here the White Balance Shift option, because it is the next selection on the Shooting menu. This option lets you fine-tune the color bias of your White Balance setting after you have selected it using the WB button. I'll discuss this menu item in more detail in Chapter 5, along with the general discussion of white balance.

Color

The Color option on the Shooting menu gives you one more tool to control the look of your images. This menu item lets you adjust the color density of your images to one of five levels: High, Medium High, Mid, Medium Low, or Low. The default value is Mid. You can use this feature to increase the saturation, or intensity, of the colors in your images. I consider this option to be one tool in the sophisticated set of adjustments offered by the X10 to let you fine-tune the appearance of your images in very precise ways.

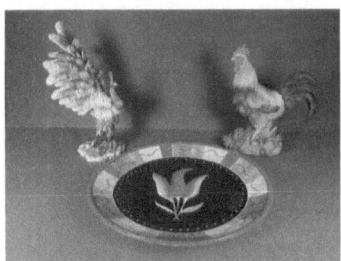 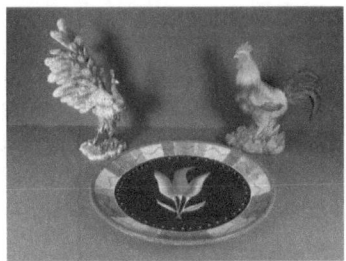

In the examples shown above, the image on the left was taken with Color set to High; the one on the right had Color set to Low. In my view, this option does not provide a very wide range of adjustments; the differences among the various levels of Color setting are quite subtle, at least to my eye.

Sharpness

The next selection on the Shooting menu, Sharpness, gives you another tool to craft the particular appearance for your images. Like Color, this setting comes with five levels of adjustment, but with different names: Hard, Medium Hard, Standard, Medium Soft, and Soft. You can use this parameter to vary the degree to which your images have hard, crisp outlines and edges, as opposed to "softer," smoother lines and areas.

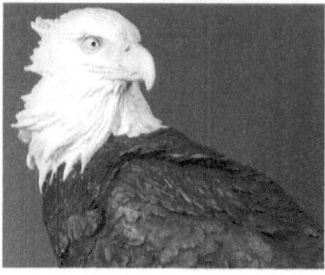 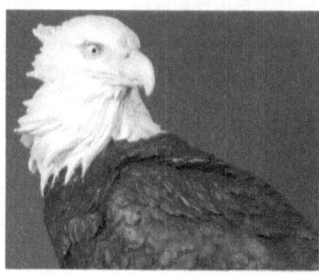

The image above on the left had Sharpness set to Hard; the one on the right had it set to Soft. This setting provides somewhat more dramatic shifts in appearance than the Color setting. However, if you use too strong a setting, you risk introducing jagged artifacts into your image.

Highlight Tone

Highlight Tone is the next menu item for establishing a distinctive look for your photos. In this case, changing the level alters the amount of contrast in the lighter parts (highlights) of your images, using the same five options as for Sharpness: Hard, Medium Hard, Standard, Medium Soft, and Soft.

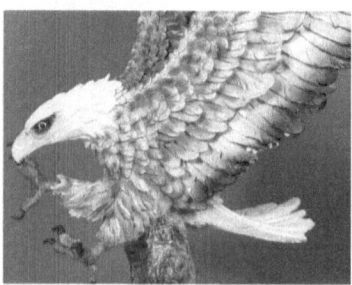 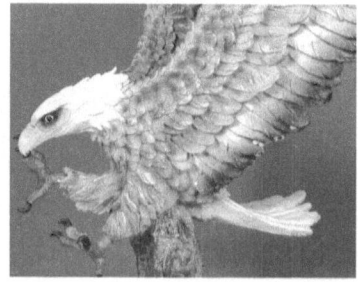

The Highlight Tone setting can cause fairly dramatic changes; on the left above, the setting was Hard; on the right, it was Soft.

Shadow Tone

The next item on the menu, Shadow Tone, gives you a tool to control the level of contrast in the darker portions (shadows) of your images, with the same five levels as for Highlight Tone, above. Here again, as with Highlight Tone, you can achieve fairly dramatic differences in the appearance of your images.

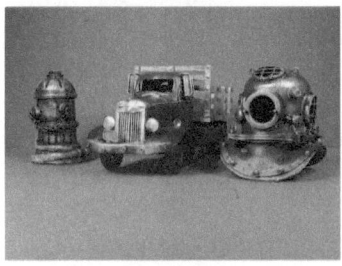 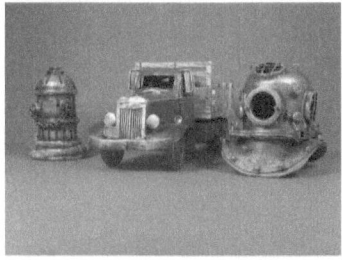

If you use a setting of Hard, as on the left above, the dark areas are sharply emphasized; the image on the right, with a setting of Soft, shows markedly less emphasis in the shadow areas.

Noise Reduction

The next option lets you control how much noise reduction the camera uses in processing your shots. I have found that the effects of this setting can be difficult to notice until you are working with images shot at high ISOs. The images below were both shot at ISO 12800; the one on the left had Noise Reduction set to High; the one on the right had it set to Low.

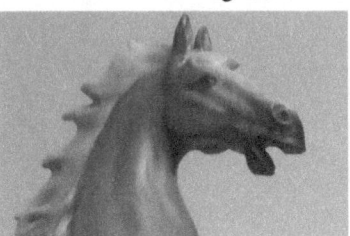 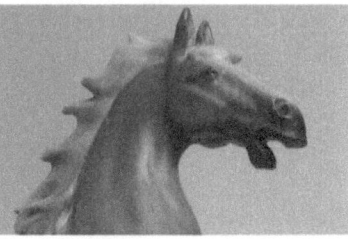

The higher the ISO, the more chance that visual noise will be introduced into the image. With standard noise reduction, the camera's circuitry reduces the noise level, but in doing so it also reduces the details that are clearly visible in the image.

If you want to preserve details and accept a certain amount of noise, you can use this option to select a lower level of noise reduction.

This feature uses the same five levels as the Color option, discussed above.

Of course, you are likely to want to combine several of the settings I have just discussed in order to develop your own "look" for your images, or, perhaps, to develop different looks for different classes of images. Using just the five adjustments discussed above, there are many combinations you can create; and, of course, you also can make adjustments to other settings, including Film Simulation, White Balance, and Dynamic Range, to create other styles. For now, I will show how these settings can be combined to create different appearances.

For all three of the following images, I used Aperture Priority mode with ISO at 800 and Dynamic Range at 100%; Film Simulation was Provia. For the first image, below, all five adjustments (Color, Sharpness, Highlight Tone, Shadow Tone, and Noise Reduction) were set to their medium settings.

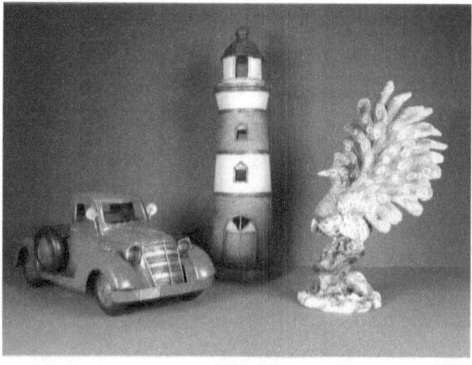

For the second image, on the next page, Color was Medium-High, Sharpness Medium-Hard, Highlight Tone Medium-Soft, Shadow Tone Medium-Hard, and Noise Reduction Medium Low. This group of settings emphasizes the shadows and edges, giving the image a somewhat dark, harsh appearance.

CHAPTER 4: THE SHOOTING MENU

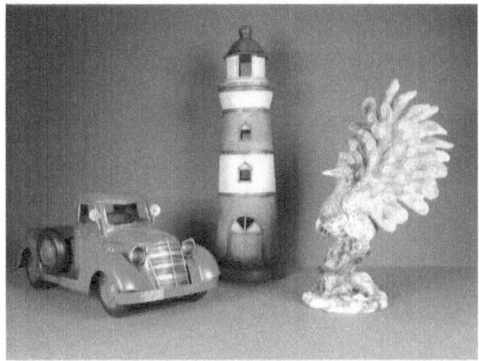

Finally, for the third image, Color was High, Sharpness Hard, Highlight Tone Soft, Shadow Tone Hard, and Noise Reduction Low. As you can see below, this combination yields a noticeably harsh and dark rendering of the scene. You might want to use settings like these for street photography in order to achieve a somewhat industrial, gritty look; you might want to consider opposite values for some of these adjustments when doing portraits or taking pictures of less serious subjects.

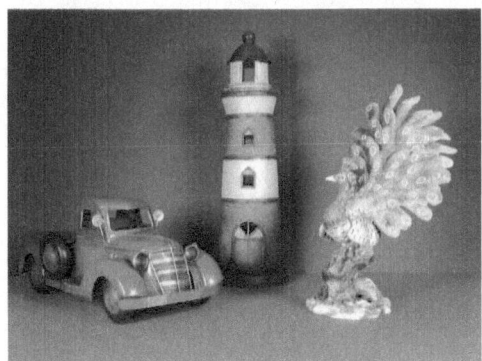

Intelligent Digital Zoom

The next option on the Shooting menu gives you the ability to double the effective focal length of the lens while shooting still images in most shooting modes. (It is not available in Movie mode or in the Advanced shooting mode, or in the Natural &

119

Flash setting of Scene Position mode.)

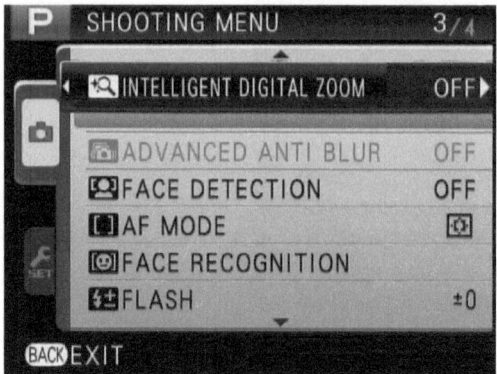

This is an interesting feature that needs some explanation. Note that this is not a pure "digital zoom" like that on some cameras, which extends the zoom range of the lens beyond its normal maximum. Instead, this feature doubles the focal length of the lens throughout its entire zoom range.

In other words, with some cameras, there is optical zoom that operates normally, and digital zoom that takes over at the upper end of the optical zoom range. If the X10 worked in that way, then, after the lens was zoomed optically from its 28mm position to its 112mm telephoto position, the digital zoom would then continue the zoom range to a focal length of 224mm, double the normal range. Instead, with the X10, when you turn on Intelligent Digital Zoom, the lens is converted to having effective focal lengths from 56mm at the wide-angle end to 224mm at the full-telephoto end. There is no longer any ability to zoom back out to the 28mm wide-angle setting.

This approach to digital zoom has advantages and disadvantages. This type of digital zoom is useful because the aperture of the lens does not change at the wide-angle end of the zoom range, even though the focal length is doubled.

Here is an example, because this concept can be confusing. Normally, as you zoom the lens in optically to a larger magnification, the maximum aperture decreases. With the X10, this decrease is not severe—the lens stops down to f/2.2, then f/2.5, and, finally, f/2.8 when fully zoomed in. So, normally, if you zoom the lens in to 56mm, which is twice the wide-angle focal length of 28mm, the maximum aperture will decrease from f/2.0 to f/2.5. However, if you turn on Intelligent Digital Zoom, that feature will automatically double the focal length to 56mm without moving the optical zoom at all. Therefore, the lens will be able to use its maximum aperture of f/2.0, allowing you to have a better chance of blurring the background or using a fast shutter speed, because the aperture is wide open.

Also, having the ability to magnify the focal length electronically can be of benefit in certain specific situations. For example, in some cases you may want to focus or evaluate exposure based on a small part of the scene, and it may be easier to do so if you can zoom in electronically on a narrow section of the subject, and then zoom back out to take the picture.

The disadvantage of using Intelligent Digital Zoom is that, as with any such electronic enhancement of an image, the camera is not really gathering additional information as it does when it uses optical zoom. Instead, it is doubling the size of an image that already exists. Although Fujifilm states that the X10 uses special processing to prevent undue deterioration of the image, I suspect that some image quality is likely to be sacrificed when using this feature. I recommend using it sparingly, and only when it provides a clear benefit.

Advanced Anti Blur

The Advanced Anti Blur option appears on the Shooting menu for all still shooting modes, but it is grayed-out and unavailable for all modes except one—EXR Auto, when you have the option of turning it either on or off. If you turn it on, the flash must either be turned off or in Auto Flash mode for the Advanced Anti Blur feature to function.

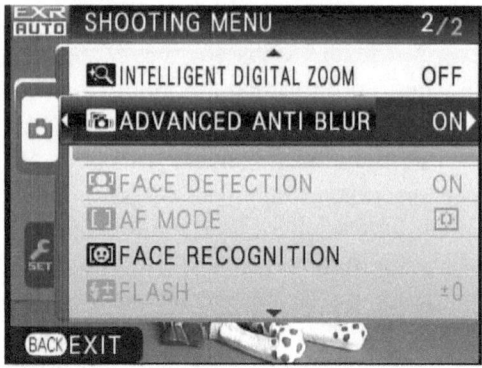

Assuming you have this feature turned on in the menu system and the flash turned off or set to Auto Flash, then, if the lighting is sufficiently dim for the camera to use this option, the camera will shoot a rapid series of images using a high ISO setting, and then combine them in the camera into a single composite image that does not suffer from the high visual "noise" that is characteristic of shots taken at high ISO values. The image will be cropped slightly at the edges, evidently to allow room for the camera to align the multiple images, cutting off areas that do not line up properly. Note that the "anti blur" part of the feature's name does not mean that it will compensate for motion by the camera or subject; it just means that the camera will use a high ISO level and then combine the multiple shots to reduce the visual noise that usually results from using a high ISO. In other words, you need to hold the camera very steady when using Advanced Anti Blur.

To test this feature, I took three identically composed shots of a model airplane with the X10 on a tripod. The first image, at the top of the next page, was taken with the camera set to EXR Auto mode, but with Advanced Anti Blur turned off. The camera took this shot at f/2.5 with a 1/4-second shutter speed, using ISO 1600.

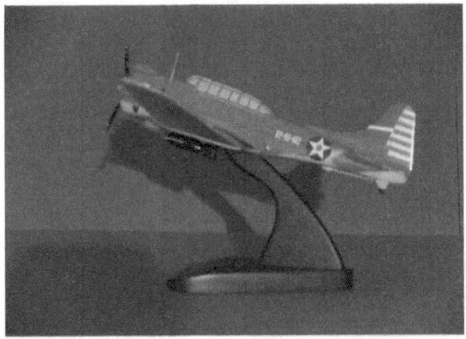

For the next shot, below, the camera was still set to EXR Auto, but this time with the Advanced Anti Blur feature turned on. The camera took four shots in a burst and then combined them to produce the image seen below. In this case, as you can see, the camera cropped the edges of the image slightly. The camera's automation made this exposure at f/2.5 for 1/9 second at ISO 3200. In other words, the camera boosted the ISO to a high level so it could use a faster shutter speed, and then combined the images internally to reduce the effects of noise.

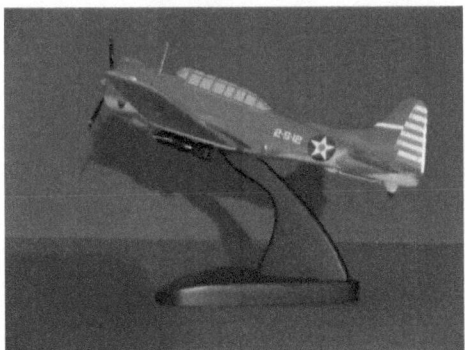

For the last image in the series, on the next page, I set the camera to the Scene Position mode and selected the Night (Tripod) setting, just for the sake of comparison. With this setting, the camera used f/2.2 for a long exposure of 1.1 second, and reduced the ISO all the way down to 200, relying on the tripod to permit the use of both a slow shutter speed and a low ISO.

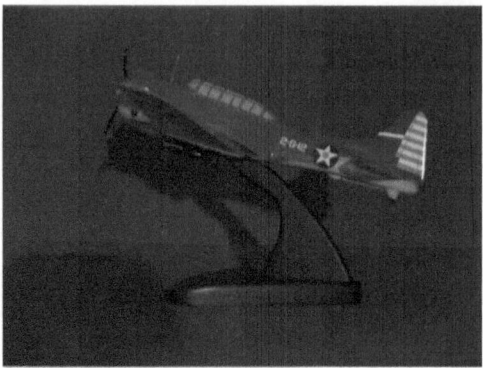

When the camera is set to EXR Auto, I recommend leaving Advanced Anti Blur turned on, because it gives you a chance to get a usable image when you are photographing at night or in other dimly-lighted settings and you cannot or do not want to use flash. Just remember to hold the camera very steady and allow for slight in-camera cropping at the edges of the image.

Face Detection

This menu option has only two possible settings—On or Off. When it is turned on, the X10 uses its programming to recognize human faces in the scene before it. If it recognizes faces, it places a green frame around the face closest to the center of the image and white frames around any other faces in the picture. Then, when you press the shutter button, the camera optimizes its focus and exposure for the primary face.

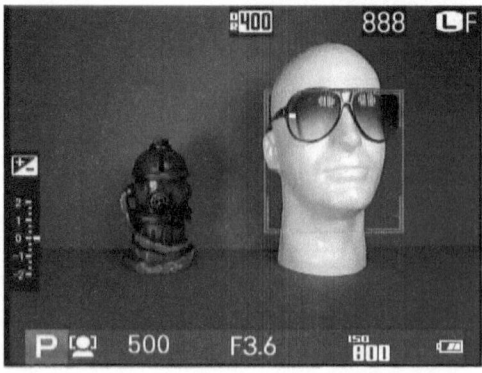

This may be a useful option if you are using the self-timer with the camera on a tripod to take a group photo, because, if the subjects shift positions after you initially set up the shot, the camera still will use the center-most face to set the focus and exposure. However, if you are really interested in using this degree of automation, you might want to just use the EXR Auto shooting mode or the Portrait Enhancer subset of Scene Position, both of which automatically use Face Detection.

AF Mode

This option gives you three choices—Multi, Area, and Tracking—for setting up how the camera chooses one or more locations in the scene shown on the display as the point to focus on for still photography. These options are available only when the camera is set to AF-S mode (autofocus-single-shot) using the switch on the front of the camera. The AF Mode options are different in Movie mode, as discussed in Chapter 8.

There are 49 possible focus points the camera can use. If you choose Multi for AF Mode, the camera will not place any focus frame on the display. Instead, it will use the whole screen as the focus area, and it will attempt to focus on the subject using any one of its focus points, according to which object in the scene appears to be the main subject. When you press the shutter button halfway down to evaluate the focus, the camera will display a green focus frame at the point that it selects for focus, which may be in the center of the screen or at any one of the 48 other focus points around the image.

If you choose Area for the AF Mode, the X10 will place a small white rectangular frame on the display. This focus frame is located initially in the center of the image, but you can move it around as you wish. The camera will focus only on a subject that falls within that frame, whose location you control as follows. First, press the AF button (the middle of the three lower buttons on the far left of the camera's back) to activate the focus frame.

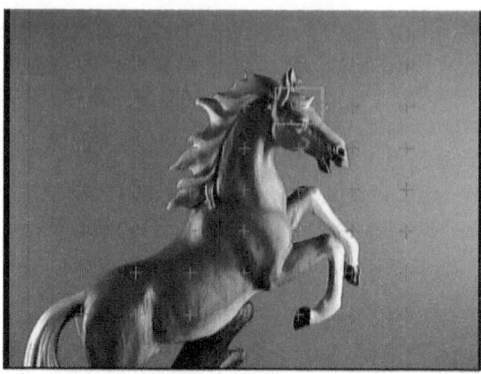

The frame will turn green with small triangles on each side and the 49 focus points will be indicated on the screen by 7 rows of 7 crosses. While the green frame is active, turn the sub-command dial or press any of the direction buttons to move the frame around the screen. The frame will wrap around from one edge of the screen to the other, such as by scrolling down past the bottom to reach the top. To return the frame to the center of the screen, press the AF button if the green frame is not already activated, and press the Menu/OK button. Once you have the green frame located where you want it, press the AF button again to turn the frame white and lock it into place.

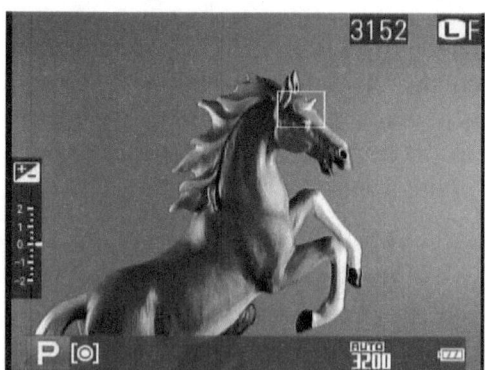

You also can change the size of the focus frame. To do this, after activating the frame by pressing the AF button, turn the main command dial (the small wheel at the top right of the camera's back) to the left to shrink the frame and to the right to enlarge it. With this action, you can reduce the size of the frame to a very small area so you can direct the camera's focus to a precise location on your subject. You can reset the size to normal by pressing in on the center of the same dial.

You also can select Tracking for AF Mode. With this method of autofocus, the camera places a double yellow focus bracket in the center of the screen. The screen shot below shows this initial stage of Tracking autofocus.

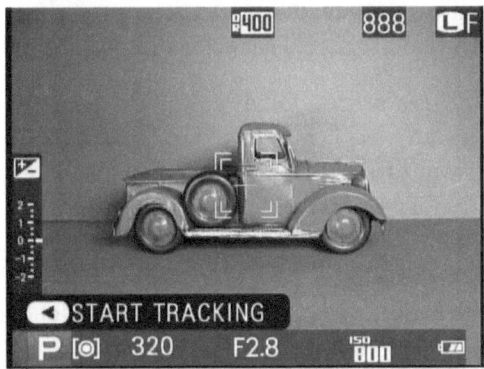

To track a moving subject, such as an active pet or child, position the yellow frame over the subject and, as prompted by a message on the display, press the left direction button. The focus frame will change to a small green frame; that green frame will "attach" itself to the subject you selected, and will attempt to keep that particular subject in focus, even as the subject (or the camera) moves.

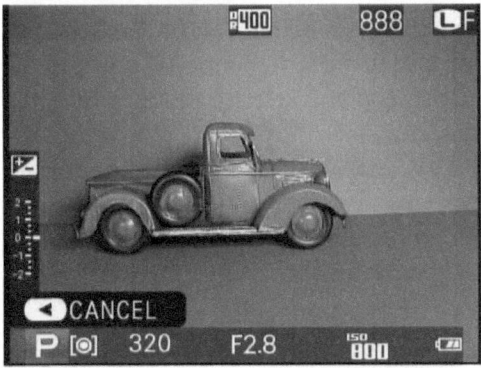

You can end the tracking session either by pressing the shutter button down to take a picture or by pressing the left direction button again, which will convert the focus frame back to its original yellow appearance, awaiting another subject to track.

This autofocus mode places a considerable drain on the battery, but it is very useful when you need to follow a subject that is moving unpredictably. You might want to consider programming the Tracking option into one of the Custom slots on the mode dial, along with other settings, such as a fast shutter speed and high ISO, that are useful for action photography.

I personally prefer the Area setting for directing the location of the autofocus system, because I can move the frame directly over the subject that I want to be in sharpest focus, and I can then be certain that the camera will focus on the right spot. However, if you are taking quick snapshots and won't have time to adjust the focus frame to the proper location, then you may want to choose the Multi option and let the camera determine where to set the focus point.

Face Recognition

This option lets you "register" a particular person's face in the camera so that it will recognize the person in the future when you take a picture, and will display the person's name and other information during playback; it will say "Happy Birthday!" if you zoom in on the person's picture on his or her birthday.

To register a face, select this menu item, choose Face Recognition from the sub-menu and turn it on, then scroll down to the Register item on the sub-menu and select it. Then, aim at the face you want to register, and place the person's eyes within the two yellow rectangles that appear, while framing the overall face within the yellow corner brackets. Take the picture and, if the camera succeeded in recognizing the face, it will prompt you to enter the person's name and other information.

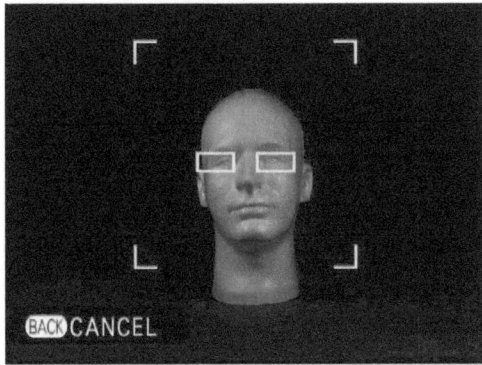

This is not an option I have much need for, and I cannot say that I have explored its operation very thoroughly. But it could be a good conversation starter, so try it out if it sounds like something your friends or relatives would enjoy.

Flash

This option, often called flash exposure compensation on other cameras, works like standard exposure compensation, discussed in Chapter 5. That is, you can dial in an amount of flash exposure compensation up to plus or minus 2/3 EV unit, in increments of 1/3 EV. (EV stands for exposure value, or f-stop, in this context.) When you do that, you are telling the camera, in effect, "Okay, you go ahead and calculate the correct exposure with the flash, but then add in (say) 1/3 EV extra, to make the picture brighter."

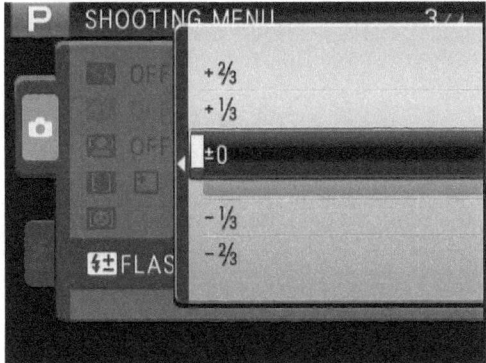

To select this setting, go to its entry on the menu screen and press the OK button or the right direction button to get to the adjustment screen. At that screen, turn the sub-command dial or use the up and down direction buttons to dial in as much as +2/3 EV or -2/3 EV, to make your flash exposures that much brighter or darker. Press the OK button to confirm your selection when the value you want to choose is highlighted by the selection rectangle. Any value you set for flash compensation will remain in effect even after the camera has been powered off and back on, so be sure to cancel it by setting it back to zero when you no longer need the adjustment. This setting also works when you have a compatible external flash unit attached to the hot shoe.

You may find it useful to experiment with negative exposure compensation in the range of -2/3 EV to soften the look of fill flash, especially when taking portraits outdoors.

External Flash

The next menu option is provided so you can set the X10 to work properly with an external flash made by a third-party company. You don't need to use this menu item—and, in fact, it will be grayed out and unavailable—if you are using either of the two Fujifilm external flash units that are designated for use with this camera, the EF-20 or the EF-42. The X10 will automatically connect to either of them and disable the built-in flash unit. You do not have to pop up the built-in flash to activate the external Fujifilm flash; the camera should recognize it and place the appropriate flash symbol in the upper left of the display. (Of course, you have to select a flash mode using the Flash button, which is also the right direction button on the sub-command dial.)

If you are using any non-Fujifilm external flash unit, Fujifilm's instructions say that you must select this menu option so that the camera will disable the built-in flash and trigger the external one. This process can be a bit tricky in practice, because you have to make sure you are using a compatible flash unit. I tried using a Metz 36 AF-4 flash, a model designated for Olympus and Panasonic cameras. It fired only once out of multiple attempts when I had the External Flash option turned on.

I also tried a Panasonic DMW-FL220 flash unit. That one worked as expected; it fired when I turned on the External Flash option, and did not fire when that option was turned off. I had to set the flash unit to its Manual mode to get it to work, which is what I expected. I then tried a Canon 430EX II flash unit, the most powerful one I had available. It also worked perfectly in its Manual mode, firing when the External Flash option was turned on, and not firing when it was turned off.

With both the Panasonic and the Canon flash, the X10's built-in flash fired when the External Flash menu option was turned off, and it did not fire when that option was turned on.

So, the process of attaching and using a third-party external flash should work well, provided you have selected a compatible unit. You should set the flash unit to its Manual mode, and you may need to set the camera to Manual exposure mode as well, because the automatic exposure features of the flash likely will not function with the X10. When you have this menu option activated, you will see an icon of a flash gun in the upper left of the display, instead of the normal flash mode icon.

The easiest option for using external flash with the X10 is to use one of the Fujifilm units that are designated for use with it. I discuss external flash options further in Appendix A.

Custom Set

This option is used for storing the camera's current settings to one of the two Custom shooting modes, C1 or C2. I discussed this process in Chapter 3, in connection with the discussion of those shooting modes.

Display Custom Setting

This final option on the Shooting menu, which also has "Custom" in its title, has nothing to do with the previous item. This one lets you select the items of information displayed on the camera's LCD screen. There is one important point to be aware of here: Even when items are selected in this menu option for viewing on the LCD, those items will not appear on the camera's display unless you have the Custom display option selected, using the Display/Back button on the camera's back.

In shooting mode, the LCD has five different display screens, including the Standard display, Information Off (showing the live image but no shooting information), the Custom display, and the Information display. You also can choose to turn the display completely off while leaving the camera on. You alternate among these five display modes by pressing the Display/Back button, at the bottom left of the control area on the right of the camera's back. The items that are selected for display using the Display Custom Setting menu item are selected for the Custom display only, and not for the Standard or Information display. So, if you have used the Display Custom Setting menu option to set a particular item, such as the framing guideline, to be displayed on the LCD but you don't see it, press the Display/Back button to select the Custom display screen, and all of the items you have selected will now be visible.

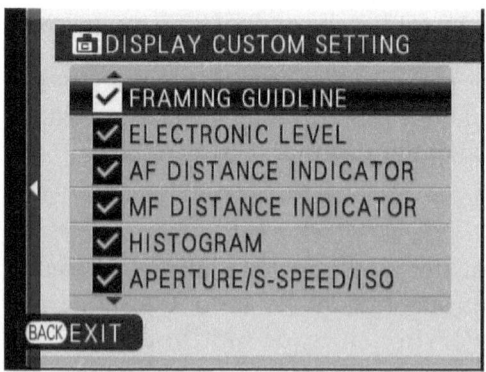

This menu item is easy to use. Just select this option and press the right direction button to move to the screen that lists all items that can be displayed. When the line you want to change is highlighted, press the Menu/OK button to check or uncheck the box to the left of the listed item. All items with check marks will be displayed on the Custom display screen.

The items that can be selected are: Framing guideline; electronic level; autofocus distance indicator; manual focus distance indicator; histogram; aperture, shutter speed and ISO; exposure compensation; photometry; flash; white balance; film simulation; dynamic range; frames remaining; image size and quality; and battery level. Most of these are self-explanatory, but a few need some explanation.

The framing guideline is placed on the display to help you compose your shots, as seen in the following image; you select the style of grid on the Setup menu, as discussed in Chapter 7.

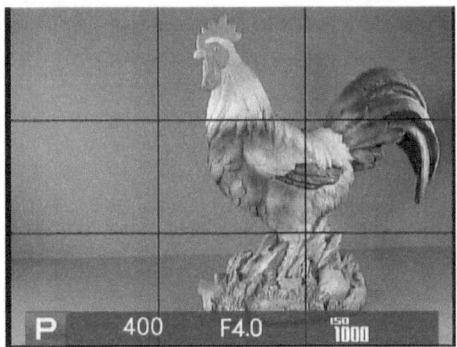

The electronic level is what Fujifilm calls a "virtual horizon."

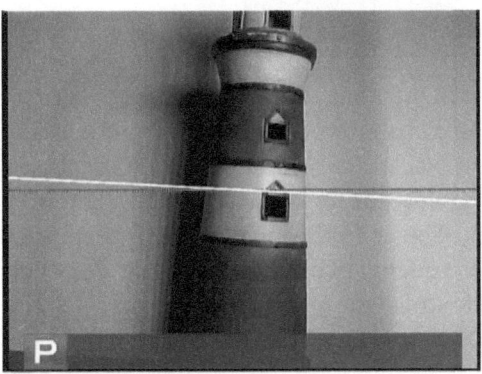

You will see a blue line that extends across the middle of the display and a white line of the same length that rolls up and down as the camera moves in and out of level status. When the blue line covers the white line, a single green line appears, indicating that the camera is level. For the image on the previous pate, I eliminated all items from the Custom display screen except for the electronic level.

The autofocus distance indicator, like the manual autofocus indicator, consists of three parts: a light-blue scale at the bottom of the display that is marked in distance units (meters or feet, selectable through the Setup menu); a vertical red line that appears on the scale when autofocusing is accomplished, to show the approximate distance from the subject that the camera focused on; and a small white area surrounding the red line, which expands and contracts to indicate the depth of field at the current settings. The image below shows only the blue scale, because focus had not yet been achieved.

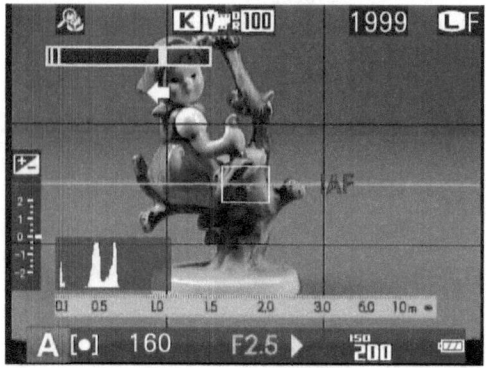

The histogram, shown in the image above, is a chart of vertical white bars showing the distribution of dark and bright areas in the image. The darkest blacks are represented by vertical bars on the left, and the brightest whites by those on the right, with gradations in between. You should generally set the exposure so the histogram looks roughly like a mountain that slopes up gradually from the left and right of the chart to a peak in the center. A histogram that is skewed too far to the left or the right of the chart indicates likely underexposure or overexposure. The histogram on the previous page is skewed slightly to the left, indicating underexposure. I'll discuss the histogram further in Chapter 6.

The next item that needs some explanation, Photometry, is the term that Fujifilm uses for the light-metering method used by the X10. There are three such methods—Multi, Spot, and Average, which I will discuss in Chapter 5.

Finally, the Flash item in the context of the Display Custom Setting menu option is the flash mode that is in effect, such as Forced Flash, Suppressed Flash, or Auto Flash.

One note about the Custom display screen: It is not available at all when the camera is set to the EXR Auto shooting mode; that screen is omitted from the cycle of display screens in that mode. The Custom display is available in all other shooting modes for still images, including the EXR modes other than EXR Auto.

Chapter 5: Other Controls

One welcome feature of the X10 is that it has more physical control dials and buttons than many other compact cameras. With some cameras, you have to probe deeply into menu systems to set some of the fairly basic settings, like white balance, autofocus mode, or metering mode. With the X10, although you still need to do a fair amount of work in the menu screens, there is an assortment of buttons, switches, and dials that let you make quick adjustments to several of the most important settings. And, as an added bonus, two of the buttons are programmable, so you can set them up to control whatever functions you most need. In this chapter, I will discuss the operation of each control and explain how you can use it to help you achieve excellent images. I will not discuss items, such as the strap eyelets, microphone openings, and built-in flash, whose functions are obvious or are discussed in connection with other topics.

Focus Switch

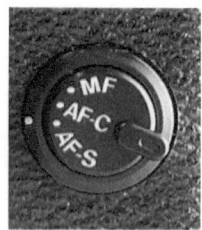

This rotating switch on the front of the camera has three positions: MF for manual focus, AF-S for autofocus-single, and AF-C for autofocus-continuous. The operation of the switch is as simple as it gets: Just rotate the switch to the position you want and leave it there. There are no menus to deal with, and no further choices to make. But there are some considerations to be aware of, which I will discuss for each of the three options.

136

Manual Focus

First I will talk about manual focus, the mode in which you have to focus the lens yourself and judge the sharpness of the image with your eyes rather than relying on the camera's autofocus system. Why would you want to use manual focus when the camera will focus for you automatically? Many experienced photographers like the amount of control that comes from being able to set the focus exactly how they want it. And, with some situations, such as dark areas or areas behind glass, extreme close-ups, or objects at various distances from the camera, it may be useful for you to be able to control exactly where the point of sharpest focus lies.

For example, not too long ago my wife and I visited a local park that has many photographic opportunities, including a small collection of animals, some of them behind chicken-wire fencing. When I used autofocus to get pictures of a rooster, I found that the camera would sometimes focus on the wire, rather than on the animal behind it. I eventually realized that using manual focus could solve this problem, because I could take full control of setting the focal distance. And, as I discuss in Chapter 9, certain other types of photography, such as capturing images through a telescope, also require the use of manual focus because of the difficulty of using autofocus.

To activate manual focus on the X10, set the rotating switch on the front of the camera to its top position, marked with the letters MF. Then adjust the focus by turning the sub-command dial (the dial in the center of the right side of the camera's back) to adjust the focus—counter-clockwise to decrease the focus distance, and clockwise to increase it. (You can reverse those directions using the Focus Control Dial option on the Setup menu.) A red indicator bar will appear in the blue distance scale at the bottom of the display to show the approximate focus distance being set. If you look closely at that indicator you will see a small white area surrounding it, which gives an approximate idea of the depth of field at the current settings.

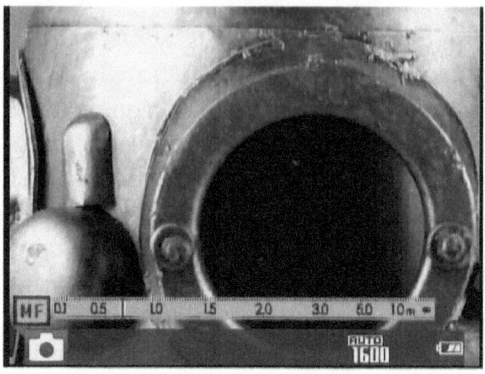

If you have difficulty seeing the screen to judge the sharpness of the focus, you can enlarge the display, as seen in the above image. To do this, go to the Setup menu and set the Focus Check option to On. Then, whenever you turn the sub-command dial to adjust the manual focus, the image will be enlarged to help you focus sharply. Unfortunately, the image stays enlarged only as long as you are actually turning the dial, and for about two seconds afterwards, so you have to be quick if you are in a situation in which you need to take your hand off the sub-command dial to adjust the subject, for example. I had this problem when I was taking photographs with the X10 through a telescope and had to adjust the focus on the telescope while checking the manual focus on the camera.

While the image is magnified, or while it is at normal size, you can at any time press the AEL/AFL button, which is just below the main command dial, to cause the camera to autofocus on the scene. In this way, even though you are using manual focus, you can get the benefit of the camera's autofocus system. If the camera is able to focus, it will beep to confirm the focus (if sounds are turned on), but the focus frame will not turn green as it does in autofocus-single-shot mode. Once the camera has used its autofocus, you can then continue to adjust the focus manually until it is fine-tuned to your satisfaction.

One problem you will likely notice with manual focus is that it can take quite a few turns of the sub-command dial to change the focus distance substantially, so it can feel as if you are turning and turning the dial with not much in the way of results. Pressing the AEL/AFL button to bring the image roughly into focus can help lessen the impact of this situation, because you will then probably only have to make a few minor adjustments with the sub-command dial to finish the focusing process.

Note that, even though manual focus is set with a physical switch, the camera will override that setting and use autofocus regardless of the switch's position, when the camera is set to EXR Auto mode, Advanced mode, Movie mode, or the Portrait Enhancer setting in Scene Position mode.

Autofocus–Single Shot

When the focus switch is turned to the AF-S position, the X10 is placed into the autofocus mode for single shots. The camera does not attempt to focus until you press the shutter button. When you press the shutter button down halfway to lock focus (and exposure), the autofocus system attempts to find a subject that it can focus on sharply.

If it is successful, you will hear a beep (unless beeps are turned off in the Setup menu), and you will see two indicators: a green focus frame will appear on the display, and the camera's indicator light, high on the center of the camera's back, just below the flash shoe, will glow green or blink green. If the light glows green steadily, focus is locked; if it blinks green, that means there may be an issue such as the risk of blur from a slow shutter speed, but the picture can be taken. Once the focus is set, it stays locked as long as you keep the shutter button pressed halfway down. If the subject moves, focus may be lost, because, in this focus mode, the camera will not adjust the focus distance to track the subject. (I'm assuming Face Detection is turned off and AF Mode is set to Multi or Area, not Tracking.)

One disadvantage of using the AF-S mode for focusing is that you cannot set the camera to enlarge the image to check focus, as you can when using manual focus.

Autofocus—Continuous

If you turn the focus switch to the AF-C position, the camera is placed into the autofocus mode for continuous focusing. When the camera is in this mode, you may hear continuous sounds from the camera as the autofocus mechanism adjusts to keep the subject in focus as the subject or the camera moves. (These sounds are very faint, so you may not hear them unless you place your ear near the camera.)

You will see a white crosshair rather than a focus frame in the center of the image, and the camera will focus on whatever object is in the center of the image, under that crosshair. Then, when you press the shutter button down halfway, the camera will lock focus and the continuous focusing will stop. When focus is confirmed, the crosshair will turn green, the indicator light will turn green, and the camera will beep.

The theoretical usefulness of the AF-C setting is to get the approximate focus set before you press the shutter button, so the final focusing operation will finish more quickly when it's time to take the picture, though it is not clear that focus times are much improved with this focus method. Also, this focus mode does not provide continuous focusing on a moving subject after the shutter button is pressed; in other words, there is no "tracking" autofocus in this mode. However, it is possible that the AF-C mode provides more accurate focusing than the AF-S mode, particularly in low light and with low-contrast subjects, so it is worth at least experimenting with. Of course, any sort of continuous autofocusing will drain your battery more quickly than normal, so be careful not to use it excessively if you are running low on battery power.

If you use the AEL/AFL button to lock focus while in AF-C mode, the crosshair will change into a green box, like the box that appears when focus is locked in AF-S mode. (The box does not appear if Face Detection is turned on.)

When AF-C mode is active, the AF Mode option on the Shooting menu is grayed out and cannot be selected, though Face Detection is still available. In addition, with AF-C active you no longer have the option to turn off the LCD display with the Display/Back button. That option does not appear when you cycle through the various display options after pressing that button when the camera is set to this focus mode.

Lens Assembly

The X10's lens and its associated items are among the most important items on the camera.

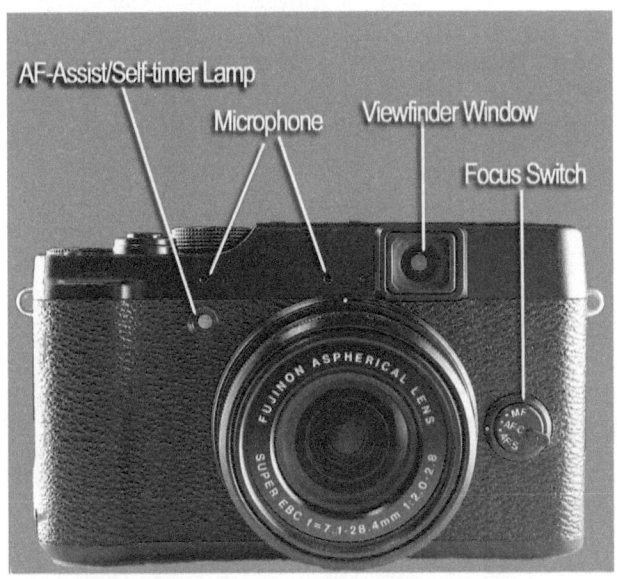

The lens itself is a high-quality Fujinon lens with an actual focal length range of 7.1mm - 28.4mm. Because the X10 has a sensor that is smaller than the size of a frame of 35mm film, these focal lengths are usually stated in the "35mm-equivalent" values, which are the focal lengths that would be needed in order to provide the same angle of view as this lens, if the camera were a traditional 35mm SLR camera.

Using the 35mm-equivalent values, the focal length range of the X10's zoom lens is 28mm - 112mm. In other words, the

X10's lens provides a field of view that is equivalent to that of a 28mm – 112mm zoom lens on a camera that uses 35mm film. A "normal" focal length is often thought of as about 50mm, and 35mm or lower is usually considered wide-angle. At the zoomed-in end of the range, the lens has a focal length of 112mm, which is a moderate telephoto range. That focal length is good for portraits and for any other shots in which it may be desirable to blur the background while keeping the main subject in sharp focus. At the 112mm focal length, the lens has a relatively shallow depth of field, so blurring of the background, or "bokeh," can be achieved fairly easily.

It also is a positive feature, in my view, that the lens is zoomed by hand, rather than electronically, giving the photographer complete control of the rate of zoom, and minimizing the drain on the battery.

The X10's lens has a maximum aperture of f/2.0, which is a "fast" aperture for any lens. In other words, the lens gathers a good deal of light, making the camera useful for low-light photography. In addition, the wide f/2.0 aperture contributes to the shallow depth of field, which also helps make it possible for the camera to capture images with blurred backgrounds, as discussed in Chapter 3. And, one excellent feature of the X10 is that, even when zoomed fully in to its 112mm focal length, the camera still maintains a respectably wide aperture of f/2.8. With many other compact cameras, the widest aperture at the maximum zoom range of the lens is considerably more narrow, such as f/5.6. In those cases, it is difficult to gather enough light for many sorts of images when the lens is zoomed in.

One other point to note about the lens assembly is that you have to turn the zoom ring (the knurled area around the lens barrel) to turn the camera on and off. Personally, I prefer using a power button or switch for this purpose, but I have not had many problems using the Fujifilm X10's system; it works well, and it ensures that the lens is retracted when the camera is powered off. The only issue I have encountered is the risk of turning off the camera in the middle of recording a video, by zooming the lens out too far. (There is a detent to help prevent this action, but I have accidentally powered off the camera in this situation, so it's something to bear in mind.)

Finally, if you look closely at the lens, you will see that there are threads around the inside of the outer part of the lens. These threads are where you attach an optional adapter ring, which then lets you attach a lens hood and filters. I will discuss that system in Appendix A.

Autofocus Assist/Self-timer Lamp

The lamp on the front of the camera, near the top part of the lens, has two important functions. First, it serves as the AF Illuminator. In that capacity, the lamp sends out a beam in dim lighting conditions to assist with autofocusing. The light cast by this lamp lets the autofocus mechanism "see" clearly enough to detect the contrasting edges it needs in order to evaluate the focus.

The lamp also acts as the indicator for the self-timer. When the self-timer is set for two seconds, the lamp blinks several times and then glows steadily as the countdown ends and the picture is taken. When the timer is set for ten seconds, the lamp glows steadily for several seconds and then finishes with a pattern similar to that for the two-second countdown.

Both uses of the lamp can be controlled through the Setup menu. The AF Illuminator menu item can turn the lamp off, in which case it will never illuminate, either for autofocus or for the self-timer. You can achieve the same effect by setting the Silent Mode item to On in the Setup menu. That feature cancels the camera's beeps as well as all uses of the lamp and the flash. You also can turn Silent Mode on or off quickly by holding down the Display/Back button for about two seconds.

The lamp is quite bright and can be distracting to your subjects. Also, it can call attention to your camera if you are doing street photography in dim lighting, or if you are shooting in any other location where you don't want to cause a disturbance. So, consider disabling it using the Setup menu or just by holding down the Display/Back button. If you find that the lack of the lamp hampers the camera's ability to autofocus, you can use manual focus or zone focusing as an alternative.

Now it's time to discuss the top of the camera, where several important controls reside.

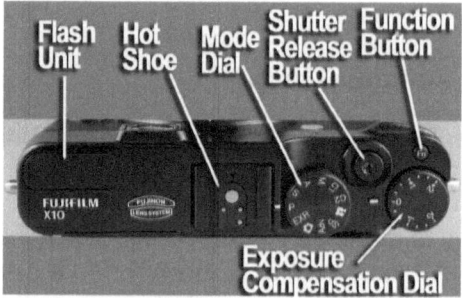

Shutter Release Button

The shutter release button is the single most important control on the camera. When you press it halfway down, the camera evaluates exposure and focus (unless you're using manual focus). Once you are satisfied with the settings, you press the button all the way down to record the image. When the camera is set for continuous shooting, you hold this button down while the camera fires repeatedly. For movies, you press this button and release it to start recording, and then press it again to stop recording.

The button also can be half-pressed to switch the camera back to shooting mode when you have been reviewing images in playback mode, and it can be half-pressed to bring the camera back to life when it has gone to sleep after a set period of time because of the Auto Power Off setting in the Setup menu. Also, you can use a half-press to exit from menu screens after you have confirmed your selections.

Finally, Fujifilm has provided a useful feature that is in line with the "retro" styling of the X10: The shutter button is threaded to accept a standard, mechanical cable release, which can be used to trigger the camera to avoid camera shake that may be caused when you press the button with your finger. This system is particularly useful when you are photographing small items, in which case the focus distance is critical and you do not want to nudge the camera out of place by even a small amount. You also can screw in a "soft release," a small, smooth button that serves as a smoother surface for your finger to press when actuating the shutter. There is more discussion of cable releases and soft releases in Appendix A.

Exposure Compensation Dial

This dial on the top right of the camera is an aspect of the X10's "retro" styling and a welcome convenience. With many cameras, you have to press a tiny button and then turn a dial or press other buttons to adjust exposure compensation. With the X10, you just turn this dial to your chosen setting and you're done. The dial has clear designations from -2 to +2 EV (exposure value) in increments of 1/3 stop. As you turn the dial, the setting appears on the vertical scale at the left of the display, unless you are using a display mode with no information.

Let's consider a specific situation in which you might use this control to adjust the camera's exposure to account for an unusual, or non-optimal, lighting situation. For example, consider the first image on the next page, which shows the X10's view of a miniature diver's helmet. Because the helmet is in front of a white background, the camera's autoexposure system makes the exposure much too dark, to account for the large expanse of white. One solution to this problem is to use the exposure compensation dial to decrease the overall exposure of the image so that the helmet will not be underexposed. To accomplish this, I dialed in 1 2/3 EV on the positive side.

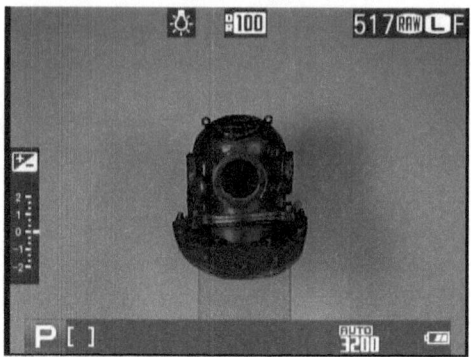

If you do this, you will see a white indicator extend above the zero point on the white scale at the far left side of the display. With this positive value, the image will be brighter than it otherwise would. (With a negative value, of course, it would be darker.) The LCD display will grow brighter or darker to indicate the effect of the adjustment.

With positive exposure compensation of 1 2/3 EV, the helmet becomes lighter and is no longer underexposed, as seen below.

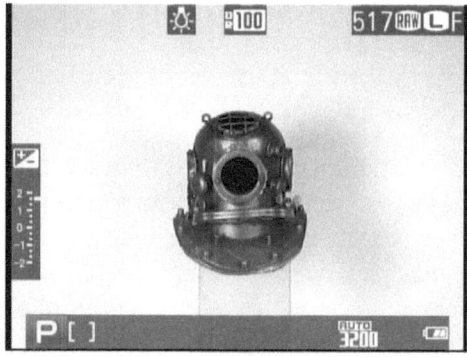

Once you've taken the picture, you should turn the exposure compensation dial back to the zero point, so you won't inadvertently change the exposure of later images that don't need the adjustment.

Exposure compensation is not available in a few shooting modes: Manual, EXR Auto, Auto, and the Fireworks setting of Scene Position mode. So, if you turn this dial when the camera is in one of those modes, nothing will happen to the camera's settings. However, if you turn the dial to a positive or negative value while in one of those modes and leave it there when you switch to another mode, such as Program, that does use exposure compensation, the value on the dial will take effect in that new mode. So, it's a good idea to check the dial whenever you start a shooting session to make sure the value is set where you want it.

Function Button

This button, marked with the letters Fn for Function, is a very small control, just to the right of the shutter button. It is hard to see, but it sits in a perfect spot for your index finger to find it by sliding off of the shutter button. It performs the very helpful task of providing you with instant access to one operation of your choice, which can be selected through the Setup menu.

By default, the Function button gives you access to the ISO setting. Just press the button, and the camera lets you change your ISO value quickly without having to press the Menu button to get access to the ISO setting through the Shooting menu. If you prefer, you can set the Function button to control any one of several other values or operations: Image Size; Image Quality; RAW; Dynamic Range; Film Simulation; AF Mode; Face Recognition; Face Detection; or Intelligent Digital Zoom. You can assign a selection to the Function button in one of two ways—either by using the Setup menu item called Function Button or by holding down the Function button until the screen for assigning a function to it appears.

The choices for the Function button are self-explanatory, because pressing the button produces the menu screen that is associated with the item in question. For example, if you assign the Image Size option to the button, when you press the button, the screen for selecting an image size appears, and you can proceed to choose the image size just as if you had called up the menu by pressing the Menu button.

Note that, when you want to use the function that is assigned to the Function button, such as ISO or Image Size, you have to press and release the button quickly; if you hold it down for too long a time, the camera will produce the menu for assigning a function to the button.

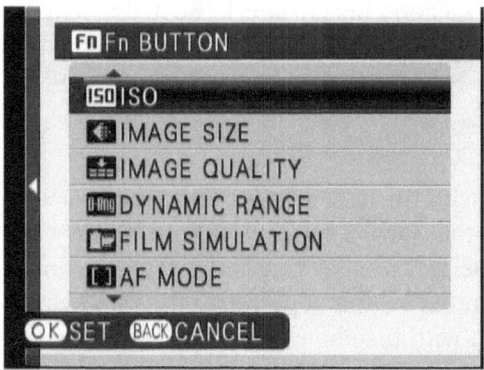

The other major location for controls is the back of the X10, as seen in the diagram below.

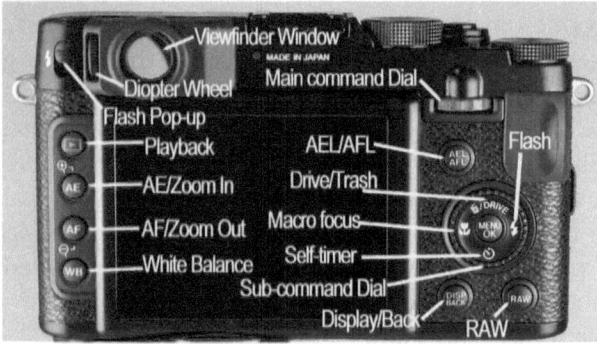

Viewfinder Window

Although not a "control" that you can manipulate, the viewfinder window is an important feature of the camera that merits some discussion. This small window provides you with an optical view of the scene the camera is aimed at. The window has some good points: It gives a high-quality view of the scene, and it zooms along with the zoom mechanism of the lens. Also, it may be easier to view a scene in bright sunlight through this window than on the LCD display.

On the negative side, the viewfinder does not show you any information about the camera's setup or the current shot, such as shutter speed, aperture, and the like. Also, the window provides only an 85% view of the scene. In other words, when you look through this window, you are seeing only 85% of the view that is reaching the sensor. Therefore, if it's critical to know exactly what parts of the scene will be recorded in your image, you will need to use the LCD display or take a test shot and then check it in playback mode before proceeding with your actual shots. Finally, when you are viewing a subject at a short distance from the camera, parallax error will make it difficult to frame the subject accurately in the viewfinder; in that case you should use the LCD display to compose your shot.

Diopter Adjustment Wheel

The small wheel to the left of the viewfinder lets you dial in optical correction so you can see a sharply focused image in the viewfinder window. Just turn this little wheel in either direction until the image is at its clearest for your eyesight. In some cases, if you normally wear glasses, you may be able to dial in enough of an adjustment that you can take your glasses off and still see the image clearly through the viewfinder.

Playback Button

This button to the lower left of the viewfinder, marked with a small green triangle, puts the camera into playback mode, which allows you to view your images on the LCD and gives you access to the Playback menu. If you press this button while the camera is in playback mode, the camera will switch to shooting mode, unless you turned the camera on using this button. You can turn the camera on using the playback button, which is the only way to power on the camera without turning the lens. If you do this, the camera will start up in Playback mode, so you can view your images. However, if you turn the camera on in this way, you cannot switch it into shooting mode by pressing the shutter button; you have to then turn the camera fully on by turning the lens, in order to get into shooting mode. I discuss your options for playback in Chapter 6.

AE/Zoom-in Button

This button, just below the Playback button, has different functions in shooting and playback modes. In shooting mode, as the AE (for autoexposure) button, when the X10 is set to one of the shooting modes that allow this setting, it lets you select the light metering system to be used by the camera for determining the proper exposure. Press the AE button and the camera will display its screen for selecting the metering method. The camera will display the heading Photometry at the top of the screen. To select one of the choices, turn the main command dial or the sub-command dial to the left or right until your selection is highlighted. Then press the Menu/OK button to make the selection, and an icon representing the selected method will appear in the lower left corner of the display, just to the right of the icon representing the current shooting mode.

The three choices for metering method are Multi, Spot, and Average. With Multi, the recommended setting for general shooting, the camera evaluates the brightness throughout the scene, but takes into account factors such as composition, colors, and how the brightness values are distributed throughout the scene. In other words, it tries to make an intelligent assessment of which part of the scene is most important and should be used to determine the correct exposure.

With Spot, the camera considers only the light inside the two percent of the scene in the very center of the display. (The camera does not display any frame or circle to mark the area used by the Spot setting.) When you set the metering method to Spot, you can observe the effects of the exposure system quite dramatically by setting the camera to Program exposure mode and aiming the center portion of the screen at various points, some bright and some dark, and seeing how dramatically the brightness of the scene in the camera's display changes. If you try a similar experiment by moving the camera around to aim at differently lit areas in Multi or Average mode, you will still see changes, but much more subtle and gradual ones.

With Average mode, the camera measures the amounts of light through all areas of the display and averages them to obtain the value for the exposure setting. In this mode, the camera does not attempt to determine what parts of the scene are most important. This method is useful for scenes that do not have great variations in lighting, such as landscapes.

In playback mode, this button is used to zoom in on an image that is being viewed on the LCD display. Once playback mode is in effect, press this button repeatedly to zoom to higher levels of magnification; a horizontal bar will appear at the upper left of the display to show how high the magnification level is, and an inset image will appear at the lower right to show what part of the image is being displayed at the zoomed level. Also, if you have displayed index screens using the zoom-out button, pressing this button will cycle through those screens until the normal display is reached again. Playback functions are discussed in more detail in Chapter 6.

AF/Zoom-out Button

The next button down on the camera's left side also has different uses in shooting and playback modes. In shooting mode, the AF button is used to alter the position and size of the autofocus frame, but only when the focus mode is set to AF-S (for single autofocus) and the AF Mode option on the Shooting menu is set to Area. When these settings are made, there will be a white rectangular focus frame in the center of the display.

If these conditions are in place, press and release the AF button to activate the movable focus frame. You will see 49 crosses appear, representing the possible focus points, and the focus frame will turn green, meaning it is active and now can be moved and/or re-sized. Then, turn the sub-command dial or press the direction buttons to move the frame to any one of the 49 focus points on the display. To return the frame to the center, press the Menu/OK button. To resize the frame, while the focus frame is active, turn the main command dial left or right. To immediately return the frame to its normal size, press in on the main command dial, treating it as a button rather than a dial. When you have finished making adjustments to the focus frame's location and size, press the AF button again to lock in the changes. The focus frame will turn white, indicating that it is ready to focus on your subject. Whenever you need to move or re-size the frame again, just press the AF button to activate the frame and repeat the above process.

In playback mode, if you have enlarged an image by pressing the Zoom-in button as discussed earlier, you can press the Zoom-out button to return the image to normal size through decreasing degrees of magnification. Once it is at normal size, pressing this button again calls up an index screen that shows five images arranged in inset blocks. Use the sub-command dial to scroll through those images and on to other images on your memory card. Pressing the button again will bring up screens showing four images, then nine, then 100. Move through these screens with the sub-command dial. There is more information about playback functions in Chapter 6.

White Balance Button

The final button on the camera's left side has a single and very important function—to let you select the white balance setting for the X10. One issue that arises in all photography is that film, or a digital camera's sensor, reacts differently to colors than the human eye does. When you or I see a scene in daylight or indoors under various types of artificial lighting, we generally do not notice a difference in the hues of the things we see depending on the light source. However, the camera does not have this auto-correcting ability. The camera "sees" colors differently depending on the "color temperature" of the light that illuminates the object or scene in question. The color temperature of light is a numerical value that is expressed in a unit known as Kelvins (K). A light source with a lower Kelvin rating produces a "warmer" or more reddish light. A light source with a higher Kelvin rating produces a "cooler" or more bluish light. For example, candlelight is rated at about 1,800 K; indoor tungsten light (ordinary light bulb) is rated at about 3,000 K; outdoor sunlight and electronic flash are rated at about 5,500 K; and outdoor shade is rated at about 7,000 K.

What does this mean in practice? If you are using a film camera, you may need a colored filter in front of the lens to "correct" for the color temperature of the light source. Any given color film is rated to expose colors correctly at a particular color temperature (or, to put it another way, with a particular light source). So if you are using color film rated for daylight use, you can use it outdoors without a filter. But if you happen to be using that film indoors, you will need a color filter to correct the color temperature; otherwise, the resulting picture will look excessively reddish because of the imbalance between the film and the color temperature of the light source.

With a modern digital camera, you do not need to worry about filters, because the camera can adjust its electronic circuitry to correct the "white balance," which is the term used in the context of digital photography for balancing color temperature.

The X10, like most current cameras, has an Auto White Balance setting, which lets the camera choose the proper balance to account for any given light source, and it also has preset settings for the most common types of lighting situation, as well as a custom setting and a color temperature selection that lets you specify the Kelvin value for your lighting source.

Here is how to set the white balance on the X10. First, you have to have the camera in shooting mode, and set to a mode in which the camera will allow you to set white balance. In the EXR Auto, Auto, Advanced, and Scene Position shooting modes, the camera sets itself to Auto White Balance. If you want to set it yourself, the camera must be in one of the other (non-Auto) EXR modes, or in the Program, Aperture Priority, Shutter Priority, Manual exposure, or Movie mode.

When the camera is in one of these modes, press the WB button, and a menu pops up on the right listing all of the options. (This menu does not disappear quickly, as some other menus do; it will stay on the screen as long as you need it.)

By pressing the up and down buttons or by turning the main command dial or the sub-command dial, scroll through the list until the selection you want is highlighted. One nice feature is that the image on the LCD changes to show the effect of each setting as you highlight it. All of the selections other than Auto, the first one, are represented by icons; as you highlight each one, a label for that setting appears to the left of the icon.

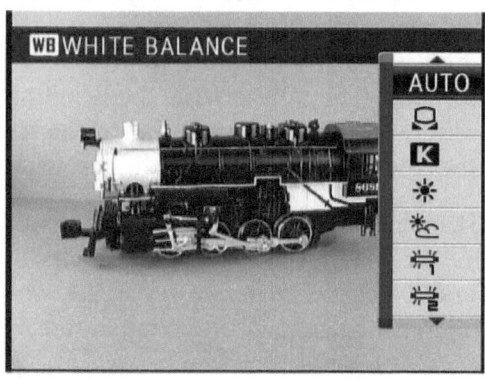

The choices for white balance are Auto, Custom, Color Temperature, Fine, Shade, Fluorescent Light-1, Fluorescent Light-2, Fluorescent Light-3, Incandescent, and Underwater. (In Movie mode, Custom is not available.) All of them are self-explanatory except, perhaps, for Fine, which is the term Fujifilm uses for daylight or direct sunlight. You do need to know a few details about how these settings work, though.

First, the three Fluorescent settings are for different varieties of lamps: Number 1 is for "daylight" lamps; number 2 is for "warm white"; number 3 is for "cool white." You may see one of these labels on the lamp or on the packaging it came in. If not, some test shots may be in order to figure out which setting is best for the particular fluorescent bulbs you are dealing with.

Next, if you select Custom, it is up to you to set the white balance manually. Use this option when you are faced with mixed lighting from multiple sources, or from a reddish or otherwise unusual light source. To make this setting, highlight Custom, and then press the OK button or the right direction button. The next screen will display messages advising you to press the shutter button to measure the white balance or to press OK or the Display/Back button to cancel.

Aim the lens at a white (or gray) surface that fills the white square on the screen and press the shutter. The camera will then display a message at the top of the display: either Completed!, Under, or Over. If Completed! is displayed, you have succeeded; press the OK button to set the new white balance.

If you see Under or Over, that means the lighting was too dim or bright to register the white balance properly; you can try again with exposure compensation adjusted for the lighting, or try with less or more light or in a different area. Once you are finally successful, the new setting will be available by choosing the Custom option for white balance, even after the camera has been powered off and back on.

Note: You can use the Custom setting to add a color tint to a scene for creative effect. For example, you can set white balance manually using a red surface for the measurement, which will result in a pronounced blue tint for pictures taken under the light source that you used when setting that white balance value. Just be careful to turn the white balance setting back to Auto or another more normal setting when you don't want that special effect for your images. (You also might want to recalibrate the Custom setting using a white or gray surface.)

The Color Temperature setting can be useful also. Once you highlight that selection, the camera displays a menu listing all of the possible values, from 10,000 Kelvin at the top to 2500 Kelvin at the bottom. If you have a meter to read the color temperature of your light source, you can use that value here.

I use a Sekonic Prodigi meter, shown below, which is very helpful in measuring the color temperature when I am using a lighting mixture such as daylight from a window and artificial lights. Or, you can use a known figure for various types of lighting, as set out at page 50 of the Fujifilm user's guide (candlelight at 2,000 K; sunlight at 5,000 K, for example).

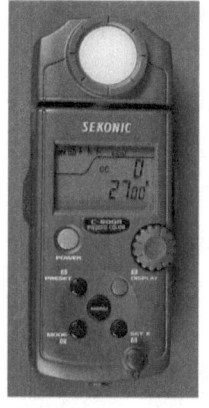

As you scroll through each numerical value, the LCD display changes to show the effect of the setting on the image. You can use the Color Temperature option to achieve a particular look. For example, if you set the color temperature in the 2500 K range when the actual color temperature is higher, you will get a "cooler" look than normal—with bluish, wintry tints. If you select a value closer to 10,000 K when the actual color temperature is lower, the image will appear considerably "warmer" than normal, with reddish, sunset-like hues.

The chart on the next page shows how white balance settings change the look of your images. The same scene was shot each time under consistent incandescent lighting; the only thing that changed was the white balance setting on the X10.

Here are a few things to point out about these white balance illustrations. First, the Custom setting was calibrated on the gray object near the front of each image; that is a photographic "gray card," which has a neutral gray shade designed for setting white balance. The Color Temperature setting was set at 2700 Kelvins. As you can see, the Auto setting did not get the colors quite right; only the Custom, Color Temperature, and Incandescent settings did a good job with the incandescent lighting that was illuminating the scene.

Fujifilm X10 White Balance Sample Images

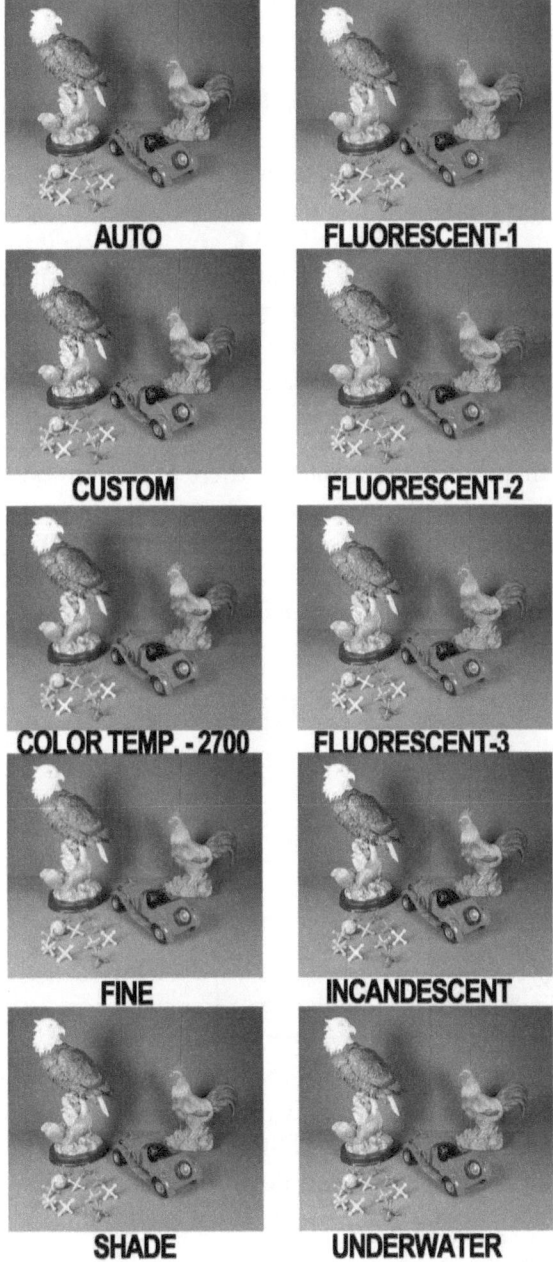

There is one more point about white balance on the X10 to be aware of. Somewhat oddly, there is no white balance setting for Flash, as there is on many other cameras. The Fujifilm user's guide at page 50 says that the white balance system adjusts for flash lighting only with the Auto and Underwater settings, and that you should turn the flash off in other cases. I have found that the Fine setting usually works quite well with the built-in flash, and you can also use the Color Temperature selection, setting it to about 5000 K and adjusting it from there as needed. However, given Fujifilm's admonition, it may be smarter just to use the Auto setting when shooting with flash. Of course, if you shoot using the RAW image quality setting (or RAW plus JPEG), you can always adjust your white balance later, in your RAW processing software.

Finally, as I mentioned in Chapter 4, there is an item on the Shooting menu called White Balance Shift. With this option, you can fine-tune the white balance setting by adjusting it along two axes—red–cyan and blue–yellow. Once you select this menu item, press the OK button or the right direction button to move to the adjustment screen.

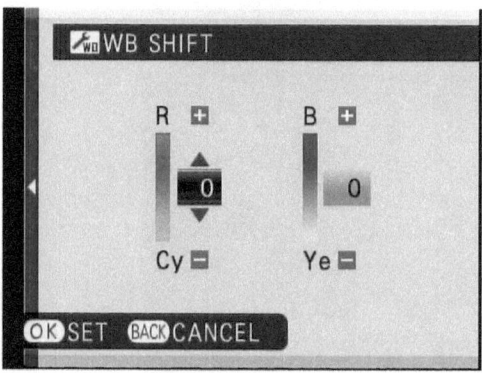

Then use the left and right direction buttons to move the selection block to either the left (red-cyan) or right (blue-yellow) axis. When one of those blocks is highlighted, turn the sub-command dial or use the up and down direction buttons to adjust the colors as you want them. There are nine levels of adjustment available, both positive and negative, so you can achieve a dramatically different color effect, depending on how much of an adjustment you dial in. In fact, if you want, you can use this feature for creative effects, such as imposing a distinctly reddish or bluish tint on an image. However, this menu option is not available for shooting movies, so any adjustment you make will not carry over for movie-making.

Main Command Dial

The main command dial is the small black wheel that sticks out of the back of the camera, just to the right of the top edge of the LCD screen. It has many uses, including adjusting settings such as shutter speed and aperture. You can turn this dial to select different settings for aperture and shutter speed using the Program Shift feature, as described in Chapter 3. Also, when you have pressed one of the buttons that calls up a selection screen, such as the self-timer button, the AE button, the Flash button or the Drive button, you can turn this dial to navigate through some of the selection screens. And, when you have pressed the AF button to activate the focus frame when the AF Mode is set to Area, you can re-size the focus frame by turning the main command dial right or left.

The main command dial also can function as a push-button, which may not be immediately obvious from looking at it. To use it in this way, you push firmly in on the dial, and it will trigger a function in certain situations. The dial has this function in Manual exposure mode; press in on the dial to change the functions of this dial and the sub-command dial for controlling shutter speed and aperture. Also, when you have been adjusting the size of the focus frame in the Area AF Mode, pressing in on this dial will return the frame immediately to its normal size.

In playback mode, you can press in on the main command dial to zoom in on the active focus point in the image being displayed. This function is very convenient for checking the sharpness of your recorded image. Press in again to zoom back out. Note that, if the image was taken with manual focus, a press of the button will zoom into the center of the image, because there is no active focus point as there is with images taken with autofocus.

Also, when an individual image is displayed on the screen in playback mode, turning the main command dial will bring up two screens with detailed information about the image. I'll discuss that operation further in Chapter 6.

AEL/AFL Button

This button directly below the main command dial has two important functions. First, it lets you lock either exposure or focus, or both. You can choose which function or functions the button locks through the AE/AF-Lock Button item on the Setup menu. Depending on how you set that menu item, a press of the button will lock just focus, just exposure, or both focus and exposure. You also can use the AE/AF-Lock Mode item on that menu to determine whether you need to hold down the button to lock the setting(s), or whether the button acts as a toggle switch that you can press and release.

To use the button, aim at your subject and press and hold the AEL/AFL button, or press and release it, depending on how it is set up, as discussed above. The focus and/or exposure value measured by the camera at that time will remain locked for as long as the button is held down (or until it is pressed again, if it is set up as a toggle switch). The exposure will be measured when you press the AEL/AFL button and locked while the button is active. However, focus is not measured until you press the shutter button down halfway to evaluate the focus. You have to press the AEL/AFL button after evaluating focus with the shutter button, and then the AEL/AFL button will lock in the focus setting. It probably makes more sense to evaluate both focus and exposure with the shutter button, and then press the AEL/AFL button to lock them both in.

Here is one example of how to use this button. Suppose you

are at an historic site and you want to make sure your focus is set on an antique chest at one side of a display table. With the AEL/AFL button set for locking focus only (through the Setup menu), aim the X10 so that its focus frame is on the chest, press the shutter button halfway down to evaluate the focus, and press the AEL/AFL button, with the result that the camera displays a green frame showing that the focus is set at that point. With the focus still locked by the button, aim the camera back in the direction of the other items, with the chest off to the side. Now, when you press the shutter button down to take the picture, the focus will remain locked on the chest off to the side, even though the camera likely would have focused on some other point with the current composition.

The second job performed by the AEL/AFL button is to allow the quick use of autofocus when the camera is set to manual focus. As I discussed earlier in talking about manual focus, when the focus switch is on the MF setting, the normal way to focus is by turning the sub-command dial on the back of the camera. But, if it is taking too many turns to do that, or if you want the camera to give you a head start on focusing, just press this button in, and the camera will, if possible, focus automatically as well as it can. You can then continue the process by adjusting focus manually with the sub-command dial.

Indicator Lamp

This small lamp, positioned high up on the back of the camera just under the flash shoe, is hard to see until it lights up. It glows a bright green, orange, or red at various times to announce processes or problems. Some of the main signals to be aware of are a steady green when focus is locked; steady orange when images are being recorded; and blinking rapidly orange when the flash is charging. The complete list of signals is at page 21 of the official Fujifilm user's manual for the X10.

Sub-command Dial and Buttons

The most prominent set of controls on the back of the camera is contained within the perimeter of the circular control pad, which includes the sub-command dial, with a ridged rim, in the center. Turning the sub-command dial serves multiple purposes, as discussed below. The four edges of this dial function as buttons; you press in on the ridged edge at the top, bottom, left, or right of the dial to activate those buttons. Each of these four buttons serves as a direction button to move through menus, images, and other items in some contexts. Each of the buttons also has another purpose designated by a white icon or label next to the button. Finally, in the center of the sub-command dial is the Menu/OK button. I will discuss each of these controls in turn.

Sub-command Dial

The sub-command dial is the ridged dial that surrounds the Menu/OK button. It serves various purposes when you place your finger on the raised edge and turn the dial left or right. One of its major functions is to focus the lens when the camera is set to manual focus mode. You just turn this dial left to focus nearer, and right to focus farther away. (You can reverse those directions using the Focus Control Dial item on the Setup menu.)

When you are navigating through the camera's menu screens, turning the dial moves the selection block from item to item. The dial also can be used to set the shutter speed when the camera is in Shutter Priority mode and to set the aperture in Aperture Priority mode. In Manual exposure mode, the sub-command dial can be used to set either aperture or shutter speed; that function is switched by pressing in on the main command dial. Also, when the camera is in Program shooting mode, turning the sub-command dial carries out the "Program Shift" function of selecting an aperture-shutter speed pair that is equivalent to the settings selected by the camera's autoexposure system, as described in Chapter 3.

Turning the sub-command dial left or right also selects items from the small menus that pop up on the display when you are using the camera's physical controls, such as the Flash, Macro focus, White balance, or Drive mode button.

In normal playback mode, you can turn the sub-command dial left or right to scroll through your images in either direction.

Menu/OK Button

This button, which is one of the most-used controls on the camera, serves as a selection, confirmation, or "set" button when you choose certain options. For example, whenever you use the camera's menu system and highlight a desired menu option, you can press the Menu/OK button to confirm and set your selection. You also press this button to get access to the menu system.

The button also has some more specific functions. When you are using the Area autofocus mode, in which the focus frame can be moved around the screen, you can return the frame to the center of the screen immediately by pressing the Menu/OK button. In addition, you can use this button to lock the RAW button so it won't operate and to limit the functioning of the buttons on the sub-command dial so they can't accidentally be pressed to active the Drive mode, Flash mode, self-timer, or Macro focus settings. To do this, press and hold the Menu/OK button for about two seconds until a padlock icon appears on the screen. The four direction buttons on the sub-command dial will still continue to work as navigation controls; they just won't perform their secondary functions. All of these controls will now remain locked until you hold the OK button down again to remove the lock.

In playback mode, the OK button will return a zoomed image immediately to normal size, and you can use it to display an image that is highlighted on an index screen. Also, the OK button will un-zoom the magnified display on the Focus Check screen. In addition, you can press the OK button to take a still picture while the camera is recording a movie.

Direction Buttons

Each of the four edges—top, bottom, left, and right—on the sub-command dial is also a "button" that you can press to get access to a setting or operation. This may not be immediately obvious, and sometimes it can be tricky to press them in exactly the right spot, but these four direction buttons are very important to your control of the camera. You use them to navigate through menus and through screens for settings, whether moving left and right or up and down.

You also use the direction buttons in playback mode to move through your images and, when you have enlarged an image using the AE/Zoom-in button, to scroll around within the magnified image.

In addition to these navigational duties, the direction buttons are used for several miscellaneous functions. For example, the down direction button is used to start playback of a movie, and the up button is used to stop playback. The down button also is used to "open up" a sequence of shots taken in continuous-shooting mode so the images in the sequence can be viewed individually.

Finally, each of the direction buttons also has its own separate identity, as indicated by the icon or label that appears next to each of the buttons, as discussed below.

Up Button: Delete/Drive Mode

When the camera is in playback mode, pressing the up button while an image is on the display brings up a message asking if you want to erase the image; highlight OK or Cancel in response, as prompted on the screen.

When the camera is in shooting mode, the up button gives you access to the multiple options for Drive mode, which are

CHAPTER 5: OTHER CONTROLS

among the most powerful features of the camera.

A press of this button brings up a menu of options for continuous shooting. When you press the button, a vertical menu appears at the left of the screen with seven choices represented by icons: still image, burst shooting, Best Frame Capture, AE bracketing, ISO bracketing, film simulation bracketing, and dynamic range bracketing.

The details for each of these Drive modes are discussed below. Before discussing them, though, I will provide a brief introduction to the concept of continuous shooting.

With film cameras, continuous shooting involves the use of a special motor to advance the film rapidly, and often the use of an extra-large cassette to hold a large quantity of film. This sort of equipment is bulky and expensive, and, of course, shooting and developing large numbers of exposures is itself quite expensive. With digital cameras like the X10, expense is no longer a factor. Continuous shooting is literally available at your fingertips whenever you want to take advantage of it.

The usefulness of shooting rapid bursts of exposures is more obvious in some contexts than in others. For example, when you're shooting sports events, it's clearly worthwhile to fire off a swift sequence of shots in order to catch the perfect instant when a baseball player tags a runner heading for home plate, or to catch a soccer ball as it bounces off a player's head towards the goal. But continuous shooting also can be helpful in more ordinary shooting, such as when you're taking pictures of children at play. You have a better chance of capturing a fleeting smile, laugh, or cute gesture if you keep the exposures rolling. And, even when your subject is not moving noticeably at all, it can be advantageous to take multiple shots. For example, when you're taking a portrait, there may be subtle changes in the subject's expression, or in the way sunlight falls on a cheek, or in the subject's posture. Taking a series of shots gives you some insurance against coming away from the photo session with no winning shots.

With that introduction, let's take a look at the terrific assortment of continuous-shooting options that the X10 provides. To get access to these options, press the up direction button, which is marked Drive, and a menu will pop up on the screen showing the menu of available settings. If you don't choose an option within about 3 seconds, the menu will disappear.

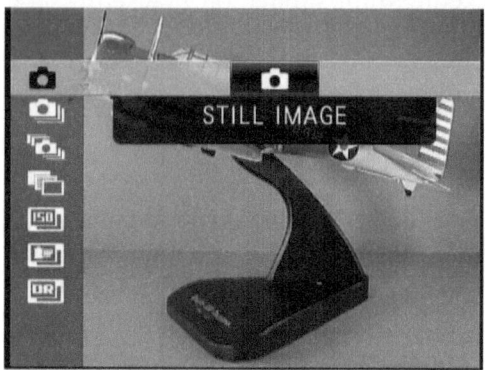

All of the settings (except the first one, for single shots) offer various ways to take multiple shots, with a press (or press and hold) of the shutter button. For burst shooting, the exposure and focus settings are fixed when the first image is taken, and they will not vary for later shots, even if the conditions would require different settings.

You cannot use the flash for any of the multiple-shot settings. Neither ISO, Film Simulation, nor Dynamic Range bracketing will operate when the camera is set to take RAW or RAW+JPEG images through the Setup menu. Autoexposure bracketing, however, is still available with RAW or RAW+JPEG. Continuous shooting options are not available with all shooting modes; see page 126 of the X10 User's Manual for the complete chart of restrictions.

Following are details for each of the options on the Drive menu.

CHAPTER 5: OTHER CONTROLS

Still Image

This is the normal mode for shooting images. Select this option to turn off all continuous shooting. Note that, in some cases, having one of the continuous Drive mode options will make it impossible to make other settings. For example, you cannot use flash when any of the continuous-shooting options are in effect. Therefore, you need to select the still image setting if you want to use the flash. Also, you cannot shoot in the RAW format with some of the continuous-shooting options, as noted below. So, if you want to have access to the full range of selections, turn off the RAW setting on the Setup menu.

For the discussion below, I will assume you have the flash retracted and the RAW option turned off.

Burst Shooting

This second option on the Drive mode menu is one of the most useful and powerful settings on the X10, because it gives you the ability to shoot a series of rapid-fire images as you hold down the shutter button. This capability is, of course, extremely useful in many contexts, from shooting an action sequence at a sports event to taking a series of shots of a portrait subject in order to capture his or her changing facial expressions.

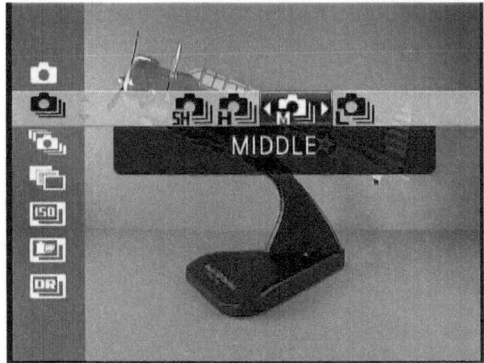

When you scroll down to this line, you will see four speed choices in a gray bar extending across the display, from left to right: Super-High, High, Middle, and Low. These labels mean

167

that you have the choice of setting the camera to shoot at varying frame rates with these general descriptions. The frame rate is the number of images the camera can take as you hold down the shutter button. For Super-High, the maximum frame rate is 10 frames per second; for High, the maximum is 7; for Middle it is 5; and for Low it is 3. Of course, as you might expect, those maximum rates can be achieved only under ideal conditions; in other cases, such as when dim light requires a slow shutter speed, the rates will slow down. The camera can take a maximum of 200 images in any one burst, but, as noted, it will not maintain its full speed for that duration.

Using the left and right buttons on the sub-command dial, or turning the main command dial left or right, highlight either one of these options. (I find it easier to use the buttons.) Once you have highlighted one of the choices, you can just let the selection screen disappear, which it will do quite quickly. (You have to move fast to get your selection made.) An icon will appear in the upper left corner of the display announcing your selection, unless you select still image, which is the default choice, for no burst shooting.

As I noted earlier, focus and exposure are locked in with the first shot for all of the burst modes. There also are some other limitations for certain options. With the Super-High setting, the Image Size is automatically set to no more than Medium. Also, if Dynamic Range was set above 100%, it will automatically be reduced to 100%. With the High selection, Image Size can still be Large, but not at the maximum pixel count of the 4:3 aspect ratio, and Dynamic Range will be reduced to 100%.

Once you have finished taking a burst of shots, you will notice that it can take the camera quite a while to record them all to the memory card; you will see the orange indicator light glowing at the upper middle of the camera's back. If you need to take a new picture during that time, you can cancel the recording operation by pressing the Display/Back button at the bottom of the camera, below and to the left of the sub-command dial. If you do that, though, you will lose the images that had not yet been written to the memory card.

Because the shots you take in a burst have to be sent to the camera's memory buffer and then written to the memory card, there is a limit to the number of shots that can be taken at the maximum speed; after several shots the rate of shooting will slow down to a considerably lesser rate, but the shooting will continue on at a reasonably rapid pace, roughly one or two frames per second. In my experience, the maximum rate only lasts for a second or two before settling into a slower burst.

Also, somewhat oddly, the camera will allow you to turn on the self-timer and burst shooting at the same time, but, after the self-timer counts down, the camera will take only one shot, no matter what frame rate you have selected. In other words, you can take a "burst," but it will consist of only one shot. If you want to take multiple shots using the self-timer, you need to use the Best Frame Capture feature, discussed next.

Best Frame Capture

The next icon down on the Drive mode menu, which looks like a camera surrounded by two sets of frames, represents the burst mode called Best Frame Capture. With this option, the camera will record several images during the time when you are pressing the shutter button down halfway to evaluate focus and exposure. Then, when you press the shutter button down all the way to capture images, the camera takes a further burst of images. This mode is intended to be used when you are taking pictures of an event that is unpredictable, so you will have a pre-capture buffer that helps you avoid missing the first few instants of the event. For example, if you are watching a child at bat in a baseball game, you might be half-pressing the shutter button each time a pitch comes in, but you would not actually press the button all the way down to capture the images until he or she swings, or maybe only if the bat hits the ball. At that point, the camera will record the images that came before you pressed the button all the way down, as well as the images that occurred after you pressed it down.

To use this feature, select its icon; the camera will prompt you to press the right direction button for "set-up." Press that button, and you will see a screen that lists options to select the shooting speed and the number of frames. First, press the right button to get to the sub-menu for shooting speed, and select Super-High, High, Middle, or Low, just as with the normal burst mode. Then, press the left button or the Display/Back button to return to the previous screen; on that screen, highlight the option for Number of Frames, and press the right button again. On the next screen, use the up and down buttons or the sub-command dial to choose either 16 or 8 as the total number of frames. You will then see either 16 or 8 dots inside a black band on the screen. (If you select 16 shots, the maximum image size is reduced to Medium.) Use the left and right direction buttons to move that band left or right, dividing the white dots between shots taken before the shutter is pressed all the way and those taken after it is pressed all the way.

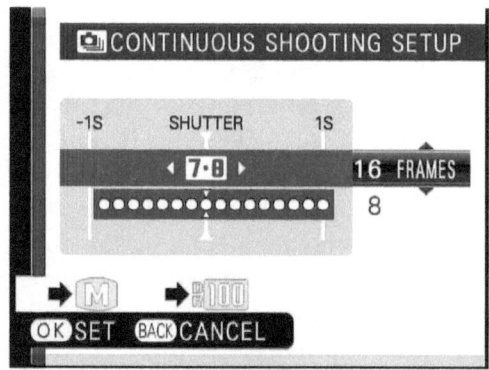

When you are done, those two numbers will appear in a white box above the band with the white dots. For example, with the setup shown above, the X10 will take 7 shots before the shutter is pressed and 8 shots afterwards. The total, including the shot taken with the shutter press, is 16. Press the Menu/OK button to confirm these settings, then press the left button or the Display/Back button to return to the shooting screen.

CHAPTER 5: OTHER CONTROLS

Once you are ready to shoot, press the shutter button to evaluate focus and exposure, and press the shutter button down all the way at the appropriate time; the camera will record the two bursts from before and after the full shutter press.

This feature has its limits; if you press the shutter button all the way down too soon, the camera won't record all of the pre-shutter images, and if you hold it down halfway for too long, it may record only pre-shutter images. But, as a way to let you get the jump on an event and not miss the first second or two of the action, this feature can be of considerable use.

One final note about Best Frame Capture: Although, as noted above, the camera will not take a burst of shots in the standard burst mode when the self-timer is in use, it will take a burst of shots in Best Frame Capture mode after the self-timer counts down. In fact, using Best Frame Capture is the only way to accomplish multiple shots when using the self-timer. This feature can be very useful when you need to take a group portrait using the self-timer; you can place the camera on a tripod, set the self-timer for 10 seconds, turn on Best Frame Capture, and let the camera take as many as 16 shots, to increase your chances of getting good expressions from every subject. The camera will take all 8 or 16 shots, regardless of how you have them divided up between pre- and post-shutter capture.

Exposure Bracketing

This next option on the Drive mode menu lets you set up the camera to take three images continuously with one press of the shutter button, but with different exposure levels for each image, thereby giving you a greater chance of having one image that is perfectly exposed. This feature also can be used for taking three exposures at different values that you can later combine in editing software to create a composite HDR image.

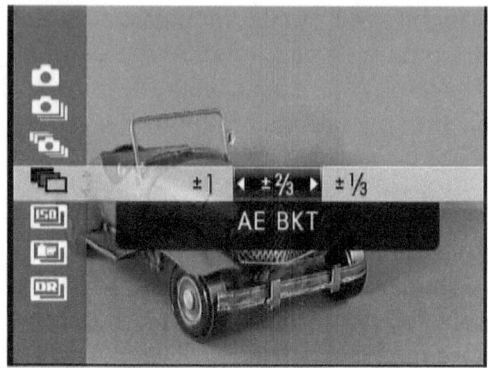

Once you select this option, the fourth one down on the left side of the screen, you will see a gray bar similar to the one for the continuous shooting option. In this case, there are three options to select from using the right and left buttons on the sub-command dial, or by turning the main command dial: intervals of 1, 2/3, and 1/3 stop. Highlight the option you want, which will set the amount by which the three bracketed exposures will differ in their exposure levels. You can then just leave the chosen interval highlighted, and the menu with these choices will soon disappear.

Once you have set this option as you want it and composed your shot, press the shutter button and the camera will take three shots in rapid succession. In this case, unlike the situation with burst shooting, you do not have to hold down the shutter button, because the camera is programmed to make three exposures no matter how long the button is held down.

The first exposure will be taken at the metered value, the second one overexposed by the selected interval, and the third one underexposed to the same extent.

The image shown at left on the next page is an HDR composite, created with Photomatix software, made from three shots by the X10 with autoexposure bracketing, at an interval of 1 full stop between exposures. The image on the right is an HDR composite of the same scene using seven shots taken in Manual exposure mode, at considerably greater exposure intervals.

In my opinion, the version created from the bracketed images is just about equal to the other version in its HDR effect.

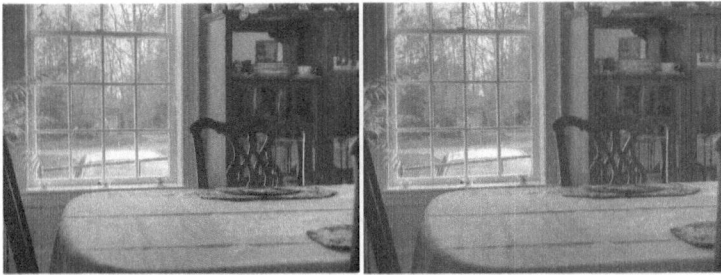

ISO Bracketing

ISO bracketing works in the same way as exposure bracketing, except that, instead of varying the level of exposure, the camera varies the ISO setting for the three images. You have the same choices for the interval of stops between shots as with exposure bracketing. In this case, the camera actually takes just one shot and then internally creates two more shots, one with the ISO setting raised to produce overexposure and one with the setting lowered to produce underexposure. Therefore, you will hear the shutter operate only once. In other ways, the bracketing is just like exposure bracketing.

For example, I just used this feature to take a bracketed series; the first image was taken at ISO 1600, the value chosen by the camera for proper exposure, and the next two images were internally processed at ISO 2000 and ISO 1250.

Film Simulation Bracketing

Next, the X10 can produce a series of images using the three choices for color film simulation: Provia, Velvia, and Astia. In this case, there are no settings for you to adjust—the camera takes one shot and then produces three images using the film simulation settings to produce those three different film styles. Here again, as with ISO Bracketing, you will hear the shutter activate only once. This is a good option to use for comparing the effects of the three major Film Simulation settings, especially when you are first starting out with the X10; it may help you develop a feel for which setting is most appealing to you for various subjects.

Dynamic Range Bracketing

The last type of bracketing available with the X10 lets you see the effects of three different Dynamic Range settings—100%, 200%, and 400%. As with film simulation bracketing, there are no adjustments for you to make. In this case, the camera takes three separate shots with the three different Dynamic Range settings. This option can be quite useful in situations where there is a mixture of shadows and bright light, but you are not certain how strong a Dynamic Range setting would be best.

Right Button: Flash

The right direction button, with the lightning bolt icon next to it, also is the control for changing the flash mode. There are a couple of important preliminary points to note about this button: First, it will not function as the Flash button unless you have first popped up the built-in flash unit using the flash pop-up switch, or you have attached a compatible external flash unit. Also, in certain shooting modes, including the Advanced mode and the Landscape or Fireworks subsets of Scene Position mode, among others, the flash is disabled and this button will have no effect.

In addition, the flash is not available if you have selected any of the continuous shooting or bracketing options using the Drive button. It also is not available if you have turned on Super Macro mode for focusing. Finally, flash will be deactivated if you have turned on the camera's Silent Mode, either through the Setup menu or by holding down the Display/Back button for a couple of seconds.

For the following discussion, I assume you have a flash unit (built-in or external) activated, have the camera set to the Program shooting mode or another one that is compatible with the use of flash, and do not have Silent Mode in effect.

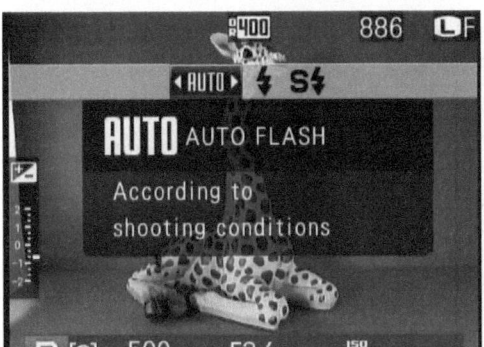

When you press the Flash button, a small menu pops up displaying the available options for the flash, with one of them selected. These will change depending on the current shooting mode.

To select an option, you have to quickly move to your desired choice by using the left and right buttons on the sub-command dial, or by turning either the main command dial or the sub-command dial. I find it easiest to just keep pressing the right (Flash) button until the option I want is selected. Once your chosen option is highlighted, you can just let the button go, and the selection will be complete.

When the camera is set to Program mode, all three possible options are available: Auto Flash, Forced Flash, and Slow Synchro. (A fourth option, Flash Off, is not needed, because you can just retract the flash unit to turn the flash off.)

When Face Detection is turned on through the Shooting menu and the Red Eye Removal option is turned on in the Setup menu, the three flash options change to include the red-eye removal icon—a small image of a human eye next to the flash icon.

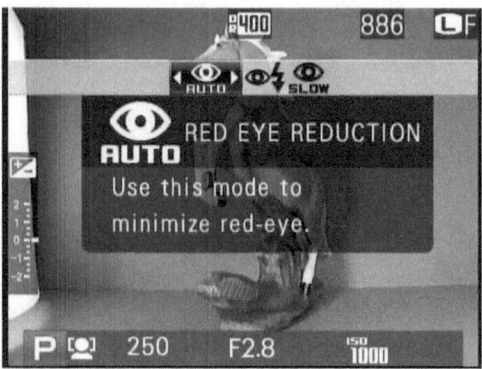

With the Red Eye Removal versions of the Auto Flash, Forced Flash, and Slow Synchro options, when you press the shutter button, the camera will fire a pre-flash before it fires the "actual" flash to take the picture. The idea is to force your subject's pupils to contract, so light cannot bounce off the retinas and produce the eerie glow of "red-eye."

In Aperture Priority mode, all flash modes are available except Auto Flash. In Shutter Priority and Manual modes, the only options available are Forced Flash and having the flash turned off. Slow Synchro is not available in those modes, because you are choosing the shutter speed, and for Slow Synchro to function, the camera has to choose the shutter speed. I'll discuss the Slow Synchro feature further in Chapter 9.

Down Button: Self-timer

The down button is labeled with the clock-dial icon that represents the camera's self-timer. When you press this button, the camera displays a horizontal menu of the three available choices for setting the self-timer: Off, 10 seconds, and 2 seconds.

CHAPTER 5: OTHER CONTROLS

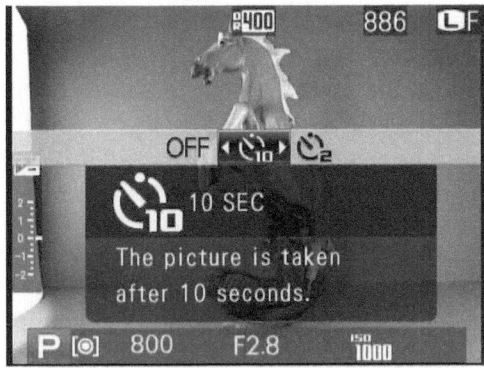

If you set a delay of either 10 seconds or 2 seconds, the camera will delay for that amount of time before taking the picture, after you press the shutter button. Choose 10 seconds if you need a substantial delay so you can get into a group picture after pressing the shutter button; choose 2 seconds if you just need to avoid touching the camera during the exposure, so as to minimize the camera shake that can accompany a shutter press. You might need to use the 2-second delay when you're taking extreme close-ups, because any camera motion could be magnified by the closeness to the subject. Or, the 2-second delay could help when you're shooting in dim light and a slow shutter speed is needed because any camera motion during the long exposure could blur the image.

Note that, once you have selected a self-timer setting, it will remain in effect until you cancel it using this menu option or until the camera is turned off. So, if you find there is an unusual delay after you press the shutter button, you may have turned on this option and forgotten to cancel it. Note also that the X10's unusually bright lamp next to the lens blinks as the self-timer counts down. If you want to avoid having this glaring light flash in your subject's eyes, you can disable it by pressing and holding the Display/Back button to activate Silent Mode, or by turning off the AF Illuminator option in the Setup menu, as discussed in Chapter 7.

One good feature of the X10 is that you can use the self-timer in conjunction with the Best Frame Capture feature of Drive mode. Therefore, you can, for example, set the camera on a tripod with the camera set for shooting 8 or 16 frames, turn on the self-timer for a 10-second delay, and join a group, with the camera taking a rapid-fire series of shots after the delay, making it more likely that at least one image will be a keeper.

You also can use the self-timer in connection with the various Bracketing options. However, you cannot use it when shooting panoramas or movies, and you cannot use it with the normal continuous-shooting option on the Drive mode menu. (To be more precise, you actually can turn on the self-timer and the normal continuous-shooting option at the same time. However, because you will not be holding down the shutter button after the self-timer counts down, only one image will be captured by the "continuous" shooting.)

Left Button: Macro Focus

This final button around the rim of the sub-command dial is labeled with the flower icon that represents macro, or close-up, focus. This button's only purpose is to switch the X10 into Macro mode or Super Macro mode, so you can focus more quickly on subjects that are close to the camera.

The normal focus range of the X10's lens is from 1.6 feet (50 cm) to infinity at its wide-angle position, and 2.6 feet (80 cm) to infinity at the telephoto end. In other words, if you're not using the Macro focus mode, the lens will readily focus on objects as close as 1.6 feet from the lens. If an object is closer than that, the camera will still focus, but it will take longer, because its focus system is calibrated for the more distant objects.

If you press the Macro button and switch into Macro focus mode, the focus range drops down so the camera will focus on objects from 3.9 inches (10 cm) to 9.8 feet (3.0 m) at wide-angle, and 1.6 feet (50 cm) to 16.4 feet (5 m) at telephoto. Using this much more limited range, the camera can more quickly zero in on closer objects.

If you choose the other available option, Super Macro, the focusing range switches to 0.3 inch (1 cm) to 3.2 feet (1 m); Super Macro focusing is available at the wide-angle position only. The camera will still focus on distant objects when set for Macro or Super Macro, but it may take longer to focus.

In order to activate Macro or Super Macro mode, just press the left button and then, as with the other buttons, quickly use the left and right buttons, the main command dial, or the sub-command dial to move the selection block to the right to select the flower icon (Macro) or the flower icon with the magnifying glass (Super Macro).

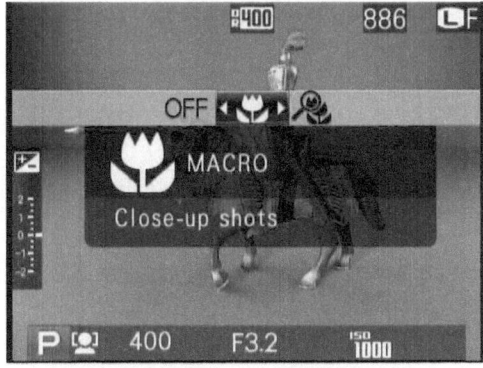

(My preference is just to press the left button two or three times quickly.) You will then see the Macro or Super Macro icon appear in the upper left corner of the display.

You cannot select either macro focus option when the camera is set to EXR Auto mode, though the camera can detect macro scenes and set macro focusing itself in that mode. Macro also cannot be set in Movie mode, or in most of the Scene Position modes. However, in the Flower and Text subsets of Scene Position mode, Macro mode is automatically activated, and you can select Macro with the Natural & Flash and Natural Light options. Also, when Super Macro mode has been selected, the flash will be disabled and cannot be used. I will discuss macro shooting further in Chapter 9.

Display/Back Button

The button marked DISP/BACK, at the very bottom left of the area below the sub-command dial, is used in several ways.

Display Button

First, this button switches among various displays of information on the camera's screen, in both shooting and playback modes. The shooting displays are for still images only; in Movie mode, there is only one display screen that appears in all situations.

There are five shooting displays that are called up by successive presses of this button: Information Display; Standard; Information Off; Custom; and LCD Switched Off. The Custom display is not available in EXR Auto shooting mode, and LCD Off is not available when the focus switch is set to AF-C.

To change displays, press the Display button to bring up the horizontal menu at the bottom of the screen that shows all five choices. Then navigate to the one you want using the main command dial, the sub-command dial, the left and right direction buttons, or, the easiest in my view, by pressing the Display button repeatedly to move through the menu. Once you have highlighted the choice you want, just let the button go and the selection will take effect. The Standard display is shown below.

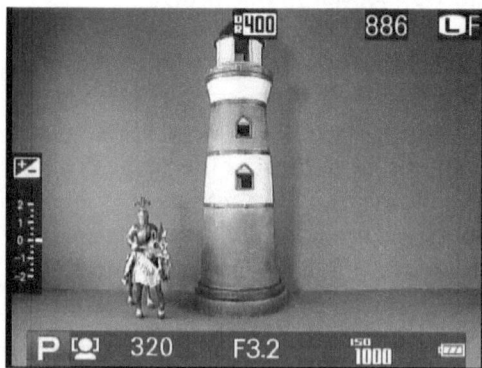

The Standard display overlays the live view of the scene with basic shooting information, including shooting mode, metering mode, shutter speed, aperture, ISO, exposure compensation, Dynamic Range setting, number of images remaining, image size and quality, flash mode, and battery status. Of course, the items displayed vary somewhat according to the shooting mode and factors such as whether the flash is in use.

A press of the Display button changes the Standard display to the Information Off screen, which shows only the live view, with no information displayed on the screen. After that display comes the Custom display, shown below, which I discussed in Chapter 4 in connection with the Shooting menu item that lets you choose what items are displayed on this screen.

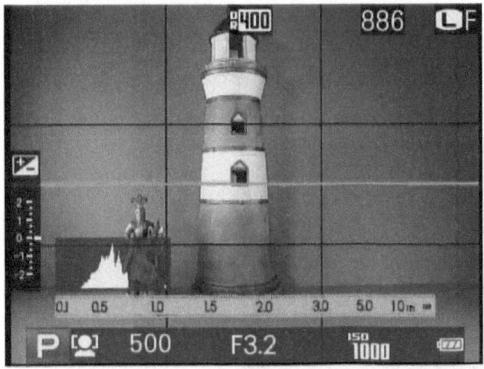

If you check all of the boxes for that menu item, you will have a display like that shown above, which provides a considerable amount of information, along with helpful features such as the histogram and the electronic level. If you uncheck all of the boxes, the only bit of information left on the screen will be an icon announcing the shooting mode. Personally, I like to include every item except the framing guideline and the AF and MF distance indicator scales.

The next view in the display cycle, LCD Off, is self-explanatory. Choose this option if you want to conserve battery power or avoid attracting attention to your camera and yourself by keeping the screen completely dark. Note, though, that the small indicator light up on the camera's back below the flash shoe will still glow green when focus is confirmed, and, if you have set the Image Display item on the Setup menu to any value other than Off, the LCD will display each of your images as soon as you capture it. So, if you want to maximize the darkness of the LCD, you need to turn off that menu item as well as select the LCD Off display for shooting mode. When the camera is connected to a TV with the AV cable, the LCD Off option is disabled.

Finally, there is another option—the Information display—that does not present a live view of the scene, the histogram, or the electronic level, but provides much of the information that can be included on the Custom display as well as one other item—a detailed representation of the focus area, showing which focus point is in use if one has been selected, whether chosen by the photographer (in Area AF mode) or by the camera in (Multi AF mode).

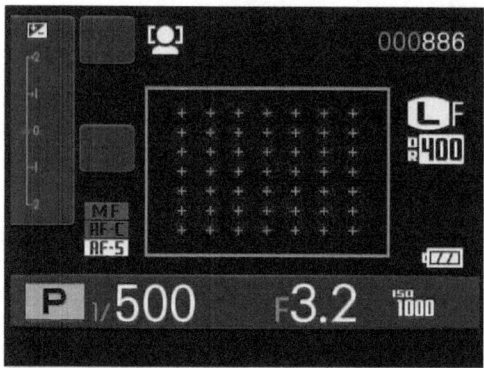

This display is intended for use when you are using the camera's optical viewfinder to compose your shots, so you can see detailed information about the camera's status even though you are not using the LCD to compose the shot. (The viewfinder, of course, displays no information about the camera or the shot.)

In playback mode, there are four screens available through presses of the button.

CHAPTER 5: OTHER CONTROLS

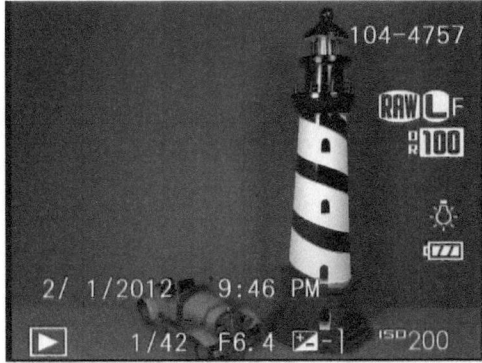

The first playback display option, shown above, the Information On screen, shows the recorded image overlaid with icons and figures showing the date and time the picture was taken, its identification number, image quality and size, aperture, shutter speed, ISO, and Dynamic Range setting. The battery status icon also is shown. The second view is of the image only, with no information overlaid on it.

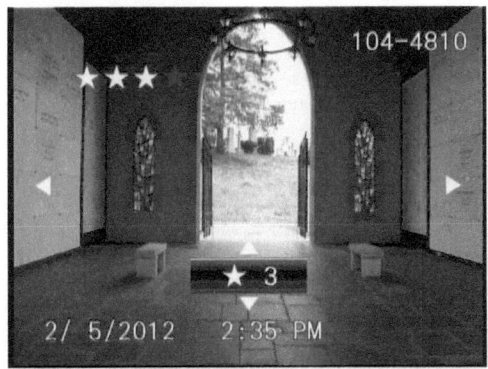

The third view, seen above, is the Favorites screen, which includes only the image number, date and time, and your rating, along with a selection box for changing the image's rating (number of stars). I will discuss Favorites in Chapter 6.

183

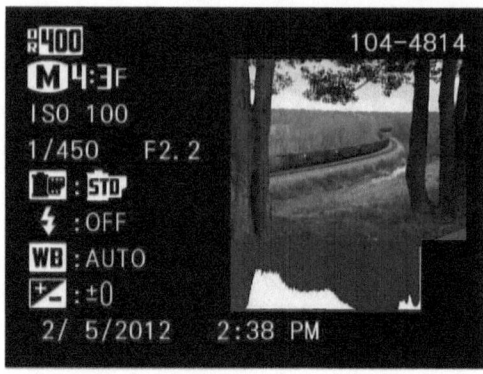

The fourth and final view in playback mode, shown above, is the most detailed view. It includes a thumbnail version of the image, a histogram below that, and, on the left side of the display, considerable details, including the Dynamic Range setting, image quality and size, ISO, shutter speed, aperture, Film Simulation mode, Flash mode, White Balance setting, exposure compensation, and date and time the image was made.

Also note that, no matter which of the four playback displays is selected, you can call up a detailed series of information screens for any image by repeated turns of the main command dial. I'll discuss that function further in Chapter 6.

It also should be noted that all four playback display screens, as well as the detailed information screens, are available for videos as well as for still images, though there is not very much information available for videos, because the camera uses automatic settings for the most part.

There is one other function of the Display/Back button in playback mode that should be mentioned. When you are viewing an index screen with multiple images, once you have highlighted an image, you can bring it up on the screen to view individually by pressing this button. (You also can press the OK button to do the same thing.) Similarly, when an image is enlarged in playback mode, you can return it instantly to normal size with this button (or the OK button).

CHAPTER 5: OTHER CONTROLS

Back Button

The Display/Back button also has a second identity as the Back button. In this capacity, the button serves to exit from menu screens or other selection screens. You will see a message on the display indicating that you use the Back button to exit from a particular screen. It also has a more specific duty when you are viewing the individual shots from a burst of continuous shots. To return to normal playback mode, in which you view just one shot from any burst, you press the Back button, as prompted by a message on the display.

Silent Mode

The very versatile Display/Back button has another function that is not obvious, but is quite important. If you press and hold the button for about two seconds, the camera enters Silent Mode, which also can be invoked through the Setup menu, as discussed in Chapter 7. In Silent Mode, the camera not only suppresses all operational sounds, it also disables the Autofocus Assist lamp and the built-in flash, so there is little risk of attracting unwanted attention to yourself. To cancel Silent Mode, just press and hold the button for two seconds again.

Checking and Updating Firmware

Finally, the Display/Back button has one more function that you won't need often, but that can be critically important. This button is used to check the firmware version that is installed in your X10, and to update that version to a newer one when an updated version is made available by Fujifilm. Firmware is a term for something that is somewhat like both software and hardware; it is the programming for the camera's circuitry, which is electronically recorded into the camera either at the factory, or through your computer if you upgrade the firmware with an update provided by Fujifilm. A new version of the firmware can fix bugs and can even provide new features, so it's well worthwhile checking the Fujifilm web site periodically for updates. Instructions for installing an update are provided on the web site. Essentially, the process involves downloading a file to your computer, saving that file to an SD card formatted for the camera, then placing that card in the camera so the firmware can be installed.

To check the current version of your firmware, hold down the Display/Back button while turning the camera on. The display will show a message stating the current version of the firmware and tell you to press the OK button to proceed to upgrade to a newer version; you can then press the Display/Back button again to cancel the upgrade process, if you were just checking the current version of the firmware.

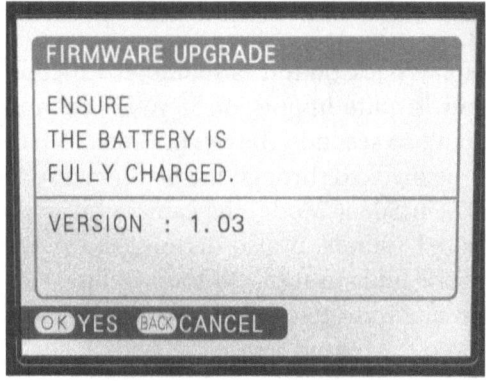

My camera currently has version 1.03, as seen above. This upgrade was important; it fixed some bugs, attempted to address the "orbs" problem (discussed in Chapter 9), and added a completely new function—the ability to program the RAW button to call up a function, just like the Function button. If you have any version with a number lower than that, you should look into downloading the latest version and upgrading. At this writing, the latest firmware can be downloaded at http://www.fujifilm.com/support/digital_cameras/software/#firmware.

RAW Button

This control, directly to the right of the Display/Back button, has functions in both shooting and playback modes. In shooting mode, the button's function was changed with the upgrade

CHAPTER 5: OTHER CONTROLS

of the X10's firmware to version 1.03, as discussed in the previous section. In case you have not upgraded your camera's firmware, I will discuss the operation of the button under earlier versions as well as the current version.

Under versions of the firmware prior to version 1.03 (released in February 2012), pressing this button switches the image quality setting for the next shot you take. If you are taking a series of images with the camera set to Fine (JPEG) quality, for example, you can press this button and the next image will be of the Fine+RAW image quality. Here is how this works.

Under the earlier firmware, this button acts as a one-time toggle switch. That is, if the camera has its image quality set to Fine, a press of this button toggles the setting to Fine+RAW. If the image quality is set to RAW or Fine+RAW, a press of the button switches the image quality to just Fine. The same thing works with the Normal setting.

When you press this button, it only affects the next shot you take. If you want to cancel its effect before taking that shot, you can press the RAW button again to undo the effect of the previous press of the button.

However, with the upgrade of the X10's firmware to version 1.03, the operation of the RAW button has changed rather dramatically. It can no longer be used to toggle the format of the next single shot. Instead, the button acts like a clone of the Function button, which can be programmed to take on any one of several functions, as discussed earlier in this chapter.

To program the RAW button, select the Setup menu item named Fn Button. With the upgrade to firmware version 1.03, Fujifilm added a sub-menu item to this menu. So, select Fn Button from the Setup menu, then press the right direction button to move to the next screen, and select RAW. Then, another press of the right button takes you to the screen for selecting one of the ten possible settings for this button.

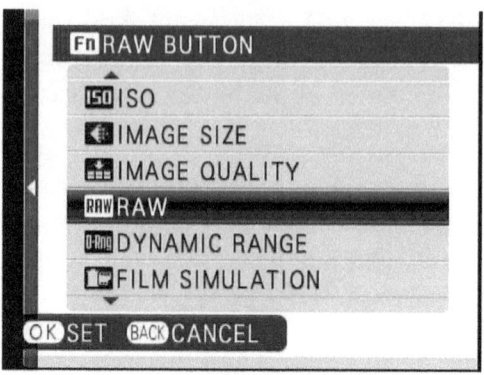

Note that, as shown above, RAW is one of the settings that can be assigned to the RAW button. However, it's important to note that that setting does not just set the camera to take the next single shot in a different format, as the button did under the original firmware. That one-shot toggle of the RAW format is no longer available under the newer version of the firmware.

When the camera is in playback mode, pressing the RAW button has a single specific function, which has not changed with the firmware upgrade. If you press the button while a single RAW quality image is displayed, the camera calls up the RAW Conversion option from the Playback menu and gives you a powerful set of options for converting that image to a JPEG version. That is, you can alter the exposure, White Balance, Dynamic Range, and other aspects of the image right inside the camera, and produce another version of it without affecting the original. I will provide details about this option in Chapter 6, in the discussion of the Playback menu. (If you press the button while a JPEG (non-RAW) image is displayed, nothing will happen; the button will not function.)

Because, with the original firmware version, there was some danger that you could press this button unintentionally while in shooting mode and thereby lose the chance to capture a RAW image that you needed, or thereby record a RAW image that you didn't need, Fujifilm included a way to lock out the use of the button. That capability is still present with the new firmware version. Just press and hold the Menu/OK button for about two seconds, and the use of the RAW button, as well as the use of the four buttons on the sub-command dial for their selection of Macro focus, Drive mode, Flash mode, and the self-timer will be disabled until the process is reversed by pressing and holding Menu/OK again. Note that this locking stays in effect even after the camera is powered off and back on again.

Chapter 6: Playback and Printing

If you're like me, you take the images you've created and import them into your computer, where you manipulate them with software, then post them on the web, print them out, e-mail them, or do whatever else the occasion calls for. In other words, I don't spend a lot of time viewing my pictures in the camera. But that doesn't mean it's not a good thing to know about. Depending on your needs, there may be plenty of times when you take a picture and then need to examine it closely in the camera. Also, the camera can serve as a viewing device like an iPod or other gadget that is designed, at least in part, for storing and viewing photos. So it's worth taking a good look at the various playback functions of the X10.

Normal Playback

Here is a brief rundown of basic playback techniques. First, you should be aware that, when you take a new photo, your image may stay on the screen for a few seconds for review, depending on the setting for the Image Display option in the Setup menu, as discussed in Chapter 7. You can turn this function off, or you can set the camera so the image stays on the display until you dismiss it by pressing the OK button or pressing the shutter button halfway. If your major concern with viewing images in the camera is to check them right after they are taken, this feature is useful. However, you cannot do much with the image while it is displayed in this mode—you cannot display detailed information for it, delete it, or mark it as a favorite. You can enlarge the image using the AE/Zoom-in button, and shrink it back down with the AF/Zoom-out button, but only if you have the Image Display option set to Continuous.

If you want more control over how your images are viewed, you need to work with the settings that are available in playback mode.

To review your images in playback mode, the basic process is very simple. Just press the Playback button, marked by a right-facing triangle at the upper left of the line of buttons on the camera's back. Once you press that button, the camera is in playback mode, and you will see the most recent image saved to the memory card that is in the camera (or, if no card is inserted, to the internal memory). To move back through older images, press the left direction button or turn the sub-command dial to the left. To move through the increasingly more recent images, use the right direction button or turn the sub-command dial to the right. To speed through the images in either direction, hold down the right or left direction button.

Different Playback Screens

When you are viewing an image in single-image display mode, pressing the Display button repeatedly cycles through the four screens that are available: the full image with basic information, including date and time it was taken, image number, image size and quality, and basic shooting information; just the full image with no information displayed; the Favorites screen, where you can mark or unmark an image as one of your Favorites; and a reduced-size image accompanied by detailed recording information, including aperture, shutter speed, ISO, recording mode, exposure compensation, and other data, plus a histogram. I included examples of the information screens in Chapter 5; I discuss the histogram immediately below.

Histogram

As noted above, the most detailed information screen that is summoned by pressing the Display button includes a histogram for the image being displayed. The histogram is a graph, or chart, representing the distribution of dark and bright areas in the image in question. The darkest blacks are represented by vertical bars on the left, and the brightest whites by vertical bars on the right, with continuous gradations in between.

If you have a histogram in which the pattern looks like a tall ski slope coming from the left of the screen down to ground level in the middle of the screen, that means there is a large amount of black and dark areas (high points on the left side of the histogram), and very few bright and white areas (no high points on the right). A ski slope moving from the middle of the screen up to the top of the right side of the screen would mean just the opposite—too many bright and white areas.

A histogram that is "just right" would be one that starts low on the left, gradually rises to a medium peak in the middle of the screen, then moves gradually back down to ground level at the right. That pattern indicates a good balance of whites, blacks, and medium tones. The three images shown below and on the next page include histograms that illustrate the different results for shots that are underexposed, normally exposed, and overexposed.

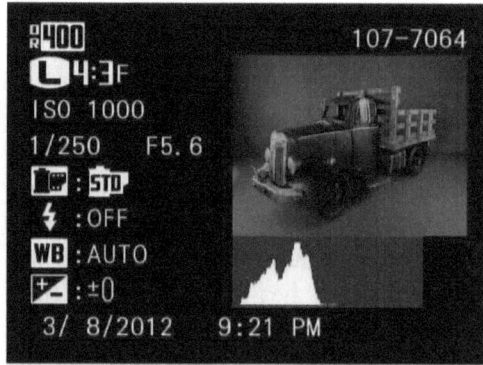

CHAPTER 6: PLAYBACK AND PRINTING

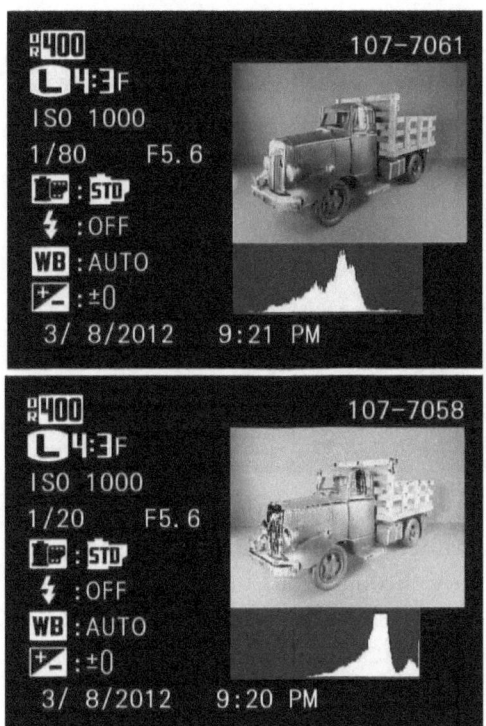

The histogram is an approximation, and should not be relied on too heavily. It may be useful to give you some feedback as to how evenly exposed your image is likely to be. Of course, there may be some cases in which you want to have an image with a histogram skewed to the left or right, because you are striving for an overall low-key (dark) or high-key (bright) appearance.

One additional note about the histogram display on the X10: If the image is overexposed, the overexposed highlight areas on the thumbnail of the image will blink, indicating that those parts of the image are excessively bright.

Index View and Enlarging Images

In playback mode, you can use the AE/Zoom-in and AF/Zoom-out buttons to the left of the LCD screen to view index screens of your images or to enlarge a single image. When you are viewing an individual image, press the AF/Zoom-out button once, and you will see a screen showing five overlapping images, one of which, in front is outlined by a thin gray frame.

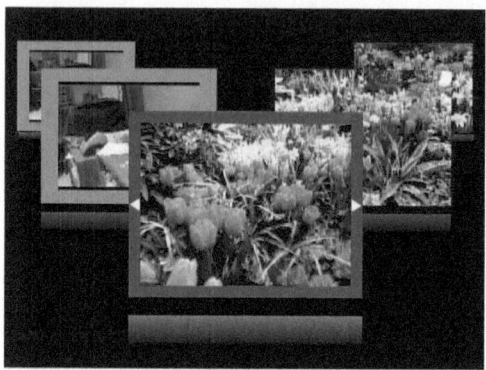

You can then press the OK button or the Display/Back button to bring up the outlined image as the single image on the screen, or you can move through your images with the five-image index screen by pressing the left and right direction buttons or by turning the sub-command dial. To return from the single image to the index screen, press the AF/Zoom-out button again.

In this and other index views, you can identify the images on the screen to some extent by their frames, such as the large gray frames on the two images on the left, above. Images displayed with gray frames represent movies; if you see green frames, as in the 100-frame index screen shown at the bottom of the next page, they indicate frames that represent series of continuous shots.

If you press the AF/Zoom-out button once more, the camera will display an index screen that shows just four images, but these are not overlapping, so you can see each one more clearly. (Actually, Fujifilm calls this the "Two-Frame Display" and recommends it for comparing two images taken in the Natural & Flash mode of Scene Position. There are actually four images displayed, but two of them are very small ones that are waiting to be scrolled into position for the larger views.)

CHAPTER 6: PLAYBACK AND PRINTING

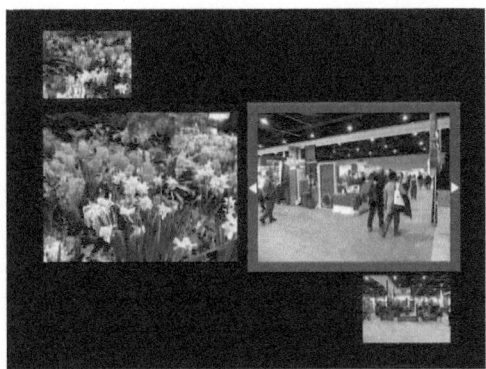

Another press of the AF/Zoom-out button brings a screen with nine images, and a last press brings a 100-image index screen (assuming in each case that you have that many images; if not, there will be blank spaces on the screen).

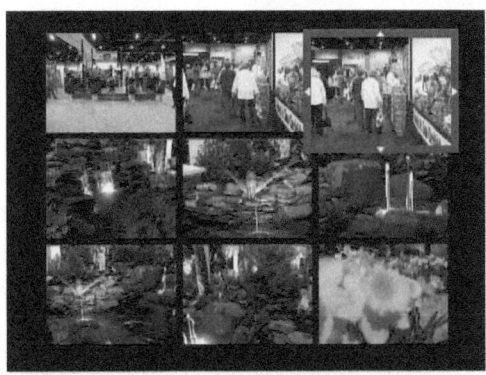

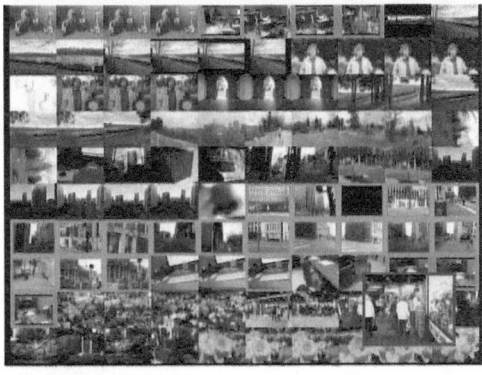

195

You can maneuver through any of these screens to select a single image for viewing. If you want to reduce the number of images per screen, just press the AE/Zoom-in button repeatedly to reverse the progression of index screens. On any of the index screens other than the first one, you can navigate using all four direction buttons or by turning the sub-command dial. (On the first one, you can use only the left and right buttons or the sub-command dial.)

When you are viewing a single image, a press of the AE/Zoom-in button enlarges your view of that image.

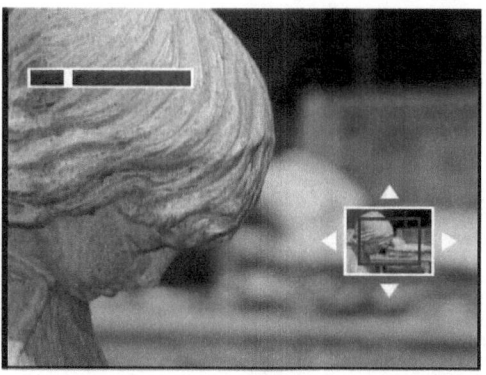

You will briefly see a bar in the upper left of the display that shows the degree of zoom, and a display in the lower right with an inset gray rectangle that represents the portion of the image that is now filling the screen in enlarged view. If you press the AE/Zoom-in button repeatedly, the image will be increasingly enlarged up to a maximum that depends on the Image Size setting. While the image is magnified, you can scroll around within it using the four direction buttons; you will see the inset gray rectangle move around within the white rectangle that represents the whole image. To reduce the image size again, just press the AF/Zoom-out button as many times as necessary, or press the OK or Display/Back button to return immediately to normal size. You can move to other images by turning the sub-command dial even while an image is enlarged, but the next image you view will be at the normal size.

Focus Point and Information Screens

There are some other things you can do when viewing a single image in playback mode. To zoom in on the focus point, press in on the center of the main command dial—the small wheel above the AEL/AFL button. The image will be enlarged to its maximum size with the focus point centered on the display. (In this context, the focus point is the place where the camera's focus frame set the focus.) To zoom back out to normal size, press in on the center of the dial again or press the OK or Display/Back button. If the image was taken with manual focus, the image will be enlarged with its center point in the center.

To see two screens of additional information about an image, while the image is displayed in playback mode, turn the main command dial left or right. If you turn it to the right, the first turn will take you to the first of two black screens with data including the settings for Dynamic Range, Color, Highlight Tone, Shadow Tone, and other items. The next turn will produce a similar screen with data about color space, metering mode, and flash mode; and the third turn will display a screen with a green cross that marks the focus point in the image, if the image was taken with autofocus. Once the first of these screens is displayed, you can also get to the next ones with the down direction button. The following series of images includes the standard information screen, the two detailed information screens, and the screen with the cross marking the focus point.

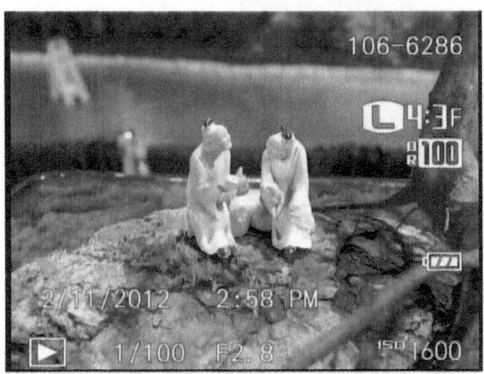

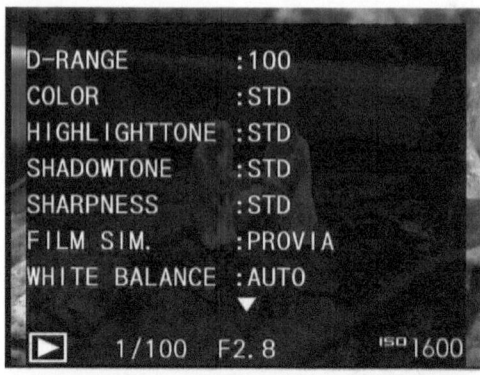

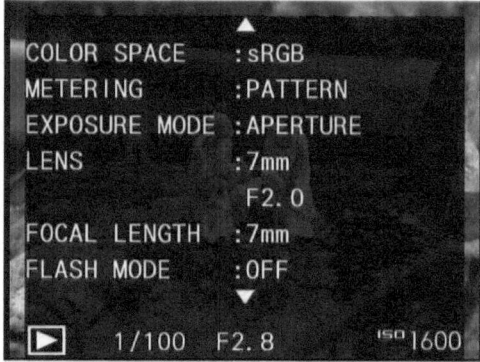

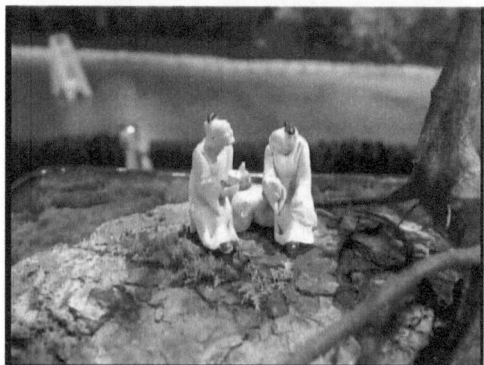

Marking Favorites

When you have a single image displayed on the screen in playback mode, you can mark it as a Favorite, which lets you search for it as such at a later time. To mark an image, press the Display button until the Favorites screen appears, with the star icon highlighted. You will then see at the bottom of the display a small black rectangle containing a star with a number, likely a zero, to its right. That number represents the rating of that image in the Favorites ranking. Now you can press the up and down direction buttons to change that rating.

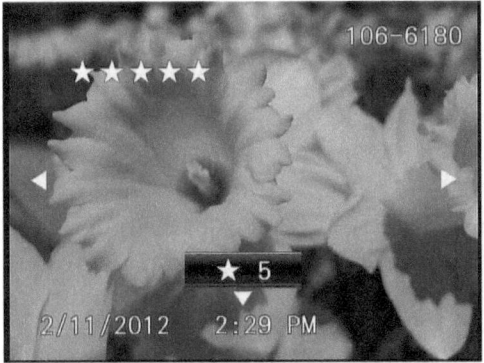

For example, you can press the up button five times to give the image the maximum rating of five stars. You can move to other images using the sub-command dial or the left and right direction buttons, and change the ratings of those images as you wish, also. Whenever you give an image a rating of at least one star, that number of stars appears in the upper left when the image is displayed with the basic information display or the Favorites display.

Later in this chapter I'll discuss how you can use the Favorites rankings to select and view images.

RAW Conversion

Another operation you can carry out while an image is displayed in playback mode—if the image was captured with RAW image quality—is to convert the RAW image to a JPEG version using the X10's built-in set of sophisticated RAW processing tools. When a RAW image is shown on the display, just press the RAW button at the lower right of the camera's back and the camera will display the RAW Conversion screen from the Playback menu. I will discuss the details of how to use this feature later in this chapter, when I discuss the options on the Playback menu.

Viewing Shots Taken in a Burst

When you view a burst of continuous photos taken with the X10, in normal playback mode the camera displays only the first shot of the burst. In other words, if you scroll through your shots, you will see only one image from this burst, even though there may have been eight or ten shots (or more) in the burst. In order to see the individual images from the burst, you have to "open up" the sequence by pressing the down direction button. You can then navigate through each of the shots in the burst, but you cannot advance beyond the burst. You will be "stuck" inside the same sequence of shots until you return to normal playback mode by pressing the Display/Back button.

Here is an example, which will make it easier to illustrate the way the X10 handles playback of bursts. Suppose you have selected continuous high-speed shooting by pressing the Drive mode button (up direction button) and selecting the SH (Super-High speed) option from the list of choices. Now, when you aim the camera at your subject and hold down the shutter button for a couple of seconds, the camera will rapidly record a sequence of shots. The LCD screen will display a message indicating that the images are being stored to the camera's memory; then the normal live view of the scene will return.

When the camera has settled back to live view, you can press the Playback button to start viewing your images. If everything worked as expected, there will be numerous images to view, depending on factors such as how long you held down the shutter button. However, when you press the Playback button, you will see only one image from this sequence. If you press the left or right direction button or turn the sub-command dial, you will move to an entirely different image, if one exists; you will not see the other images from this sequence.

CHAPTER 6: PLAYBACK AND PRINTING

Where are the other images? Well, look at the display on the screen, which has a couple of unusual aspects. (I'm assuming the Information On display is active; if not, press the Display button and select the option with the "i" icon at the bottom.)

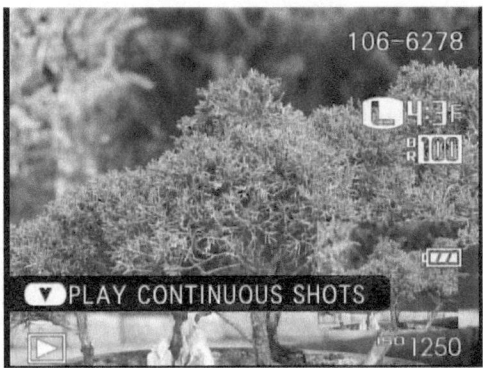

For one thing, when the image is first displayed, for about a second you will see an icon with a triangle representing the down direction button at the bottom of the screen, with a message indicating to press that button to "Play Continuous Shots." Also, in the lower right corner of the image you will see a small inset screen that contains views of the other images. That little square is almost like a movie, because it keeps cycling through all of the other shots from this particular burst. After the first second, that inset square is the only visible indication that you are viewing the first image from a burst of images, as shown below.

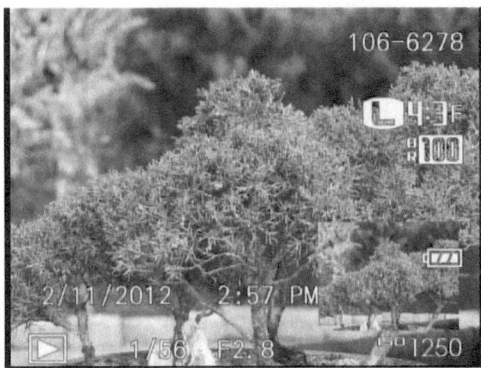

201

In this normal playback mode, you can still perform operations such as deleting, rotating, copying, and protecting. However, any such operation will affect all of the images in the burst. So, if you press the Delete button (up direction button) while an image is displayed in this mode, all images in the burst will be deleted. You won't see any message warning you that all images from the burst will be deleted, but, after you have selected OK to confirm the deletion, you will see a blue screen for a fairly long time while the camera goes through the process of deleting all of the shots from the burst.

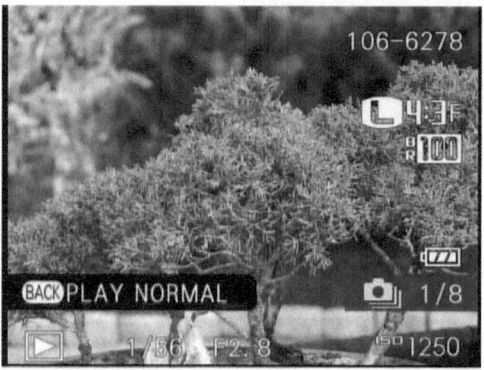

Now, go ahead and press the down direction button to enter burst playback mode, as shown above. You will see the same image as before, but the other information will change. You will now see a message at the lower left indicating to press the Back button to return to normal playback. At the lower right you will see a continuous-shooting icon next to a set of numbers such as 1/8, indicating you are viewing the first of eight images in a burst.

You can now scroll through all of the individual shots from this burst by turning the sub-command dial or pressing the left and right direction buttons. However, you will not be able to advance beyond these images—you will be "stuck" inside the burst until you press the Back button to return to single-image playback mode. While viewing the individual images inside the burst, you can magnify each individual image using the techniques described earlier. You also can perform any other operation on each image that is available using the controls or the Playback menu, such as deleting, rotating, and the like. If you delete an image, the camera will return to the burst playback mode, and you will see a reduction in the number of shots in the burst.

Also, when you copy your images to your computer, note that those that were taken in a burst have a different type of file name than individual images; the burst shots have names such as S0206219.jpg, whereas individual shots are named in the format DSCF6298.jpg. It can be confusing to locate these shots in your photo software, if it stores them alphabetically.

Playback of Panoramas

When you have taken a panorama using the Advanced shooting mode, the camera will initially display the entire image at a small size so it will fit on the camera's screen.

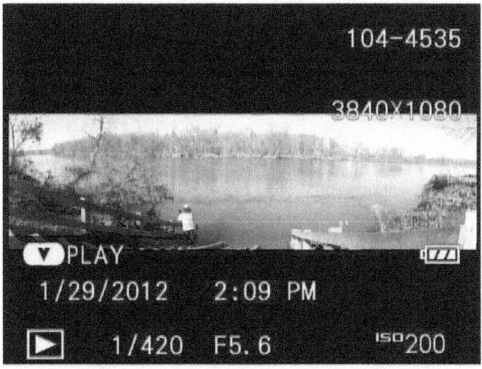

If you press the down direction button as prompted by the message on the screen, the panorama will scroll in a larger size that uses the full screen.

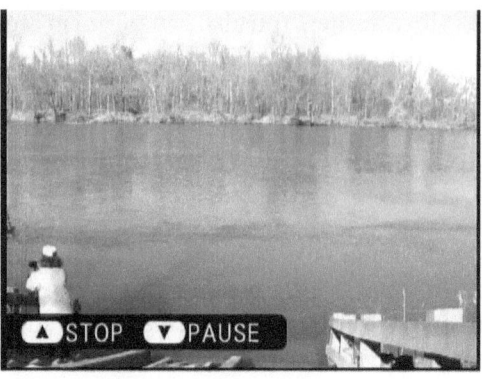

You can use the down button to pause and re-start the playback, or the up button to stop playback.

Viewing Shots Taken with Face Detection

When you have taken a shot for which the camera detected a face with the Face Detection option, in playback mode with the standard information screen, the camera will display the face detection icon, and, when the image is first displayed on that screen, the camera will display a message announcing a Detected Face, and it will indicate that you can press the down direction button to select that face. If you press that button, the camera will place a green frame on the face that was detected, and will display a message telling you to press the down direction button again to zoom in on that face.

The Playback Menu

We have just looked at the options for basic review of your images in normal playback mode as well as burst mode, and we have covered a few other playback-related topics such as information screens, the histogram, viewing burst sequences, and enlarging images on the camera's display. Now it's time to discuss the numerous options that are available through the Playback menu.

For you to get access to this menu, the camera must be in playback mode, entered by pressing the Playback button (right-facing triangle). Then press the Menu button to display the Playback menu, whose triangle icon should be highlighted on the camera's display. You can now turn the sub-command dial or press the up and down direction buttons to highlight the various entries on the three screens of the Playback menu. I'll go through the options on the menu one by one.

PhotoBook Assist

This first option on the Playback menu gives you a simple way to organize your images into PhotoBooks, the term Fujifilm uses for collections or albums of up to 300 photos each that you select and save to the memory card under one name.

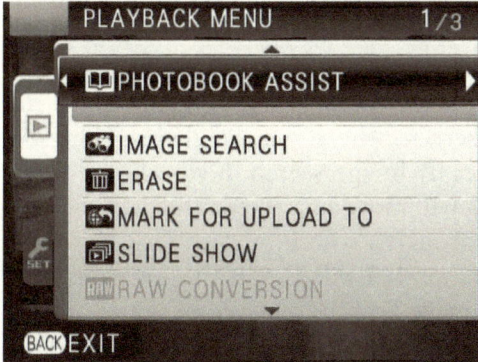

This can be a very convenient option if you accumulate a lot of photos while on a trip and you want to display them on a TV set connected to the camera. You can group your favorites into different PhotoBooks by theme, by persons who are in them, by locations, or by any criteria you choose. Here is how to work with this feature.

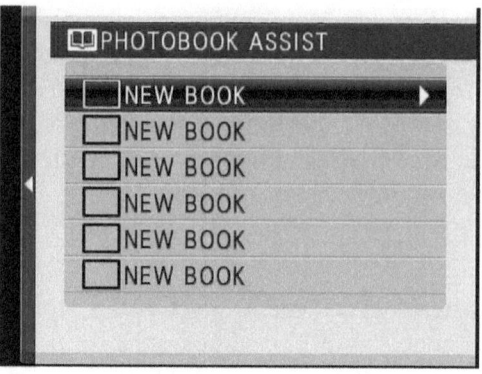

First, select this option by highlighting it on the Playback menu, then press the right direction button to move to the next screen, which has a list of books, all called New Book unless there already are some saved PhotoBooks. Navigate to a New Book line on the screen and press the right button again to move to the next screen, where you can choose either Select From All or Select By Image Search. If you choose Select By Image Search, you will move to a screen that lets you prescreen your images through a search by date, face, Favorites, type of data, or upload mark. I will discuss these options later, in connection with Image Search, the second option on the Playback menu. For now, let's use the Select From All option.

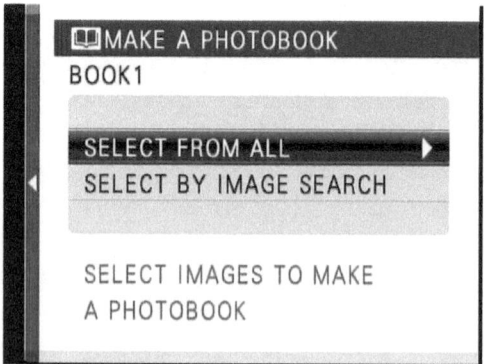

Highlight Select From All, and the camera will take you to a screen displaying one of the images on the memory card, with a message prompting you to start selecting images for the PhotoBook. At this point, you can press the up direction button to mark each image you want to include in the new book.

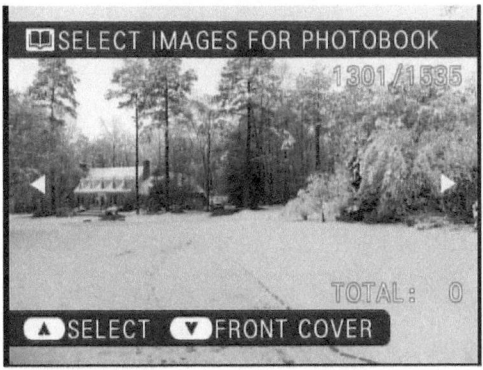

You can keep moving through all of the images in this way, pressing the up button for each image to include. As you do this, a book icon will appear in the upper left corner of the screen. To remove an image from the selection, press the up button again, and the book icon will disappear.

When the book is complete, the first image you selected will be the "cover" image, which appears along with the book's name in the PhotoBook Assist menu screen. If you want to use a different image for the cover image, just press the down direction button while that image is highlighted during the selection process.

When you have finished selecting your images, press the OK button. You will then see a screen with two choices: Select All and Complete PhotoBook. Highlight your choice and press OK to confirm. If you choose Complete PhotoBook, the camera will use the images you have marked and you will see a new entry in the list of PhotoBooks, such as BOOK1, BOOK2, etc. If you choose Select All, the camera will attempt to create a PhotoBook using all of the images on the memory card. It may not succeed, because a PhotoBook can hold only 300 images. Also, certain images, such as very small ones, as well as movies, cannot be included in PhotoBooks.

If, instead of Select From All, you choose Select By Image Search when creating the PhotoBook, you need to use the Image Search procedures, which are discussed below in connection with the next menu item.

Once the PhotoBook is complete, you can view it at any time. Just go to the PhotoBook Assist menu item, press the right direction button to go to the book selection screen, and select that book by name from the list that appears. You can then use the sub-command dial or the left and right direction buttons to scroll through the images, which are displayed with a nice-looking white border that simulates the page of a photo album. You cannot enlarge or delete images, or perform other operations on them, when viewing them in a PhotoBook.

A few other notes about PhotoBooks: If you have one or more PhotoBooks saved to your memory card that contain large numbers of images, it will take a while for the camera to enter playback mode after you press the Playback button; you will likely see a pattern of dots as the camera gathers the images into the PhotoBooks again. This performance might improve with a faster memory card, but I have found this slowdown to be a reason to avoid having large PhotoBooks.

If you want to change or delete a PhotoBook, display an image from it on the screen and press the OK button. You will be given the choice to Edit or Erase the PhotoBook. If you choose Edit, you can go through the image-selection process again and change the images in the book. If you choose Erase, the camera will ask you to confirm, and then it will erase the entire book, renaming it as New Book, thereby freeing up a slot for you to add a book. You can have only six PhotoBooks on any one memory card.

Image Search

The Image Search option lets you select a group of your images using one of several useful criteria: Date, Face, Favorites, Scene, Type of Data, or Upload Mark. Highlight Image Search on the Playback menu, and press the right direction button to move to the next screen; then highlight your choice of these criteria and press the right button again to move to the actual selection process.

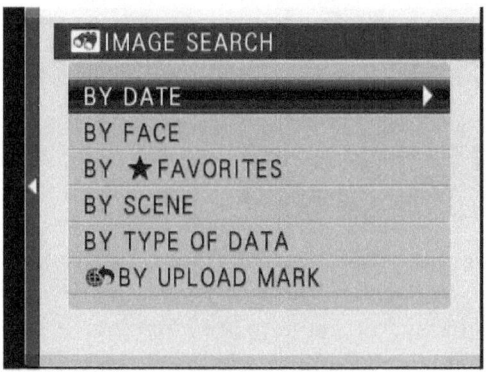

I will discuss below how to use each of the selection criteria. For all of these discussions, I am assuming that you have a reasonably large number of images on your memory card, with several for the criteria being discussed. For example, if you have images from only one date, some of the following discussion will not be applicable.

By Date

If you select By Date, press the right button and move to the next screen, which will show a date at the left along with thumbnails on that side of the screen, and another series of thumbnails along the bottom of the display.

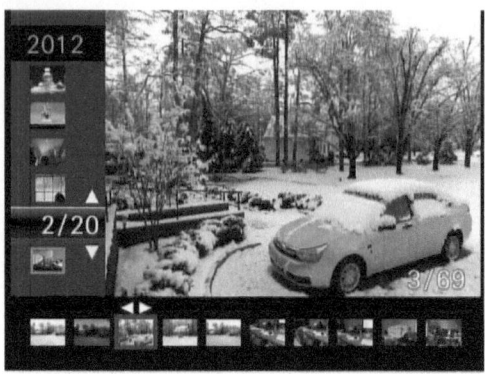

A large image appears in the middle of the screen. The thumbnails at the bottom represent the images taken on the date that is currently highlighted at the left. The large image corresponds to the thumbnail on the bottom of the screen that is currently highlighted.

Use the up and down buttons to scroll through the various dates; the earliest date is at the top of the screen and the latest one is at the bottom of the column on the left. As you reach the last date, the selection will wrap around to the top, and vice-versa. For example, right now my earliest date is 1/19. As I scroll down I reach the latest date, which is 2/20. If I press the down button one more time to scroll down, I scroll past 2/20 and wrap around to the top of the list, and 1/19 is displayed again. I can then press the up button to move back to 2/20 if I want.

Once you have highlighted the date you want, use the sub-command dial or the left and right direction buttons to scroll through the thumbnails at the bottom of the screen until you find the image you want. Or, if you want to do something with all images from that date, press the Menu/OK button to move to a screen that will display that date along with one image. Then press the Menu/OK button again, and the camera will display a screen with four options: Erase, Protect, Slide Show, and Exit Search.

CHAPTER 6: PLAYBACK AND PRINTING

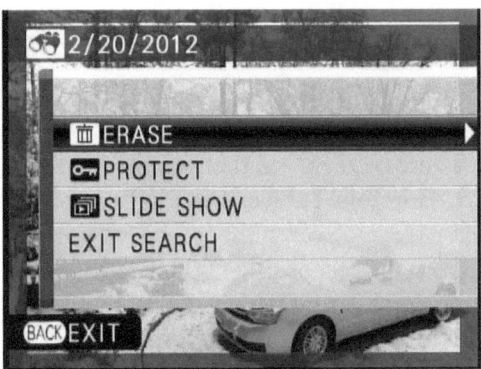

I will discuss those options later in this chapter, after I discuss the other choices for the Image Search menu item.

By Face

With the next option, the camera will search for all photos that contain what seem to be people. Once you select this option, you will see that it is not limited to faces that fill the screen; there are several sub-categories, as follows: All Image, Face Recognition, Closeup, Couple, and Group. You can choose All Image, which includes every shot that fits within any of these classifications, or you can pick any one of the individual categories, assuming there is at least one shot in the category. If there are no shots on your memory card for a category, that category will appear "grayed-out" and unavailable for selection.

This system, as you might expect, is not infallible, but the camera does a fairly good job of figuring out which of your images include people, either in closeup or otherwise. Depending on what sorts of images you have on your card, you may very well end up with some that have nothing that resembles a human or a face—to a human. In such a case, there probably is some pattern that matches the camera's programming in an unexpected way. But using this option can be an excellent way to get a first rough cut at your collection for a new PhotoBook, or just for general viewing.

211

By Favorites

This option is one of the most straightforward ones on the menu. As I discussed earlier, you can mark any image as a Favorite when it is displayed on the screen by using the Display button to select the Favorites screen and then rating the image with a number of stars, from one to five. Then, when you select By Favorites from the Image Search menu screen, you will have the ability to select images according to their ratings. The selection screen for choosing a rating lets you know how many images there are on the memory card for each rating level. In the example below, there were three frames with the 3-star rating that is selected on the menu.

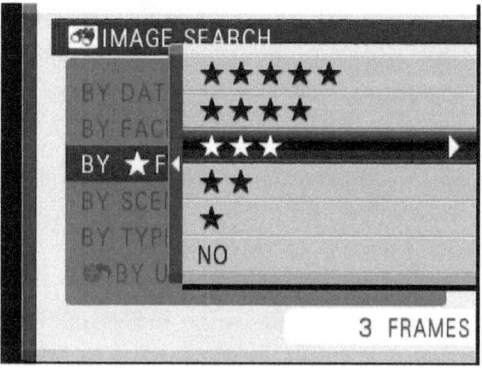

The one issue I find with this system is that you cannot select all images above a certain rating; you have to select just those with a certain, exact rating. That is, you cannot choose all images rated at two or more stars. The solution to this situation, in my experience at least, is to make sure you rate your images in a way that makes sense for the selection process later on. For example, if you know you will later be choosing the images you want to put in a slide show, just make sure you rate them all with the same number of stars, so you can select them all at once.

Finally, don't let the "Favorites" label limit your use of the ratings system. You can use this method to categorize images into any five classes. That is, if you are on a tour of a large city and you want to classify all your images of monuments in one class and those of museums in another, you could assign, say, three stars to monuments and four stars to museums so you can easily retrieve both categories later.

By Scene

With this selection, the camera gives you the option of selecting images according to their classification into scene types. There are just four basic scene types available for selection: Landscape, Night, Portrait, and Macro.

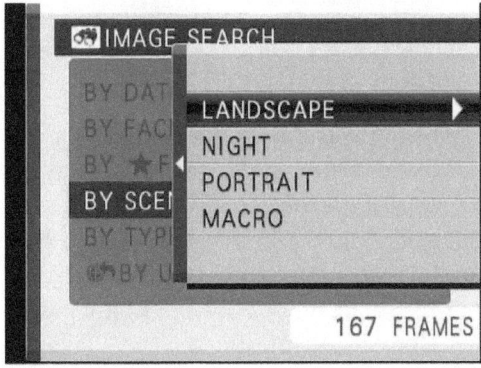

In my experience, these classifications do not necessarily match up with the camera's actual settings. In other words, if the camera selects certain scenes as being of the Portrait Scene type, that does not mean that the image was taken with the Portrait mode of Scene Position. Instead, the camera attempts to determine the Scene type by analyzing the appearance of the image, regardless of what shooting mode or other settings were used in recording the image.

By Type of Data

Here is another rather straightforward way to categorize images, though this one is of a more technical nature. In this case, the four categories available for selection are Still, Movie, Continuous (unfortunately misspelled on the menu screen), and RAW.

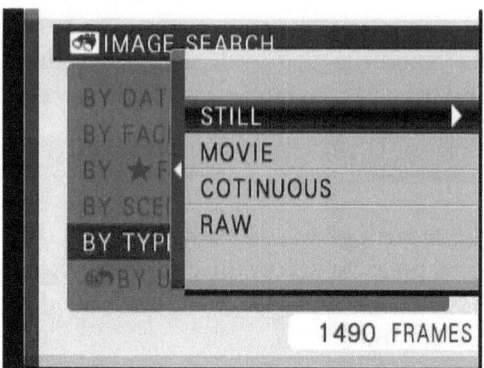

In this context, "still" means images that were taken in single-shot mode, as opposed to continuous (burst) mode.

This feature actually can be quite useful. In particular, it can be useful for finding movies, which you might want to display on a television set rather than just on the camera's display. Using Image Search, you can quickly jump to all of the movies on your memory card and find those that you want to play. Also, you may very well want to isolate all of your RAW images so you can use the RAW Conversion option on the Playback menu to make altered copies of them.

With respect to movies, it is worth noting here that you can put together a slide show of just movies, and this feature is what you use to accomplish that goal. (Slide shows are discussed later in this chapter.)

By Upload Mark

Finally, you can select images by whether they have been marked for upload to YouTube (movies only) or Facebook.

CHAPTER 6: PLAYBACK AND PRINTING

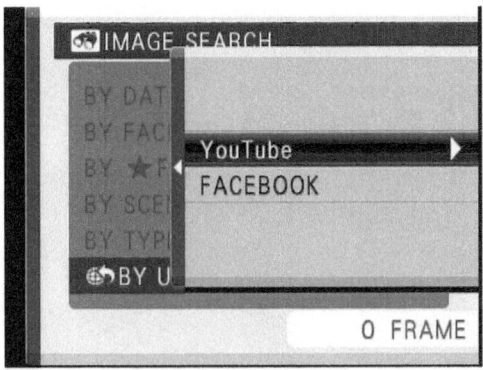

This is a straightforward option; you mark images or movies for upload to either of those internet services using the Mark for Upload To option on the Playback menu, discussed below.

Erase

The next option on the Playback menu, Erase, is used for erasing multiple images or movies at one time. This is one of the options that you can also choose once you have selected a group of images using the Image Search menu option. The Erase feature works as follows.

If you are starting from the Erase item on the Playback menu, after you have highlighted that item on the menu screen, press the right direction button to move to the next screen, which gives you the choice of several options: Back, Frame, Selected Frames, or All Frames.

215

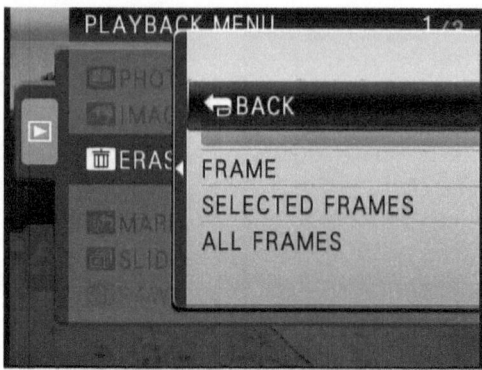

You can choose Back to cancel; Frame to erase just the frame that was displayed on the screen; or All Frames to erase all images on the memory card. If you choose Selected Frames, you are presented with an index screen displaying nine images at a time; you can navigate through those with the sub-command dial or all four direction buttons and mark (or unmark) them with the OK button. When you have finished selecting images, press the Back button, and the camera will display a message asking you to confirm the deletion of the selected frames or cancel.

If you are starting from the Image Search item on the Playback menu and move on to the Erase option after selecting images through a search, there is no need for another Selected Frames option, because you already have selected frames. Therefore, the camera presents you with only three options: Back, Frame, and All Frames. That is, you can cancel the operation by choosing Back, erase just the image being displayed using Frame, or erase all images on the card using All Frames.

Mark for Upload To

With this option, you can go through your images and mark them for upload to YouTube or Facebook. The actual uploading of the files is done later using Fujifilm's My Studio software for Windows (Macintosh users are out of luck in this area.)

Once you select this menu option, a press of the right button takes you to a screen with three choices: YouTube, Facebook, and Reset All. If you choose Reset All, the camera will de-select all images from the two uploading queues. This process can take quite a while, even if you have not selected any images at all; to cancel, press the Display/Back button.

If you choose YouTube and press the OK button, the camera will display the first image; press the OK button to mark it for upload. The camera will then display the message, "Upload to YouTube OK?" and let you confirm with the OK button or cancel with the Back button. When you are done selecting files to upload, press the Display/Back button to exit from the selection process.

Note, though, that with YouTube, naturally enough, you can upload only movies, not still images. Somewhat oddly, Fujifilm has programmed the camera to let you scroll through all of your images, even after selecting YouTube for the upload destination; for every still image, you will see the message Cannot Execute, meaning that image cannot be marked for upload to YouTube. So, if you are marking movies for YouTube, you should first use the Image Search menu option, which lets you find all movies on the memory card using the By Type of Data search feature.

If you select Facebook for the destination, the process is the same as for YouTube, except that, this time, the Cannot Execute message appears for RAW files. That is, you can upload JPEG files and movies, but not RAW images. When you are done marking the files, exit the process with the Display/Back button.

Slide Show

Like most modern digital cameras, the X10 has a capability for displaying the images on your memory card (or in the camera's internal memory) in a slide show that plays back on the camera's display or on a connected TV or HDTV set. The

X10 does not offer elaborate options such as music or a variety of transitions; your still pictures are played back with straight cuts or fades between them, and in silence. (Movies, of course, are played with their accompanying sound tracks.) There are some choices you can make for your shows, though. Here are the details.

The first decision you should make is whether to use the Slide Show menu option as opposed to the Image Search option to launch your show. If you want to show all of the images and movies on the memory card in one continuous show, then the Slide Show option will work just fine. If, however, you want to show just a subset of your images, then you should use the Image Search menu item. Once you have searched for and selected the images to show using that menu item, you can proceed directly from there to the Slide Show option by pressing the Menu button and selecting Slide Show.

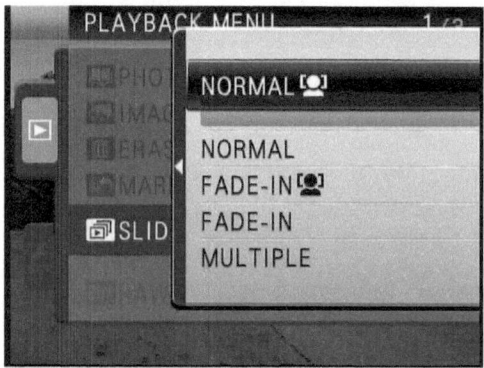

Whichever way you get there, the Slide Show option works the same. Once Slide Show is highlighted on the menu screen, press the right direction button to go to the screen with the options for the slide show: Normal (Face Icon), Normal, Fade-In (Face Icon), Fade-In, and Multiple. If you choose Normal, the images and movies will display one after another with an interval of about three seconds in between. (Movies, of course, will play fully before the next image or movie is shown.) If you choose Fade-In, the only difference will be that the images dissolve into one another. If you choose one of the menu items with the face icon added, the camera will zoom in on any faces it detects in the images (not the movies). If you choose Multiple, the camera will display several pictures on the screen at the same time, in different sizes. I find the Multiple display scheme to be distracting when I'm trying to view my images; I believe it could be useful if you want to have a background display running while people are paying attention to other things, at a conference or other event.

If you want to skip ahead or go back one image (or movie) during the show, press the right or left direction button. (This function is not available with the Multiple option.) To stop the slide show, press the OK button.

RAW Conversion

This menu item gives you a powerful set of tools for processing your RAW files right in the camera. As noted in Chapter 5, you can get access to these tools just by pressing the RAW button when a RAW image is displayed, but you also can select the RAW Conversion item from the Playback menu. In either case, this option works as follows.

This menu item will be "grayed out" and unavailable for selection unless the currently displayed image is a RAW file. If you're not certain whether a given image was shot with RAW image quality, press the Display button until the standard information screen appears; in the upper right corner, the image quality will be shown; the RAW label will appear next to the image size for all RAW shots. If you want to find all of your RAW shots so you can convert them, use the Image Search feature, discussed above, and select the By Type of Data option for the search.

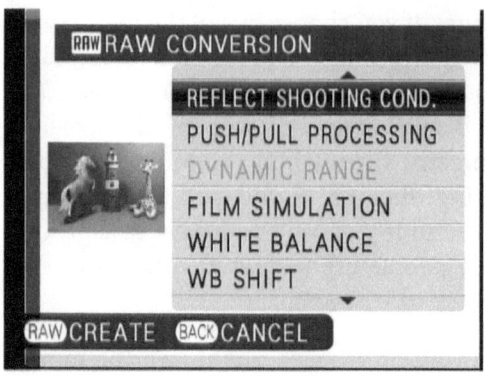

Once you have a RAW image displayed on the screen in playback mode, press the RAW button or select RAW Conversion from the Playback menu. In either case, the camera will display the RAW Conversion screen, with a large gray box that contains an impressive list of settings you can change. The box has arrows at top and bottom, meaning you can scroll up or down, wrapping around, with the up and down buttons or by turning the sub-command dial, to see all of the items in the list. If you select the first item, Reflect Shooting Conditions, that will negate any changes you have made to the other items in the list. In effect, that selection means that the camera will create a JPEG copy of the RAW file using the settings that were in effect when you took the picture. That is, if the image was underexposed, had the wrong white balance, and was using the Provia film simulation setting, all of those settings will be preserved when you finish and create the JPEG copy of the image. This option is useful if you just need to create a JPEG copy of your RAW file so you can send it by e-mail or edit it in a software program that cannot edit the RAW file, for example.

If, instead of just creating a JPEG duplicate of the RAW image as shot, you want to change some of the settings, this is where the power of RAW images and the power of this menu option come into play. I won't attempt to discuss RAW processing in detail; there are many books, videos, and articles available that provide excellent information on that topic. Here are some general guidelines.

The parameters that you can adjust in the camera using the RAW Conversion feature are the following: Push/Pull Processing, Dynamic Range, Film Simulation, White Balance, White Balance Shift, Color, Sharpness, Highlight Tone, Shadow Tone, Noise Reduction, and Color Space. What this means in practice is that you can, within some limits, change any of these settings after the fact, and fix mistakes in the settings you were using when you shot the picture. For example, if you accidentally turned the aperture dial to f/11.0 instead of f/5.6, resulting in an image two stops too dark, or you accidentally left the white balance set on Incandescent when shooting in daylight, you can change both of those settings in the RAW processing, and make the image look just as if it had been shot with the correct settings. And, of course, you also can tweak the other settings, such as Dynamic Range, Sharpness, and Noise Reduction, to achieve a look that suits your taste.

To adjust one of these settings, highlight it on the menu screen, then press the right direction button to move to the screen for adjusting it. For example, the screen for Push/Pull Processing lets you adjust the exposure value (EV, or f-stop) of your image in increments of 1/3 stop in a range from -1 EV to +1 EV. Scroll through these values, highlight the one you want to use for the adjustment, and then press the OK button to confirm the adjustment. You will be returned to the list of parameters; you can continue to adjust any or all of them as you wish.

When you have finished making adjustments, press the RAW button. Although the camera's screen indicates that you press the RAW button to "Create" a new file, actually it just produces a preview that you can still cancel out of. So, don't hesitate to press the RAW button whenever you want to see the effects of any adjustment you have made to the various parameters. When you press the RAW button, the camera will work for a while and then display a full-screen preview of the final product—a JPEG file that has had its settings altered from those in the RAW file, based on your RAW Conversion adjustments. If the preview image looks fine, press the OK button and the camera will store a new JPEG version of the image with the new settings; the original RAW file will be unaffected. If you want to keep making adjustments, press the Back button to cancel the conversion and keep working on the adjustments.

Red Eye Removal

This option is another one that involves in-camera processing of your images. In this case, though, the camera will only work with JPEG files, not RAW images. In addition, this option works only with images that were taken with Face Detection turned on, and in which the camera detected a face; those images are marked with the Face Detection icon in the upper left.

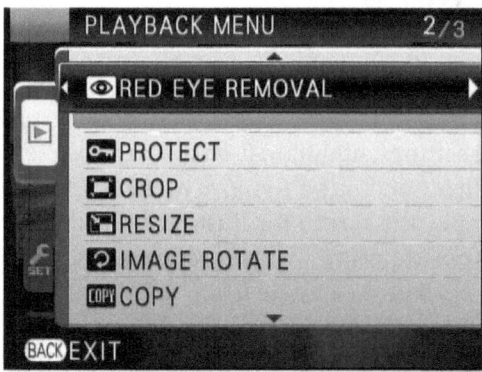

If you select this menu item, the camera will examine the current image to see if it meets these criteria and contains a face that may have "red-eye," the effect that can occur when on-camera flash bounces into the subject's dilated eyes and off the blood vessels in the retinas, giving an unpleasant reddish tinge to the person's eyes. If the camera believes this effect is present, it will process the image and create a copy of it with a new file number, with the red-eye corrected. I personally do not find much use for features of this sort, because it is easy to correct red-eye in software such as Photoshop and other editing programs. But, if you are in need of displaying a group of recent shots from a party and you want to clean up the shots that have red-eye, the X10 may be able to help you out.

Protect

With the Protect feature, you can "lock" selected images so they cannot be erased with the normal erase functions, using the Delete button or the Erase command on the Playback menu. However, if you format the memory card using the Format command, all data will be erased, including protected images. Protected images also cannot be rotated using the Image Rotate option, discussed below.

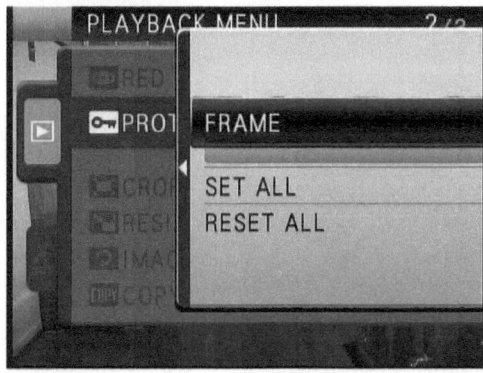

To protect images using this menu option, first press the right direction button to get to the options screen, which gives you three choices: Frame, Set All, and Reset All. If you select Frame, you then navigate through your images and use the OK button to mark or unmark any image that you want to protect or unprotect. Then press the OK button to confirm. An image that is protected will have a key icon placed in the upper left corner. That icon will be visible only when the image is viewed with the standard information screen; the icon will not appear in the image-only view, in the Favorites-selection view, or in the detailed view with the histogram.

You can use the Set All option to protect all of the pictures on your memory card (or in the camera's internal memory), or Reset All to unprotect them all.

Crop

This option for in-camera processing, which lets you save a cropped copy of any JPEG image, is quite user-friendly and it can be very useful. For example, you can crop images of people to show a close-up of a particular person's face, or you can enlarge a graphic to make it more readable if you are producing a quick presentation in your camera for a business meeting. Here is how to use this feature.

First, select the image that you want to crop. You can choose any JPEG image that is large enough to be cropped, but not a RAW image.

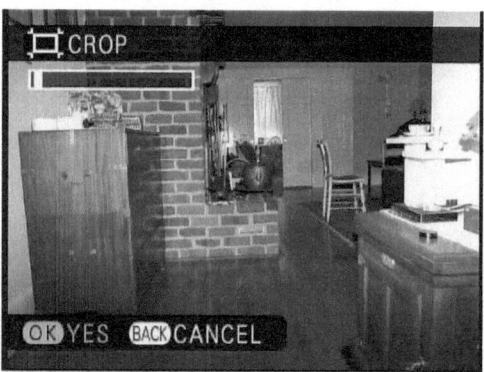

Once the image is displayed on the screen, select this menu option and the crop scale will appear at the left of the display, with the confirmation and cancel icons at the bottom. Now, just enlarge the image using the AE/Zoom-in button until the portion you want to save in the cropped image appears centered in the display. Use the direction buttons to move the image around as needed, and use the AF/Zoom-out button to reduce the image's size if necessary.

Keep an eye on the confirmation and cancel icons; if they turn yellow, that means that the cropped image will be of a small size. Once you are satisfied with how the image looks on the display, press the OK button to make the copy, which is saved as a new file.

Resize

This option provides you with another way to do a rudimentary form of in-camera editing. This feature allows you to take any of your saved images and create a new version in a small file size that is suitable for sending by e-mail or posting on the internet. This function could come in handy if you need to take a quick photo and then e-mail it to a friend or colleague. If you don't have software available on your computer to edit the image down to a smaller size, you can let the camera take over this task. (Of course, you could take the image in the small size to begin with, but you might want to have a higher-resolution version available for later editing or printing, but still be able to create a small version for e-mailing after you have already recorded the original version.)

To use this feature, you first have to navigate to the image you want to alter. Here, again, any still JPEG picture can be altered (but not a RAW image), as long as the image is not already too small to be resized.

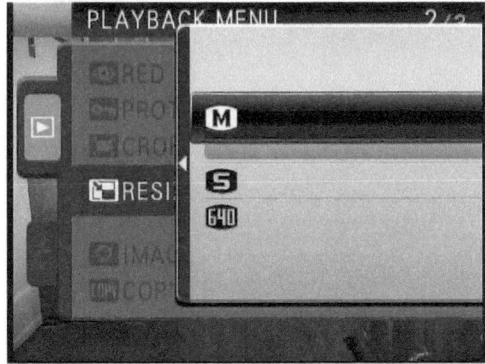

Once it is displayed, press the Menu button, then select the Resize option. On the next screen, you can choose from three progressively-smaller file-size options: M, S, and 640. Once you make your selection, the camera will ask you to confirm on the next screen; if the original image is already too small for your selected option, the camera will tell you it cannot be done at that size.

Once you have selected an acceptable size for the copy, press the OK button and the camera will make a copy of the selected image at your chosen size, and copy it to the end of the images on the memory card (or in internal memory).

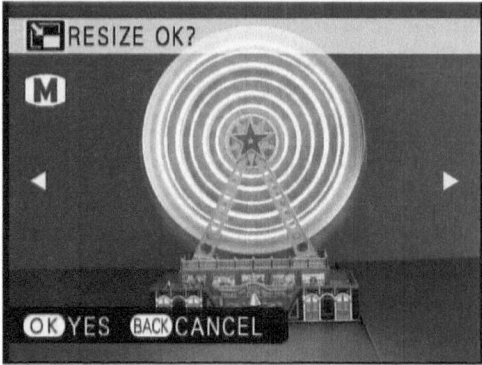

Image Rotate

Using this option, you can rotate your still photos 90 degrees clockwise or counter-clockwise. You cannot rotate images that have been protected with the Protect function, discussed above. However, you can rotate both JPEG and RAW images.

To use this feature, display the image to be rotated on the screen in playback mode, then select the Image Rotate option from the Playback menu.

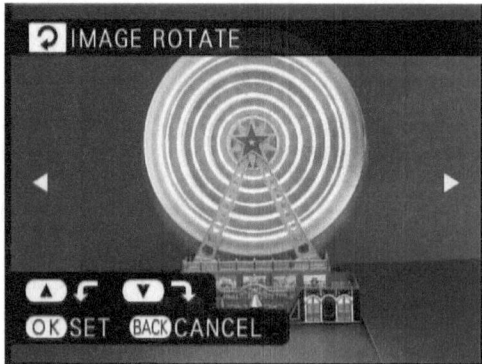

On the resulting screen, you will be prompted to use the down or up direction button to rotate the image clockwise or counter-clockwise. Press OK when it is rotated to the orientation you wish, or press the Back button to cancel the operation.

You don't have to use this function to rotate images taken with the camera held vertically; you can set up the camera to display those images in their natural orientation using the Autorotate Playback item on the Setup menu, discussed in Chapter 7.

Copy

The Copy option lets you copy your images from the camera's internal memory to the currently installed memory card, or from the memory card to the internal memory. When you choose this menu option, the camera first displays a screen with these two choices, clearly labeled on the screen.

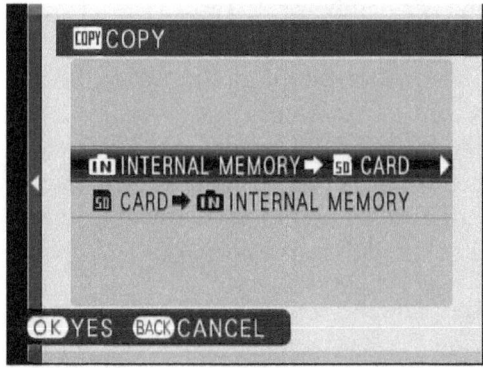

Highlight one of those options and press the OK button or the right button to move to the next screen. The camera will then give you the choice of copying all of your images ("All Frames") or just selected ones ("Frame"). If you choose the latter, the camera will display the first image and ask you to confirm the copy by pressing the OK button. Then press OK, and the camera will ask you once more to confirm the operation. The camera will then move on to other images with a similar procedure. If you choose to copy all images, the camera will ask you to confirm that operation as well.

If you regularly copy your images to a computer, you probably won't have much need for this option, but it can be a handy procedure when a computer is not available. Also, if you have taken a few images with the internal memory, it can be quite convenient to copy them to a memory card so you can save them, and then reformat the internal memory for future use.

Copying from an SD card to internal memory is not likely to be a function you need often, but it could be useful if you're at an event with another photographer who got some shots with another camera that you need copies of. You could copy a few shots from his or her SD card to your internal memory (and from there to your SD card) to take home with you.

Voice Memo

The Voice Memo option is a handy way to record a brief audio file with an image, perhaps to take oral notes about unusual shooting settings, or information about the subject of the image. You also could record a brief snippet of sound from the scene itself, such as a train whistle, though you might be better off just recording a movie in order to capture such natural sounds. You can record a voice memo with any still image, either JPEG or RAW, but not with movies or protected images.

To use this option, display the image in question on the LCD screen, go into the Playback menu, and select this op-

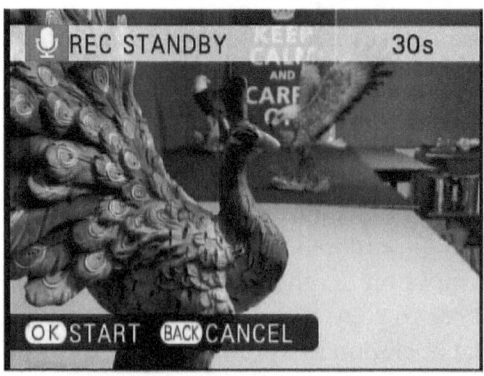

tion. Press the right button to move to the "Record Standby" screen. When you are ready to start speaking (or to start recording some other sound), press the OK button, and a red circle will blink in the upper right corner of the screen, beside a countdown from 30 seconds to zero, when the recording will end. You can end it sooner by pressing the OK button. You can then save it by pressing the OK button or press Back to re-record it.

When the memo has been recorded, the image will have a microphone icon at the left side of the screen. To play the memo back, with the image displayed, go into the Playback menu and select Play under Voice Memo.

If for some reason you would like to use the Voice Memo apart from the image it is associated with, it is saved as a separate .wav file on the memory card, and you can transfer it to your computer and edit it, add it to iTunes or some other audio management program, and manipulate it like any other sound file. These .wav files, although short, are of high quality, so you may someday find an interesting use for this capability.

Erase Face Recognition

This option is used to erase the link between an image and a face that has been registered with the camera for Face Recognition. If you have an image with such a link, and you want to erase the link, either because the face was incorrectly matched with the name or just because you don't want the link anymore, use this menu option. Display the image with the link and the camera will zoom to the recognized face. Press the OK button to remove the link.

Print Order

If you want to select multiple photographs before sending them to the printer, use the DPOF (Digital Print Order Format) function, which is built into the camera. The DPOF system lets you mark various images on your memory card to be added to a print list, which can then be sent to your own printer. Or, you can take the memory card to a commercial printer to print out the selected images.

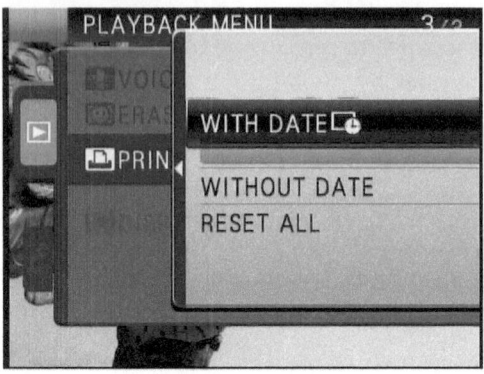

To add images to the DPOF print list, select the Print Order option from the Playback menu, then choose the With Date or Without Date option from the next screen to specify whether the pictures will be printed with the date they were taken. The camera will then display the first of your images, with a block showing in the lower left saying 00 "sheets" specified, meaning no copies of that image have been ordered yet. Use the sub-command dial or the left and right direction buttons to move through the images. When an image you want to have printed is displayed, press the up direction button to mark it for printing; press the button repeatedly or hold it down to increase the number of copies up to as many as 99. Press the down button to decrease the number of copies or to unmark the image by reducing the number of copies to zero. You can then keep browsing through your images and adding (or subtracting) them from the print list. As you add various numbers of copies for different images, a DPOF counter in the upper left corner of the display will give a cumulative total of the number of copies ordered for all images.

When you have finished selecting images to be printed, press the OK button to confirm your choices and exit from the selection screen. Then confirm the Completed message on the screen by pressing the OK button. You can then take the memory card to a service that prints photos using the DPOF system, or you can connect the camera to a PictBridge compatible printer to print the selected images.

If you want to cancel a DPOF order, you can do so quickly by going to the Print Order menu item and selecting Reset All from the sub-menu screen.

Display Aspect

This final option on the Playback menu is available for selection only when the camera is connected to an HDTV set with an HDMI cable. The purpose of this option is to specify how images that were taken in the 3:2 aspect ratio (non-widescreen) should be displayed on the HDTV. If you select 16:9, the image is cropped at the top and bottom to fit in the 16:9 format of the widescreen TV; if you choose 3:2, the image is shown in its full size, with black bands at the sides.

Printing Images

There is a lot of variation among photographers with respect to how often they print their photographs on a printer. Some people are content to view their images on the camera's screen; many save them to a computer and share them on sites such as Flickr and Facebook; others send them to friends by e-mail.

If you want to produce copies of digital photographs on paper, there are various approaches to getting that done. You can import the photographs into a program such as Adobe Photoshop or Photoshop Elements, or use the software supplied by Fujifilm with the X10, or any of many other programs that are available for photo editing. Once you have edited the images to your satisfaction, you can print the finished products from that software.

However, in some cases you may not be willing or able to spend the time to manipulate the pictures in software before printing them out. You may have access to a printer that will connect directly to the camera, and you may need or want to print out copies on photo paper without going through the time-consuming process of transferring the images to a computer first. Or, you may want to try a service that will take your memory card and produce high-quality prints directly from that card. The following discussions will cover the high points of these procedures.

Printing Directly from the Camera

The X10 camera uses the PictBridge printing protocol, which lets it communicate directly with a wide variety of printers. The procedure is quite simple: Just plug the black USB cable that came with the camera into the mini-USB port inside the door on the right side of the camera. (This is the upper of the two ports in that location.) Then plug the other end of the cable into the USB port of a PictBridge-compatible printer. (This USB port is different from the one for the cable that connects the printer to a computer; this one is rectangular; the port for the cable to the computer has more of a square shape.) The printer does not have to be made by any particular company; I plugged the camera directly into my HP Photosmart C6180 printer, and the two devices communicated with no problems.

Once the connection is made and the printer is turned on, the camera will turn on automatically and display a special screen that appears only when it's connected to a PictBridge printer.

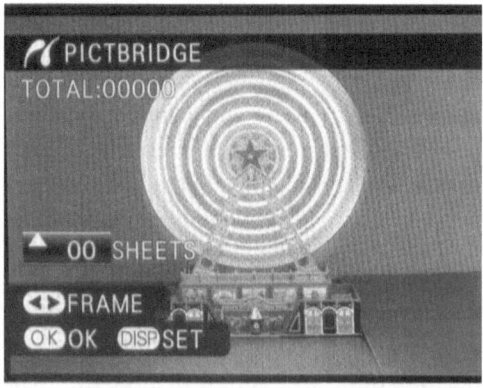

To print an individual image, navigate to the image you want to print and press the OK button; the camera will prompt you for the number of prints and the paper size. To print multiple images, when the print display screen initially displays, follow the prompts on the screen to set the number of copies of each image to print and to navigate to other images to mark. Or, you can use the DPOF selection of images, as discussed earlier in this chapter. For further details about these procedures, see the Fujifilm X10 user guide at pages 70-75.

Once you have the settings as you want them, press the OK button on the camera to print out your photographs.

Chapter 7: The Setup Menu

Now I have discussed the options available to you in the Shooting menu and Playback menu systems. The last menu system to discuss is the Setup menu, which gives you various options for housekeeping matters such as screen brightness and operational sounds, but also includes some very important settings that affect your images, including RAW, image stabilization, and red-eye settings. In addition, this menu is where you perform the crucial operation of formatting a memory card.

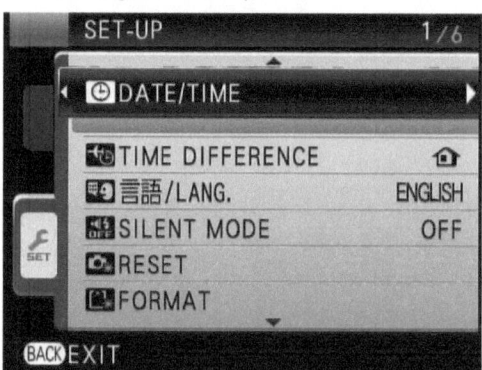

As a reminder, you enter the menu system by pressing the Menu button. The available menus change depending on whether the camera is set to shooting mode or playback mode. However, in either case, you can enter into the Setup menu. After you first press the Menu button, use the left direction

CHAPTER 7: THE SETUP MENU

button to highlight the top icon at the far left of the menu screen, which will be the camera icon if the camera is in shooting mode or the triangle if the camera is in playback mode. Once that icon is highlighted, use the down direction button to move the highlighting to the wrench icon at the bottom of the left column; that icon represents the Setup menu.

Then, use the right button to move the selection block back into the list of menu items, and use the sub-command dial or the up and down direction buttons to navigate through the various options on the Setup menu's screens. I'll discuss those choices in turn.

Date and Time

Chances are you set the date, and time when you first set up the camera. If you haven't done so or need to change them, use this option and navigate through the various selections using the left and right direction buttons; change the values using the sub-command dial or the up and down buttons.

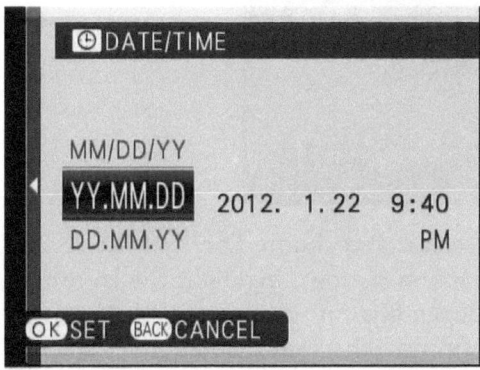

It's important to have these settings correct, because the date and time information is recorded invisibly with every picture or video you capture with the camera. That information can be printed out or retrieved through your software, and you can search for images by date, so you need to be sure these items are set properly from the outset. If you live in an area where the time changes in certain seasons (for example, Daylight

Savings Time in most parts of the United States), you will have to reset the time yourself when the time changes; the camera does not have an option for doing that automatically. (Though, if you don't travel much, you can use the Time Difference option, discussed below, and set up another time zone for the time change.)

Time Difference

The Time Difference option lets you set up a time zone, called "Local," with a different time than the one you initially set in the camera, which is called your "Home" time. Then, when you go to a different time zone, you can set the camera quickly to the "Local" setting so that images recorded during the trip will reflect the correct time and date when they are taken.

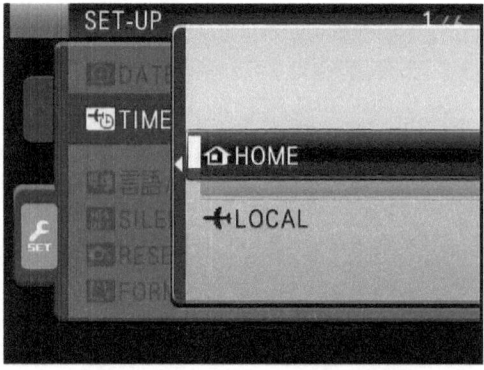

To use this option, select it and choose Local on the second screen. Using the direction buttons, highlight the large plus sign or minus sign, depending on whether the Local time is later (plus) or earlier (minus) than your Home time. Then go to the next two blocks and use the sub-command dial or the up and down buttons to enter the hours and minutes of the time difference; press the OK button to confirm.

When you arrive at your destination, go back to this menu item and make sure that Local is highlighted. When you return home, use the menu option once more to select the Home option, so that your normal time zone will be in effect.

CHAPTER 7: THE SETUP MENU

Language

This option gives you your choice of 35 languages for the display of commands and information on the camera's display.

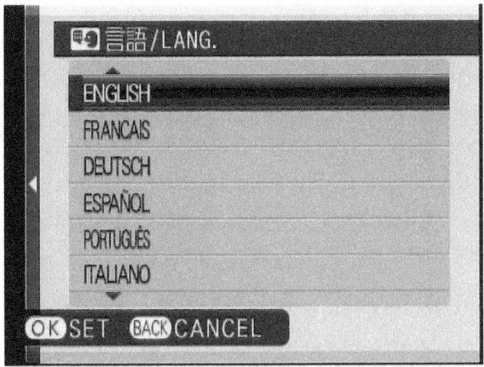

After selecting this item, scroll through the language choices using the sub-command dial or the direction buttons and press the OK button when your chosen language is highlighted.

Silent Mode

This is one of the most useful settings on the Setup menu, at least for some photographers. One of the great attributes of the X10 is its ability to operate silently and unobtrusively. With its classic slim shape and black color, the camera can easily disappear into a photographer's hands. For street photography and other forms of candid photography, it is extremely helpful to supplement this cloak of invisibility with a cone of silence.

When you invoke Silent Mode from the Setup menu, the camera suppresses the operational sound made by the shutter as well as any beeps made to confirm focus or to announce errors. In addition, the camera goes beyond the "silent" label and turns off the AF Illuminator lamp and disables the flash.

In this mode, the camera can be fairly hard to detect. However, one item that is left to alert a passerby is the indicator light high on the back of the camera, just below the flash shoe.

237

This lamp emits a rather bright glow when the camera is recording images to the memory card or internal memory. Silent Mode does not dim this lamp, but you can, with a small piece of black tape. That step is recommended for the photographer who seeks near-perfect invisibility on the streets.

Also, if you have turned on the Image Display option (discussed later in this chapter), the images that flash on the LCD after you take them can give you away. To avoid that happening, you can turn off that option. In shooting mode, you can turn the LCD display off, using the Display button to select that display mode from among the five available options.

Finally, one of the best things about Silent Mode is that you do not have to dig into the menu system to activate or deactivate it. Fujifilm has helpfully programmed the X10 so that you can press and hold the Display/Back button to toggle Silent Mode on and off. A press for about two seconds is all it takes. The camera displays a sound icon on the screen to confirm the change.

Reset

Choose this menu option when you want to reset all of the camera's settings back to their original (default) values.

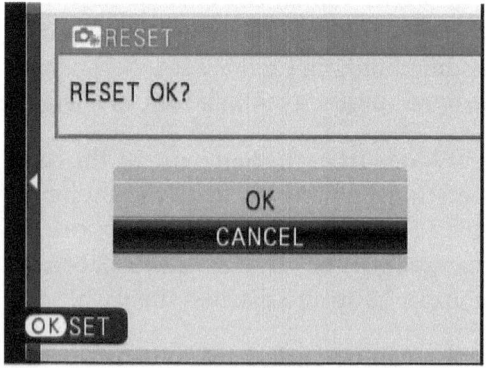

This action can be useful if you have been playing around with different settings and you find that something is not working as expected. It will give you a fresh start with known values for all of the major settings on the menus and for shooting. There are a few settings that will not be reset, including Date and Time, Time Difference, and Background Color.

Format

This is one of the most important of all menu options. Choose this process when you want or need to completely wipe all of the data from a memory storage card. When you select the Format option, the camera will warn you that all data will be deleted if you proceed.

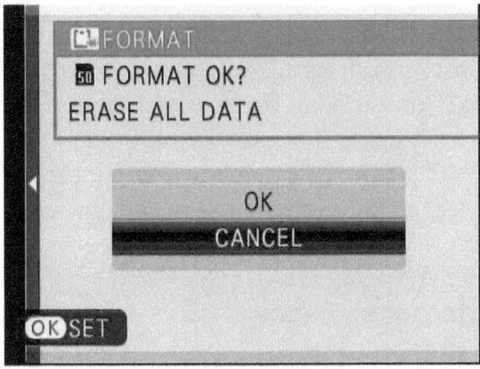

If you reply by highlighting OK and pressing the OK button to confirm, the camera will proceed to format the card that is in the camera, and the result will be a card that is empty of images and properly formatted to store new images from the camera. With this procedure, the camera will erase all images, including those that have been protected from accidental erasure with the Protect function on the Playback menu. It's a good idea to periodically save your good images and videos to your computer or other storage device and then re-format your memory card in the camera, to make sure the card is properly set up to start recording new images and videos. It's also a good idea to use the Format command on any new memory card when you first insert it in the camera. Even though it likely will work without that procedure, it's best to make sure the card is set up with Fujifilm's own particular method of formatting.

If you want to format the camera's internal memory instead of a memory card, just remove the card from the camera. Then, when you select the Format command, the camera will format the internal memory.

Image Display

This is another very useful option, which I have mentioned several times before. With this menu item, you can control whether and for how long an image appears on the display after you take it. By default, this setting causes your new images to appear for 1.5 second. If you like, you can set it to 3 seconds, Off, or Zoom (Continuous). You may want to use the 3-second setting if you are using the optical viewfinder, to allow for the time to look up from the viewfinder and examine the screen. If you choose Off, new images will never appear on the display; the camera will return you to the shooting screen as soon as possible after the image is captured.

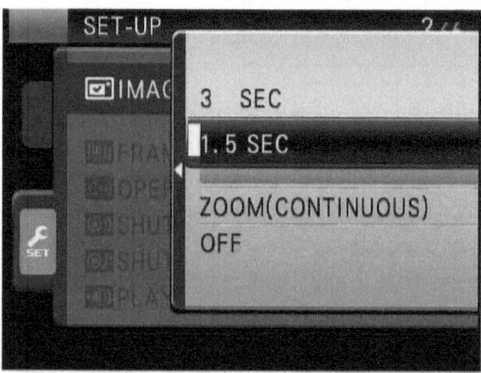

With Zoom (Continuous), a new image will stay on the screen indefinitely until you press the OK button or press the shutter button halfway down to dismiss it. When the image appears, it will immediately be magnified to its maximum level centered on the focus point, and the screen will display the controls for scrolling in the image with the direction buttons. You can adjust the magnification level using the AF/Zoom-out and AE/Zoom-in buttons. However, you cannot delete the image or call up an index screen while it is displayed in this mode. You also cannot choose what information is displayed on it using the Display button; only the image itself is displayed.

Frame Number

This option controls how the camera assigns numbers to your images and videos. The choices are Continuous and Renew.

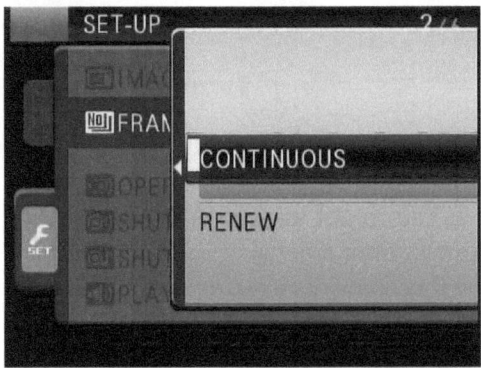

If you choose Continuous, the camera keeps numbering where it left off, even if you put in a new memory card. For example, if you have shot 112 images on your first memory card, the last image likely will be numbered 100-0112, for the folder number (100, the first folder number available), and 0112 for the image number. If you then switch to a brand new memory card with no images on it, the first image on that card will be numbered 100-0113, because the numbering scheme continues in the same sequence. If you choose Renew instead, the first image on the new card will be numbered 100-0001, because the camera resets the numbering back to the first number.

Operation Volume

This is the first of three entries on the Setup menu that let you control the volume and types of sounds the camera makes. This item sets the loudness of the artificial clicks that the camera makes as you press the control buttons. In addition, with the upgrade to firmware version 1.03, this option controls the volume of the autofocus confirmation beep.

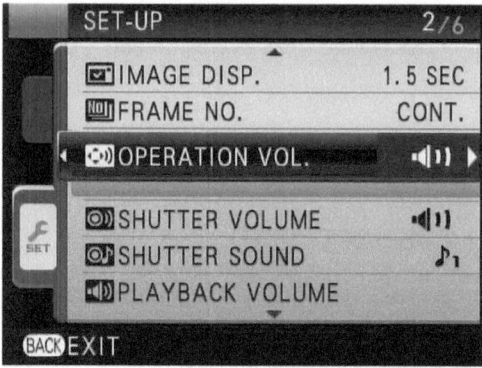

With this item, you can silence these sounds altogether, or set volume level 1, 2, or 3. You might want to silence these particular items but still maintain a quiet shutter sound with the next menu item, so you'll know when a picture has been taken.

Shutter Volume

This option controls the volume of the sound of the X10's shutter. If you want to silence the camera as much as possible but also hear when the picture is taken, you can leave the shutter sound turned on, but at the lowest possible volume.

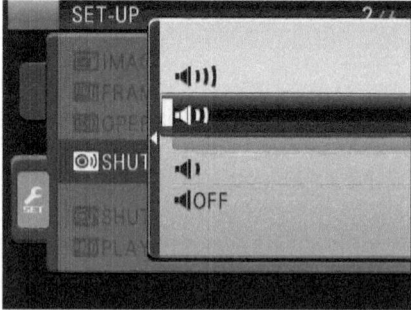

You can choose from three levels of sound, or silence.

Shutter Sound

If you like to customize your camera's operational sounds, you can choose from three different types of shutter sound.

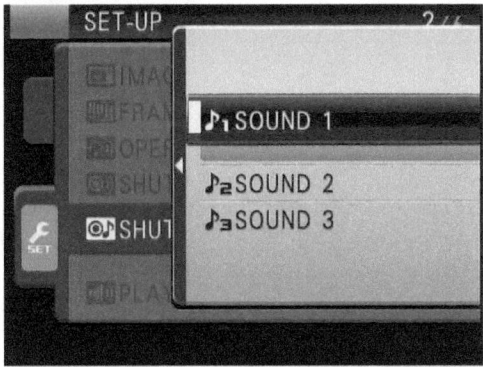

Number 1 is the sound of a leaf shutter, which has the advantage of reflecting this camera's actual construction; number 2 is the sound of a focal-plane shutter; and number 3 is the sound of a reflex camera with an internal mirror that slaps as the image is taken. I don't see a great deal of reason for selecting any sound other than number 1, but this is a matter of taste, and some photographers might prefer the other, heavier sounds.

Playback Volume

This item controls the initial volume of movies when you play them back in the camera.

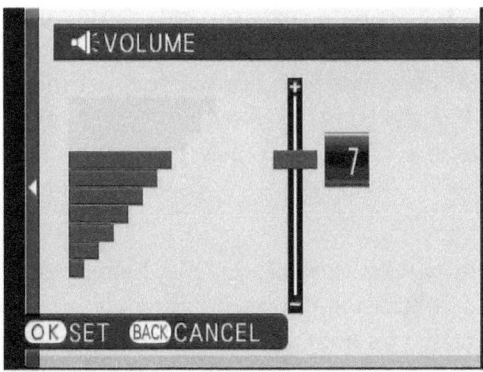

243

The values range from zero to ten; the default is seven. You can also adjust the volume while a movie is playing. To do so, press the OK button to pause the movie, then use the up and down direction buttons to adjust the volume along the vertical scale that appears along the left of the screen; press the OK button again to resume playback with the new volume setting.

LCD Brightness

This option controls the brightness of the display. It has no automatic dimming or other fancy features; it just shows you a scale that defaults to the standard brightness of zero, and lets you adjust the active display to be brighter or dimmer by setting the level to a positive or negative number from one to five.

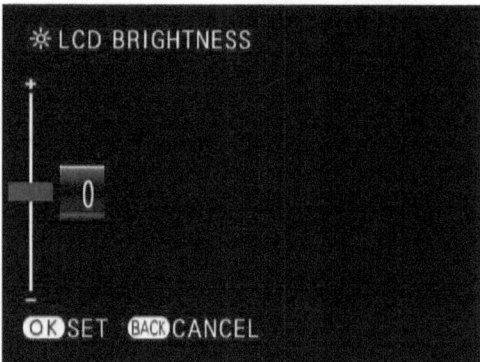

If you can manage with a dim screen, you can conserve battery life by choosing a lower brightness setting than normal. If you alter the brightness, be careful that you don't mistake the brightness of the display for the brightness of the final image. Just because the screen is brighter than normal does not mean the shots you take will be any brighter; you may want to check the histogram to make sure you are getting a good exposure.

Auto Power Off

By default, the camera powers down to save its battery after two minutes when no controls are pressed. Using this menu option, you can change that interval to five minutes or you can turn the feature off so the camera stays powered up as long as the battery lasts.

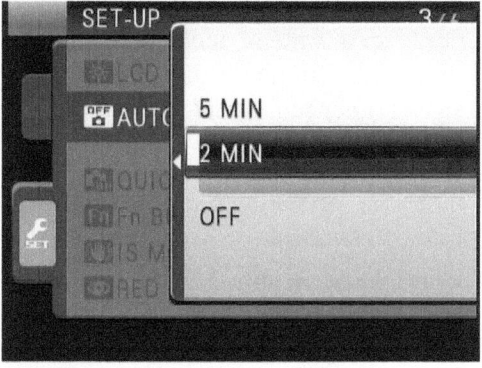

When the camera powers down in this way, you can wake it up by pressing the shutter button halfway.

Quick Start Mode

This is an option that you can use to save battery power as a trade-off against speed of operation. By default, this option is turned off, in which case the camera takes about one or two seconds to come to life after being powered off for a short time. If you turn Quick Start Mode on, the camera will activate in less than one second, but the battery will be drained faster.

In my experience, the camera turns on rapidly enough for my purposes with this option turned off, as long as the memory card is not loaded with images. As the number of images increases, I have noticed some slowdown. If you experience that slowing, you can try formatting the card (after saving your images to a computer) to speed things up, and you also might want to try turning Quick Start Mode on, if you don't mind the extra battery drain.

Function Button

With this menu option, you can choose what operation is assigned to the Function (Fn) button, the small button that sits at the far right of the top of the camera, to the right of the shutter button. I discussed all of these options in Chapter 5, in connection with the discussion of the button itself; if you press and hold the button, it calls up this menu item from the Setup menu. By default, the button is assigned to ISO, but you can choose from a wide range of other functions.

Also, with the upgrade to firmware version 1.03, this menu item includes a second option, for setting the function of the RAW button. That button can be assigned to any of the same ten functions as the Function button. My personal preference as of this writing is to have the Function button assigned to ISO and the RAW button assigned to RAW.

IS Mode

This menu option, which is called Dual IS Mode in the X10 user's manual, gives you several options for controlling how the camera uses its image-stabilization capability.

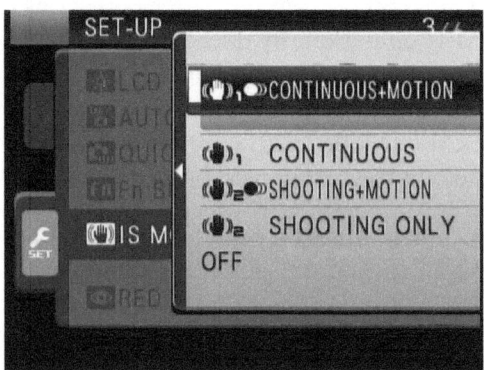

There are two items you can control, resulting in four combinations of those items on the menu screen. Those two items are the stabilization system itself, which is an optical system that shifts the lens elements to counteract the effects of camera shake, and a secondary system that detects motion and raises the ISO setting to permit a faster shutter speed.

First, you can choose between Continuous and Shooting image stabilization. If you set the system to use Continuous stabilization, then the camera constantly uses its stabilization system, rather than waiting until you press the shutter button halfway. With the Shooting option, the system does not start to function until you press the shutter button, thereby saving battery power.

The second item you can control is whether the Motion component of the stabilization system is used. On the Setup menu, the IS Mode item has four possible settings: Continuous + Motion; Continuous; Shooting + Motion; and Shooting Only. I prefer to use Continuous without the Motion option, so the camera uses its optical stabilization system but does not alter the ISO or shutter speed unless I make those settings myself.

Red Eye Removal

This next option lets you adjust the camera's approach to dealing with "red-eye" in your images—the red cast to human eyes that results from on-camera flash that lights up the blood vessels on the retina. The first line of defense is to set the flash mode to Auto Flash or Forced Flash with this Red Eye Removal option turned on. You have to have Face Detection turned on in the Shooting menu for the X10 to actually activate the Red Eye Removal function for the flash.

Once you have Red Eye Removal (and Face Detection) activated, you will see an eyeball icon next to the flash mode's lightning bolt icon when the flash is activated. In that case, the camera fires its flash unit once before the image is taken with the actual flash shot; the "pre-flash" is intended to cause the subject's pupils to narrow, thereby reducing the ability of the later, full flash to enter them, bounce off the retinas, and produce the unwanted red glow in the eyes.

In addition to firing the pre-flash, when this menu option is turned on, the camera performs in-camera processing on the image itself if the camera actually detects a face in the image. This process does not operate with RAW images, however.

My own preference is to leave this menu option turned off and to deal with red-eye effects by removing them with editing software, if necessary. However, if you will be taking flash photos at a party, you may want to use this menu option to minimize the occurrence of red-eye effects in the first place.

AF Illuminator

This menu option lets you turn on or off the white light beam that emanates from the AF Illuminator/Self-timer lamp on the front of the camera, just below the area of the mode dial. This beam comes on when the camera is trying to focus in a dark area; the light helps the autofocus mechanism find the patterns and shapes it needs to evaluate in order to achieve proper focus. You should usually leave this setting turned on, but you may want to turn it off when you're taking pictures in a place where the beam could be distracting or annoying to others, or where it might alert the subjects of your candid photography. (This light is remarkably bright, and you should avoid shining it in people's eyes if you can avoid doing so.)

The choices for this setting are On or Off. With On, which is the default setting, the lamp will fire when the camera's autofocus system determines that extra light is needed. Note that the AF Illuminator is one of the items that are turned off as a group when you set the camera to Silent Mode, either through the Setup menu or by pressing and holding the Display/Back button for two seconds. The AF Illuminator is automatically disabled for shooting panoramas and in several of the Scene Position settings, including Landscape, Sport, and Fireworks.

AE/AF Lock Mode

This option has a very narrow and specific function—to choose whether the AEL/AFL button has to be pressed and held down to do its work, or acts as a toggle switch that can be pressed and released. (You control what functions this button performs with the next menu item discussed below; this menu item controls only the behavior of the button itself.)

CHAPTER 7: THE SETUP MENU

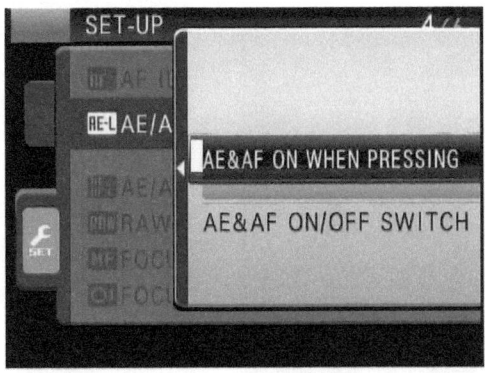

To make this choice, select this menu item and choose either AE&AF On When Pressing, or AE&AF On/Off Switch. If you choose the first option, the camera will display a P at the right side of the menu item, for Pressing; if you choose the second, the camera will display an S, for Switch.

Note that this menu item does not affect the use of the AEL/AFL button for causing the camera to autofocus when in manual focus mode.

AE/AF Lock Button

The previous option lets you choose whether the AFL/AEL button has to be held down or acts as a toggle switch; this menu item gives the choice of what function the button performs when you hold it down or toggle it. The choices here are AE Lock Only, AF Lock Only, and AE/AF Lock. With the first choice, using this button locks only exposure; with the second, it locks only focus; with the third, it locks both. As with the previous menu item, this one does not affect the use of the button for autofocus when in manual focus mode.

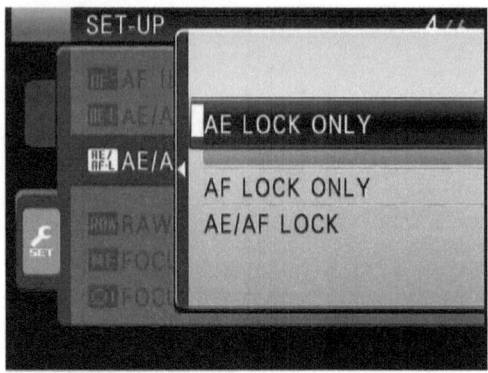

RAW

This option lets you control whether the camera captures its images in RAW format only, JPEG format only, or in both formats at once. This is an extremely important menu item, and it is somewhat unfortunate that it is buried fairly far down in the Setup menu. You might want to assign its function to the RAW button to make it more readily accessible. I will discuss the use of RAW images further in Chapter 9, but I will talk about the basic considerations here.

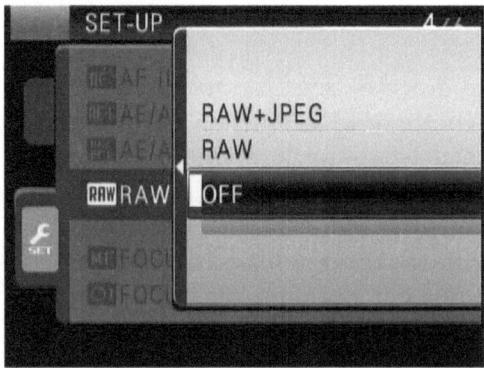

If you select RAW through this menu item, your still images will be recorded at the maximum size and quality. When using the RAW option, the camera captures and records all significant data that reaches the image sensor, and stores it in a way that can be manipulated to a great extent after the fact. Thus, if you capture in RAW, you can later alter the exposure, White Balance, and some other settings as if you were changing the settings that were used to take the photograph. However, you will have to edit the image with software on a computer (or convert it to JPEG using the RAW Conversion menu item of the X10), and you will not be able to use some features of the camera that are incompatible with RAW images.

If, on the other hand, you turn RAW off with this menu item, you will be capturing images in JPEG only. JPEG, which stands for Joint Photographic Experts Group, is an industry standard that uses compression to reduce the size of images. It also reduces the quality somewhat, and does not permit changes to the settings to the extent that RAW does.

The third option for this menu item is to select RAW+JPEG, which means that the camera will record both a RAW and a JPEG image each time a photograph is taken. In that case, the camera records two images—one RAW, uncompressed image at the largest size, and one JPEG image with whatever Image Size and Image Quality options you have selected on the Shooting menu. This setup may be useful if you want to have the RAW files for later editing on your computer, but you want the smaller, more easily shared JPEG files as proof copies that you can print out or view on a computer immediately without the processing that RAW files require. Also, some software may not be able to process the X10's RAW files at all, at least not until the software is upgraded to a later version.

There is one other very important point to note about the RAW setting. If you shoot using the RAW format, several of the other options that you set for shooting your images have no practical effect. For example, if you shoot using RAW image quality with the Film Simulation item set to Monochrome, the images will show up as black and white on the camera's display. However, when you look at them on a computer, they will appear in color, with all of the original information captured by the lens.

In other words, several of the camera's settings affect only JPEG images—those shot with Fine or Normal quality. Of course, you can shoot with RAW plus JPEG, so you will have the benefit of the X10's in-camera JPEG processing along with the ability to manipulate many of the image's parameters using the RAW file in your editing software. So, it is important to bear in mind during the discussion of the various settings for the X10 that not all of them have any effect on RAW files.

Focus Check

This option, which is turned on by default, controls whether the image on the camera's display will be enlarged to assist with focusing in manual focus mode. When this option is turned on and the camera is in manual focus mode, the center of the image enlarges to fill the display, making it much easier to judge whether the scene is in focus. The image will stay magnified while you are using the sub-command dial to adjust focus, and for one or two seconds after you stop using the dial.

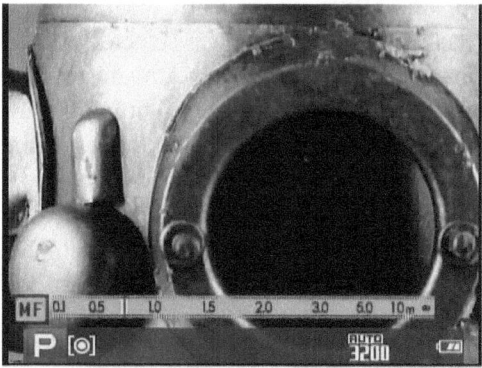

I find this feature very helpful when focusing manually, and I recommend leaving this menu option turned on.

Focus Control Dial

With this option, you can change the direction in which the sub-command dial is turned to increase focal distance in manual focus mode. By default, the ring turns clockwise to increase distance and counter-clockwise to decrease it. This item lets you reverse that situation. I have no idea why you would want to do that, but if you are more comfortable turning the ring in the other direction, this is the perfect solution.

Focus Scale Units

You can use this menu item to choose whether to use meters or feet as the unit of measurement on the focus scale.

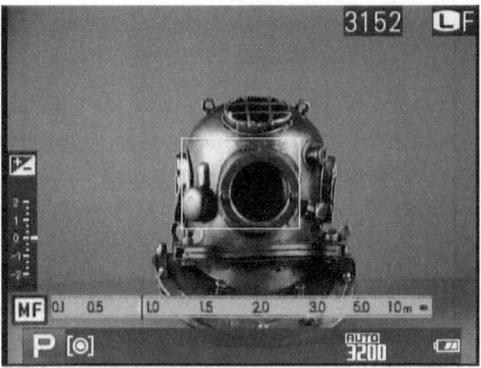

That blue scale appears across the bottom of the display; a red line appears on the scale to show the approximate point of focus, whether from your manual focusing with the focus ring or from the camera's autofocus system. In addition, a white area, which is somewhat hard to see, extends out from the red line in both directions to indicate the approximate depth of field of your shot with the current settings. Note that the autofocus indicator appears only on the Custom shooting display, and only if you have set it to appear using the Custom Display Settings option on the Shooting menu.

Framing Guideline

I hate to say it, but Fujifilm needs to get a spell-checker. Again, they misspelled the name of a feature on the menu screen.

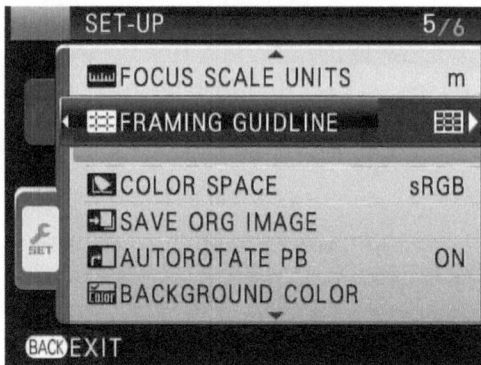

Oh, well, at least the option itself is a useful one. With this menu item, you can specify your choice of three options for the grid that appears on the shooting display to help you compose your images and videos.

The choices are Grid 9, a pattern with nine blocks; Grid 24, a pattern with six blocks across the display and four going down the display; and HD Framing, which puts only two lines on the display, resulting in a wide and narrow frame with the 16:9 aspect ratio of a widescreen (HD) image.

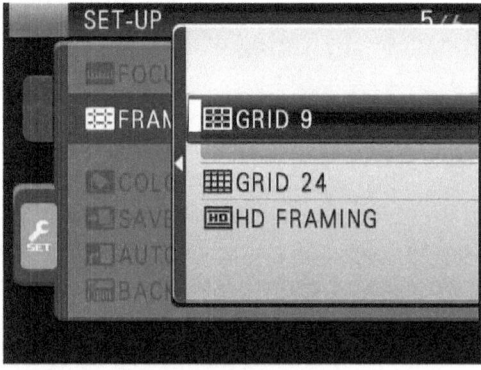

Note that the framing guideline appears on only one display —the Custom display in shooting mode, which you can select using the Display button. As you may recall from Chapter 4, you can select what items appear in the Custom display, so you can turn the framing guideline either on or off. The Framing

Guideline menu option determines what format of grid will appear if you activate that option, but you don't have to activate it if you don't want it.

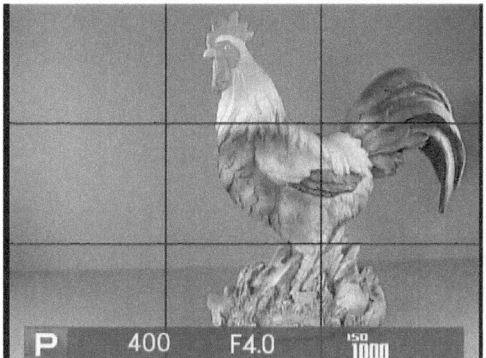

Personally, I like the nine-block grid in some situations, because it helps me compose images according to the Rule of Thirds. That rule suggests that you should place the most important subject at the intersection of the lines in this grid, which means it would be roughly one-third of the way from the edges of the image. It often seems to be aesthetically pleasing to have your subject off-center in this way.

Also, having the horizontal lines in the grid can be quite helpful in keeping your image perfectly level. Of course, you also can have the electronic level available for that purpose if you want, but the unmoving grid lines can give you a somewhat different perspective than the moving line of the level.

Color Space

With this option, you can choose whether to shoot your images using the "color space" known as sRGB, the more common choice and the default, or using the Adobe RGB color space. The sRGB color space includes fewer colors than Adobe RGB, and therefore is considered more suitable for producing images for the web and other forms of digital display than for printing. If your images are likely to be printed commercially in a book or magazine or it is critical that you be able to match a great many different color variations, you might want to consider using the Adobe RGB color space.

Save Original Image

This option controls whether or not the camera saves an unaltered copy of each image that is taken using any one of certain options: Red Eye Removal, Pro Focus mode, Pro Low-Light mode, or the seamless 360-degree motion panorama feature.

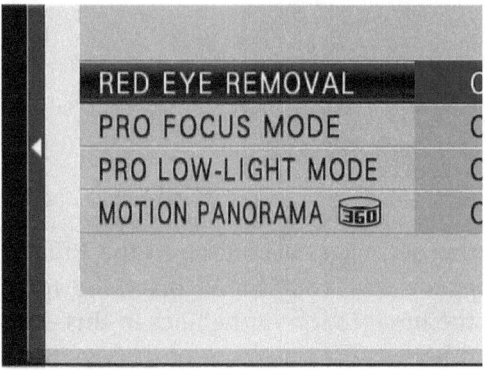

This menu option is provided because each of those features either alters an image or creates a composite from several other images. If you turn this option on, you will have an unprocessed copy of the image that was altered (by Red Eye Removal) or of the multiple images that contributed to the final Pro Focus, Pro Low-Light, or seamless panorama image.

Autorotate Playback

This option affects the way in which the camera deals with images that were taken with the camera held vertically, so that the image is taller than it is wide. By default, this feature is turned on, which means that the camera will automatically rotate any such image so that it appears properly oriented on the display. Of course, this means that the image will be displayed in a somewhat smaller size than normal, because the tall side must fit within the limits of the horizontal display. If you would prefer to have such images display without rotation, so that the image, in effect, lies down on its side, just leave this option turned off. You can always rotate such an image (or any image, except those protected with the Protect feature) manually, using the Image Rotate feature on the Playback menu.

Background Color

This option lets you select the color that appears on the edges of the menu screens and in the selection blocks that highlight the menu options you select. It might be more accurate to call it the "trim color" or "accent color"; the background color is uniformly gray.

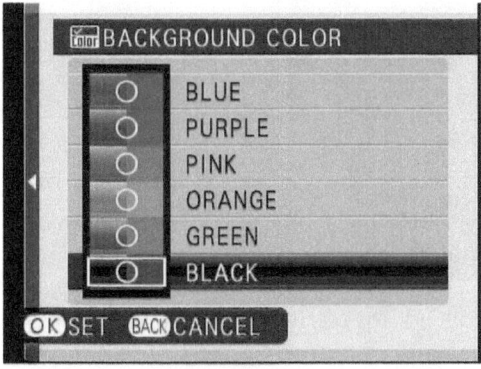

In any event, the choices here are blue, purple, pink, orange, green, and the original default of black. To the extent that you want your X10 to be a "stealth" machine you can wield without attracting too much attention, I recommend sticking with black, but you can make a fashion statement if you want to.

Guidance Display

This option does not have any impact on the operation of the camera. Its only function is to turn on or off the "tool tips," which are brief descriptive comments the camera displays when you select certain menu items.

The items I found that are affected by this setting are the Film Simulation selections on the Shooting menu, the flash mode selections called up with the Flash button, the Macro mode selections made with the Macro button, the self-timer selections, the Drive mode selections, and the various selections of sub-modes (Auto, Resolution Priority, etc.) for EXR mode. If you leave Guidance Display turned on, the camera provides brief remarks about each of the choices on the screen; for example, if you highlight Velvia for Film Simulation, the camera pops up a black box at the bottom left of the display saying, "Vibrant reproduction, ideal for landscape and nature."

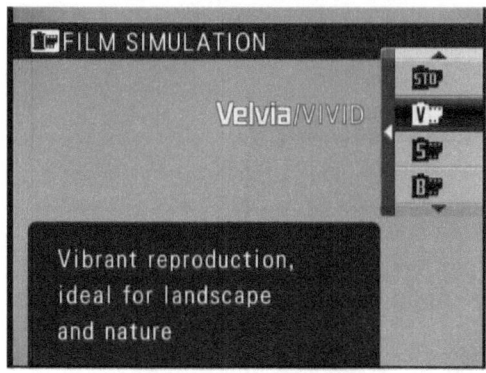

These popup comments do not really interfere with anything, so you might as well leave them turned on unless you find their mere presence annoying.

Video System

This option lets you select which set of video standards is in effect in your location. Choose NTSC for North America, parts of Latin America, and a few other areas; select PAL for the United Kingdom, much of Europe, Australia, and some other locations.

Custom Reset

This option lets you return the settings for the two Custom shooting modes, C1 and C2, to their original, default values.

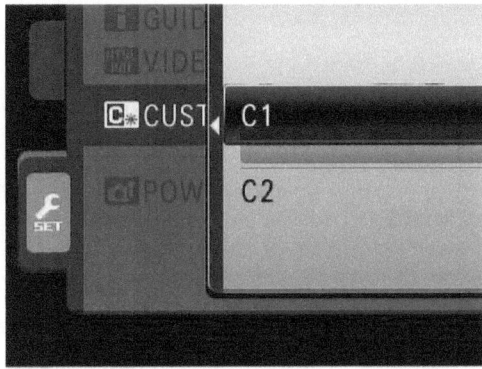

You can reset either or both of those two modes.

Power Management

You can use this option to adjust the way in which the camera's monitor dims to save power.

With Power Save, the camera keeps the display somewhat dim at all times, and dims it further after about 10 seconds when no controls have been used. With Clear Display, the camera waits about 30 seconds before dimming the display, and it keeps the display brighter and clearer while it is undimmed. If you choose to save power with this option, note that the display may be somewhat slower than normal to refresh.

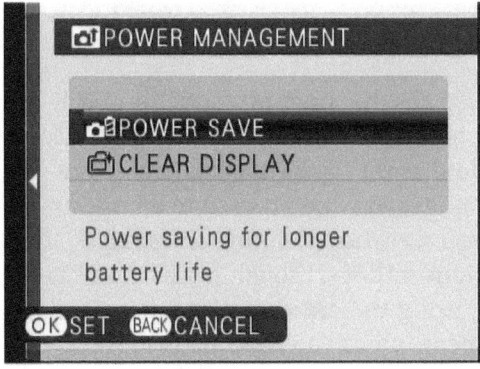

Chapter 8: Movies

Nowadays it seems that it's a necessity for any advanced compact digital camera or DSLR to include movie-making capabilities. Most recently, it's become standard practice for camera manufacturers to incorporate high-definition (HD) video recording into their premium cameras. The X10 is one example of that trend. I will explain the various options for movie-making in this chapter. Before I get into the specific settings you can make for your movies, though, I'll begin with a brief overview of the process.

Movie-making Overview

If you've used other recent models of digital cameras for movie-making, you may have seen various approaches to recording movies. With some cameras, you can press a Movie button at any time, no matter what shooting mode the camera is set to; with others, you have to set the camera to a specific Movie mode before you can record any motion pictures. There also is considerable difference among models as to what menu options and other settings are available when you record movies.

With the X10, Fujifilm takes the shooting-mode approach. So, in order to record video clips, you have to select the Movie mode using the mode dial on top of the camera. Once you have selected Movie mode, you can proceed to a large extent in the same way as you do when shooting still images. That is, you can adjust various settings, though not as many as for shooting still images, using the camera's physical controls as well as the Shooting menu. Once you have made those adjustments, you press the shutter button to record the movie.

One important point to note is that the X10 has built-in limitations on the lengths of its video sequences. Movies recorded in either of the camera's two HD formats cannot last any longer than 29 minutes in a single sequence, and movies in the 640 (non-HD) format cannot last any longer than 115 minutes per sequence. (The High Speed formats, discussed later, have much shorter limits.) You can, of course, record multiple sequences adding up to any length, depending on the amount of storage space available on your memory cards. For example, an 8 GB card can hold about one hour and 16 minutes of the highest quality HD video. If you want to fit both still images and HD video sequences on a card, you might be better off with a 16 GB card.

Quick Guide to Recording a Movie Clip

I will discuss the details of movie-related settings later in this chapter. For now, here are some suggested guidelines for quick settings when you just want to record the action, and you don't care about fine-tuning the menu options and other settings. I'll discuss these steps with a bit of extra detail, in case you have turned to this section before mastering the camera's various controls and menus.

1. Either before or after turning on the camera, turn the mode dial on top of the camera so the movie-camera icon is next to the white indicator mark on the right side of the flash shoe. This sets the camera to Movie mode, as opposed to one of the numerous other shooting modes, all of which are for still photos.

2. Press the Menu/OK button, which is in the center of the round control area on the right side of the camera's back, to activate the Shooting menu for Movie mode. Using the subcommand dial that surrounds the Menu/OK button or the up and down direction buttons on that dial, move the selection rectangle to the top item on the menu, Movie Mode.

3. Press the right direction button to move to the sub-

menu screen for selecting the format for your movies. For now, highlight the top option, 1920. Press the Menu/OK button to confirm this selection.

4. Move the selection rectangle down on the main Shooting menu screen to the next menu item, Face Detection, and ensure that it is set to Off, using the sub-menu screen to change the setting if necessary.

5. Move the selection down to the next menu item, AF Mode. Press the right direction button to move to the sub-menu screen, highlight Continuous, and press Menu/OK to confirm.

6. Move the selection down to Film Simulation and select the first option, Provia (Standard). Press Menu/OK to confirm, then press the Display/Back button, to the lower left of the sub-command dial, to exit the menu system.

7. Press the White Balance button, marked WB, at the bottom of the line of buttons on the far left of the camera's back. On the menu screen that appears, navigate to AUTO and press Menu/OK to confirm.

8. Aim the camera at your subject and compose the shot. When you are ready to start recording, press the shutter release button all the way down and release it. You can zoom the lens in and out while recording if you wish. When you are done recording, press the shutter button again to stop.

Other Settings for Movies

The steps outlined above will get you started recording video with the X10 using standard settings for movie format, autofocus, White Balance, and Film Simulation. Once you have become familiar with the basic steps for movie-making, though, you may want to experiment with some of the other available settings. There are several items that can be adjusted for recording videos with this camera.

When you are recording movies with the X10, very few of the settings that you make for still photos, either through use of the controls or through the Shooting menu, carry over to your movies. For example, even if the focus mode switch on the front of the camera is set to the manual focus position, once you have selected Movie mode the camera will focus automatically during the recording. I will discuss below the various settings you can make that will work for movies.

There are three settings that will carry over from your still shooting to Movie mode: exposure compensation, White Balance and Film Simulation. If you have been shooting still images in a mode that lets you set those items, such as Program mode, and you then switch the mode dial to Movie mode, your settings for those three features will carry over and take effect for your video recording. However, other settings, such as metering mode, Dynamic Range, Sharpness, and the like, will not carry over.

There also are a few settings that you can control while the camera is set to Movie mode. In that mode, the Shooting menu has only four items on it: Movie Mode, Face Detection, AF Mode, and Film Simulation.

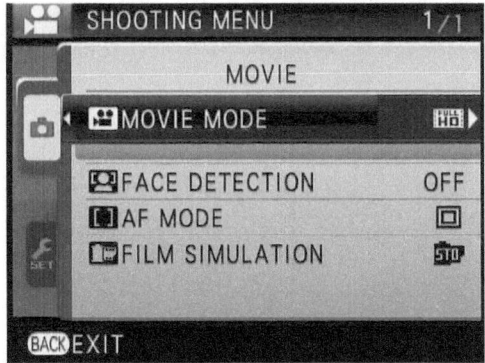

As noted above, one of those items—Film Simulation—will carry over from the camera's previous settings for still images, but you also can adjust it using the Shooting menu in Movie mode.

I will next provide some details about each of the items you can adjust while the camera is in Movie mode.

Movie Mode

The first item on the Shooting menu when the mode dial is turned to the Movie position is called Movie Mode. In this case, the word "mode" may be a bit confusing, because the Movie shooting mode is the overall framework for shooting movies. It might have been somewhat clearer to call this menu item "movie format."

In any event, Movie Mode is a very important menu item for shooting movies; it lets you select the aspect ratio, quality, and speed of your video clips. I will discuss each of the six options below.

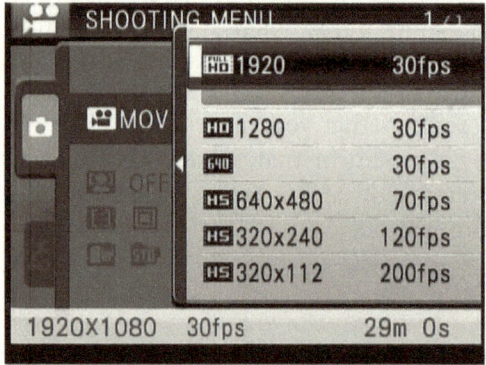

The first option on the Movie Mode menu is designated Full HD 1920. This, of course, is the highest-quality video format available with this camera; the number 1920 refers to the overall resolution of each frame of video, which is 1920 x 1080 pixels, often called Full High-Definition. This ratio of 1920 horizontal pixels to 1080 pixels is the 16:9 aspect ratio, often called "widescreen." You should select this format if you want to view your videos on an HDTV with the greatest possible resolution and quality. Of course, the video files for this format take up more space on a memory card or a computer's hard drive than the other formats.

The next option down on the list is designated HD 1280. This second-highest-quality format has a pixel count of 1280 x 720, which is the same 16:9 widescreen format as the first option. The difference is that this format has lower resolution and may not appear quite as smooth and clear as Full HD. However, its files takes up less storage space.

The third option, designated just 640 on the menu, has 640 horizontal pixels and 480 vertical ones, the same resolution as a standard VGA (Video Graphics Array) computer screen in the days before wider screens became more common. This is a relatively low-resolution format in a 4:3 "full-screen" aspect ratio. It is an excellent format to use if you need to conserve storage space on the memory card or on the computer, and the files produced by this format are quite easy to edit or send by e-mail. However, the quality of the video is noticeably lower than that of the two HD formats.

The next three formats are all designated HS, for High Speed. In this case, high speed means that the camera will record the video footage at a higher-than-normal frame rate, so that, when you play the footage back at the normal rate, the action will be slowed down.

The first of these three formats, HS 640 x 480, is of the same resolution as the lowest-resolution format for normal-speed video. However, the camera uses a frame rate of 70 frames per second (shown as fps on the menu screen), which is 2.33 times faster than the normal frame rate of 30 fps. Therefore, if you record video using this setting, when it is played back the action will appear to be 2.33 times slower than normal. To put that another way, the action will appears to be slowed down to about 43 percent of its normal speed.

The next format, designated on the menu as 320 x 240 120 fps, is of an even lower resolution in terms of pixels than the previous ones, and is recorded at four times the normal speed, resulting in footage in which the action appears to be slowed down to one-fourth of its normal speed.

The last format on the menu, 320 x 112, has the lowest resolution of all, and is recorded at a rapid 200 fps, which is 6.67 times faster than normal; the resulting footage shows the action at about 15 percent of its normal speed.

With all three of the high speed modes, no sound is recorded and the camera does not continuously adjust focus and exposure, as it does for the first three modes.

Face Detection

This second item on the Shooting menu in Movie mode lets you turn Face Detection on or off. Note that this setting does not carry over from still shooting; that is, even if Face Detection was turned on through the Shooting menu for the previously used shooting mode for still images, that setting will not stay in place when you switch to Movie mode; you need to go into the Shooting menu while in Movie mode and make this selection again.

Whether to use Face Detection is a matter of personal preference. If you are recording video of a children's play or party, it might be worthwhile to turn this option on, because you have little control of the autofocus mechanism, and this option can help ensure that the camera will focus on the children's faces rather than on the scenery or the back of the head of the tall person three rows ahead of you in the audience.

Note, however, that Face Detection is not available with any of the three high speed movie modes.

Autofocus Mode

The third item on the Shooting menu in Movie mode, AF Mode, is similar to the like-named menu item for still shooting modes, but not identical. For still shooting, AF Mode can be set to Multi, Area, or Tracking, as discussed in Chapter 4. In Movie mode, though, the only two options for AF Mode are Center and Continuous. With Center, the camera focuses just once, on the subject that is in the center of the frame when the recording starts. After initially setting the focus on that subject, the camera will not adjust its focus again until this recording sequence ends. So, if the camera is aimed at other subjects at varying distances, they are likely to be out of focus.

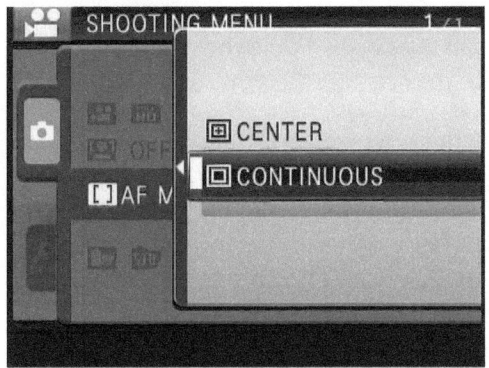

If you choose the Continuous option, the autofocus system continues to adjust the focus on whatever subject appears to be the main subject, even as the subject's distance from the camera changes or as the camera is aimed at different subjects. The Continuous option provides a greater likelihood of accurate focus for moving subjects, but, of course, it drains the battery faster than the Center autofocus method does. Also, there is some risk that the camera will record the sounds of the autofocus mechanism as it adjusts the focus.

There are trade-offs to be weighed when deciding which setting to use for AF Mode when making videos with the X10. If you are recording an event whose action is all at roughly the same distance from the camera, such as a play or concert, you may be able to do well with the Center mode, thereby minimizing battery drain and camera noise on the recording. If, on the other hand, you are recording a sports competition or some other event with action at varying distances, you should use Continuous in order to avoid scenes that are out of focus.

Here is one tip for focusing with the X10 in Movie mode: When the camera is in Movie mode, before you press the shutter button all the way down to start the recording, you can press the shutter button halfway down to force the camera to focus. In that way, you can be sure the focus is sharp when the recording starts, and you can ensure that the camera actually focuses on the subject you want it to. I have found this process to be especially helpful when using the Center option for AF Mode, because you can make sure that the camera's idea of what is in the center of the scene is the same as yours.

You cannot set Macro focus while recording a movie with the X10, and you cannot even set that mode while the camera is set to Movie recording mode. If the camera is set to Macro focus before entering Movie mode, the camera will switch back to normal autofocus mode once Movie mode is selected.

Finally, the fourth and last item on the Shooting menu in Movie mode is Film Simulation. As I noted earlier, this setting will carry over from still shooting, so whatever option you have set for Film Simulation for your stills will remain in effect for movies. You can, however, also select your choice of setting from this menu item. The choices are the same as they are for still shooting, as discussed in Chapter 4.

White Balance

As I noted earlier, White Balance is another setting that will carry over to video from still shooting, but you also can set it while the camera is in Movie mode. Just press the WB button at the bottom left of the camera's back and select the appropriate option, as discussed in Chapter 5.

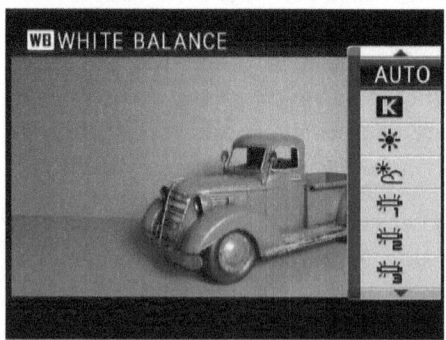

However, as noted in Chapter 5, the Custom White Balance option is not available in Movie mode, so you will need to select one of the preset choices, or, if you know the color temperature of your light source, you can use the K setting and set the color temperature to the appropriate value.

Exposure

You cannot set or adjust the basic exposure settings for the X10 in Movie mode. The camera will adjust exposure automatically, as if it were in Auto mode or Program mode. You can make one adjustment that will affect the exposure of the scene, though—exposure compensation.

To adjust this value, you use the exposure compensation dial, just as you would for shooting stills. However, for video recording, you must make any adjustment before the recording starts. You can turn the dial to your desired amount of adjustment after the mode dial has been set to Movie mode, or you can leave it set where it was for any still shooting mode, and that value will take effect once your video recording starts. If you move the exposure compensation dial during the video recording, though, the exposure compensation will not change; the value you dialed in earlier will remain in effect until the recording ends.

Film Simulation

As I noted earlier, Film Simulation is one of the few items that appears on the Shooting menu when the camera is in Movie mode. In addition, this setting will carry over to Movie mode from any value that was set for it in a still shooting mode.

The availability of the Film Simulation setting for movies is a considerable advantage, because it lets you add a distinctive style to your video footage. You can shoot in black and white, for example, or you can use a non-standard color setting like Velvia for a more vivid and saturated color look. If you are taking video of people's faces, you may want to opt for the softer look of the Astia setting.

Zoom

The X10, of course, has a mechanical zoom lens, and there is no way to disable the lens's ability to zoom during Movie recording. Therefore, you are free to zoom the lens in and out at any time, including while a video is being recorded. However, just because something is possible does not make it necessarily a good idea. In this case, there are three reasons why you should think twice before zooming the lens of the X10 while recording a video sequence. First, the zoom lens can make a mechanical sound that is quite audible on the video's sound track. So, unless you are planning to turn down the sound or replace it in the editing process, you might be better off selecting your focal length with the zoom lens before you start shooting a video sequence.

Second, zooming while recording of a video can be distracting to the viewers, especially if done repeatedly, rapidly, or with a jerky motion. Often the best approach to shooting video is to keep the camera very steady, offering the audience a stable window on the world they are viewing rather than make them feel as if they are catching glimpses from a speeding vehicle.

Third, there is a potential problem that can arise with zooming, when you zoom back out while recording a video. This problem arises because zooming the lens out involves the same action as turning the camera off. So, if you are not careful, when you zoom out, you may twist the lens far enough to turn off the camera's power, thereby bringing your video to an abrupt end. I have done this myself, and it is a fairly startling experience to realize you have just turned off the camera in the midst of a recording. Of course, you may be someone who is careful enough not to make this mistake, but one sure way to avoid it is to avoid zooming the lens while making a movie.

With those three caveats, the zoom lens is there for you to use while recording video if you feel the need to do so.

CHAPTER 8: MOVIES

Movie Playback

In Chapter 2, I discussed the fundamentals of movie playback. Now it's time to go into more detail about that topic.

When the camera is in full-screen playback mode, you can recognize the first frame of a movie by the sets of gray blocks that look like movie film sprockets on the sides of the image. When the camera shows index screens of thumbnails, you can recognize a movie by a thick gray frame around its thumbnail.

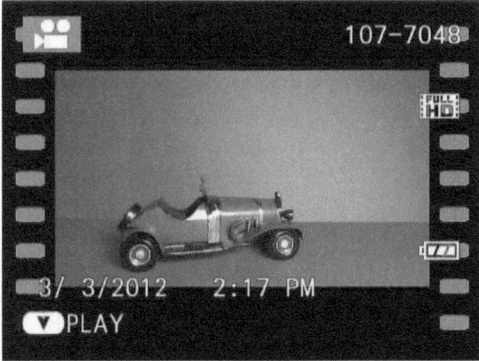

Once you have a movie's still frame highlighted on the display, press the down direction button to start the movie playing.

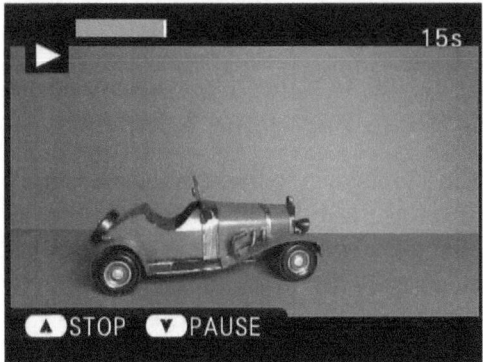

You will then see a gray progress bar that moves from left to right at the top of the screen. You will also see labels at the bottom of the screen showing that you can stop playback with the

271

up button and pause it with the down button. In addition, although no label tells you this, you can pause with the OK button and adjust the volume while paused, using the sub-command dial or the up and down buttons. If you pause in that way, you can resume play by pressing the OK button again.

When you pause the movie using the down button, you can advance or go back in the movie one frame at a time by pressing the right or left button. To adjust the speed of playback while the movie is playing, press the right button to increase speed in the forward direction or the left button to decrease speed, or to increase speed in the reverse direction. You can select from four different levels of speed in either direction, as indicated by the number of right- or left-facing triangles that appear in the top left corner of the display.

There is no way to trim or edit a movie in the camera. If you want to do any editing, you need to copy the movie to your computer and use editing software—either the software provided with the X10, or a third-party editing program such as Adobe Premiere Elements, Windows Movie Maker, or, for the Mac, iMovie, Final Cut Express, or any other program that can edit the .mov files that are produced by the X10. If you only need to make simple edits, such as trimming the beginning or end of a movie clip, you can use QuickTime Player, the free software provided by Apple.

Taking Still Photos While Recording a Movie

While you are recording a video clip with the X10, you cannot use the shutter button to take a still image, because pressing the shutter button at that point will just end the video recording. However, Fujifilm has provided a way to take a still photo while the camera is recording a movie. To do this, you just press the Menu/OK button on the back of the camera. The still image will be saved as a separate image, right after the movie file. You cannot take a great many still images in this way; the camera places limits on how many you can take. Also, there will be a brief interruption in the recording during the time when the still picture is being recorded.

This is an interesting capability, and it could be quite useful in some situations. For example, if you are recording video of your child's school graduation ceremony, you might want to snap a still photo as she receives her diploma. But the interruption in the video at this point might not be acceptable, so plan carefully before you do this.

There are not many settings you can make that will affect the appearance of this still photo. When you press the OK button to record the still image, the X10 will use the settings that are currently in use for the video recording, including White Balance, Film Simulation, and ISO (which the camera sets with no input from you). The camera will use the Image Size setting that you had set in the previous still-shooting mode, but it will set the size to Medium if you had it set to Large. (That is, Image Size will be no larger than Medium, but may be smaller.) In addition, even if you have the focus switch on the front of the camera set to manual focus, the camera will still use autofocus for any still image you take while recording video.

For example, I just set up the camera to take still images in Program mode with Image Size set to Large, Film Simulation set to Sepia, ISO set to 100, and White Balance set to Shade. I then switched to Movie mode, where I changed the settings to Provia for Film Simulation and Incandescent for White Balance. (In Movie mode, of course, you cannot set ISO or Image Size.)

Then I recorded a brief movie, and pressed the OK button to capture a still image during the recording. The resulting image had Image Size of Medium, ISO set to 800, White Balance set to Incandescent, and Film Simulation set to Provia. In other words, none of the settings for the still image carried over from the still-shooting mode except for Image Size, which was reduced to Medium, the size that the X10 uses in Movie mode when Image Size is set to Large. All of the other settings that were made for still shooting were replaced by the equivalent settings that I made on the Shooting menu in Movie mode.

To sum up this situation, if you plan to take still images while recording a movie, don't worry too much about your settings for still images, which for the most part will be the ones you (or the camera) chose for the video recording. However, do make sure that you have the Image Size set where you want it, because that single setting will carry over (in part) to the still images you take while recording in Movie mode.

Playing Movies on Portable Devices

Because the X10 records its movies in the .mov format, which is compatible with Apple's QuickTime software, the movies are compatible with iTunes. It's very easy to play these movies on your computer if you have downloaded Apple's free iTunes software. Just open a window on your computer to display the icon for a movie file (in Windows Explorer or Macintosh Finder), open iTunes on the same computer, and drag the .mov file from the Explorer or Finder window to the panel for the Library in iTunes. You can then play the movie from iTunes. If you want to play it on an iPod, iPhone, or iPad, you will need to take one more step: Select the video in iTunes, then select Advanced from the iTunes menu, and, from that menu item, choose Create iPod or iPhone version, or iPad or AppleTV version, as appropriate. Then you can sync iTunes with your device, and the movie will play very nicely on that device.

Chapter 9: OTHER TOPICS

Macro (Closeup) Shooting

Macro photography is the art or science of taking photographs when the subject is shown at actual size (1:1 ratio between size of subject and size of image on camera's sensor) or slightly magnified (greater than 1:1 ratio). So if you photograph a flower using macro techniques, the image of the flower will be about the same size as the actual flower. You can get wonderful detail in your images using macro photography, and you may discover things about the subject that you had not noticed before taking the photograph.

The X10, like many modern digital cameras, is quite capable of shooting macro photographs, such as the image at left of a toy 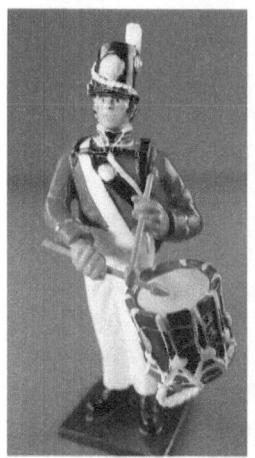 soldier. This figure is only about 2.5 inches (6.35 cm) tall, and this image, taken with Super Macro focus, is just about that size also.

As noted earlier, you can set the X10 for Macro focus as follows: First set the focus switch to AF-S. Next, press the left direction button to bring up the little menu that lets you choose whether to turn on Macro focus, then quickly press that button again to select the Macro icon (flower) or the Super Macro icon (flower with magnifying glass).

275

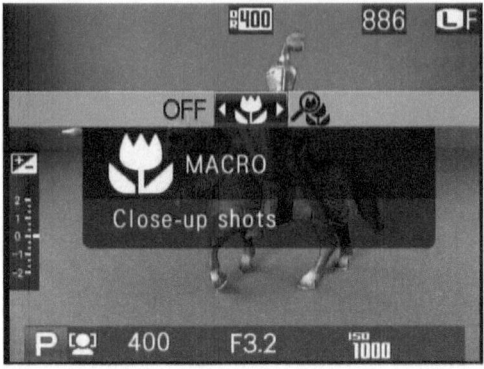

With the X10, when the focus mode is set to Macro the camera is able to focus as close as about 4 inches (10 centimeters); in Super Macro mode the camera can focus down to about 0.3 inch (1 cm). When you have selected either Macro or Super Macro mode, the camera puts the corresponding icon in the upper left corner of the screen.

In normal focus mode, when the lens is zoomed back to the 28mm wide-angle position, the camera can readily focus only as close as about 1 foot 7 inches (50 cm). However, it can still focus on closer subjects; it just takes longer to focus at that range.

You don't have to use the AF-S setting to take macro shots; if you set the camera to manual focus and then select Macro mode (or even without selecting Macro focus), you can also focus on objects very close to the lens. You do, however, lose the benefit of automatic focus, and it can be tricky finding the correct focus manually. However, if you press the AEL/AFL button while in manual focus mode, the camera will use its autofocus mechanism to help find the correct focus point. (There's not much point using the AF-C setting for macro shots in most cases, because it would be hard to achieve sharp focus on a moving subject at macro range.)

When shooting extreme close-ups, you need to use a tripod, because the depth of field is very shallow and it's important to keep the camera steady to take a usable photograph. It's also a good idea to take advantage of the self-timer or a cable release. If you use either of these, your hands will not be touching the camera when the shutter is activated, so the chance of camera shake is minimized. If you need the extra lighting of a flash unit, you might want to consider using a special unit designed for close-up photography, such as a ring flash that is designed to provide even lighting surrounding the lens.

I don't know of a ring flash designed for use specifically with the X10, but there are many flash units that could be used or adapted for this purpose, such as the AlienBees ABR800 Ring-flash unit, discussed in Appendix A.

Using Flash

Flash Modes

As I discussed in Chapter 5, pressing the Flash button (right direction button), marked with a lightning bolt, gives you access to the various settings for the built-in flash unit on the X10, or for a compatible external flash, when the camera is set to a shooting mode that allows the user to set flash modes.

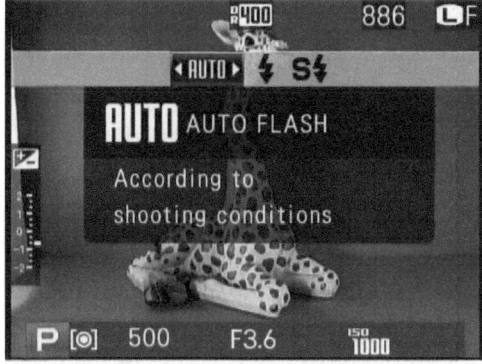

There are three possible settings for the flash unit: Auto Flash, Forced Flash, and Slow Synchro. There also are red-eye versions of all of these; the red-eye versions are available when the Red Eye Removal option is turned on in the Setup menu and Face Detection is turned on in the Shooting menu. (In a sense, there also is a fourth setting, called Suppressed Flash or Flash Off, which is listed as a setting for some Scene Position settings and for Movie mode on the chart at page 126 of the Fujifilm Owner's Manual. However, I do not consider that setting to be a flash mode with this camera, because the flash is normally turned off by keeping it retracted inside the camera, rather than by using the Flash button.)

The Forced Flash setting, with or without Red Eye Removal, is available in more shooting modes than any other flash setting. It is available in the Program, Aperture Priority, Shutter Priority, and Manual exposure modes. Auto Flash, with or without Red Eye Removal, is available only in the more automatic modes, including most of the EXR modes, the Auto mode, Program mode, and several of the Scene Position settings. The Slow Synchro setting, with or without Red Eye Removal, is available only when the camera is set to Program or Aperture Priority mode (that is, when the camera is choosing the shutter speed), as well as a few of the more automatic modes.

Apart from the shooting mode, other factors affect how the X10 uses flash. So, even if the camera is in Program mode, in which you normally have all flash modes available, there are some conditions that will disable the flash. Specifically, you cannot use the flash if you have activated any of the continuous shooting options, including burst shooting or bracketing, or if the shooting mode is set for panoramas or movies.

Also, the flash is disabled (along with the camera's operating sounds) when you activate Silent Mode, either on the Setup menu or by pressing and holding the Display/Back button for two seconds. Finally, if you press and hold the Menu/OK button for two seconds, the camera locks out the use of the Flash button, along with the other buttons on the sub-command dial. (They still function as direction buttons, but not for flash, self-timer, Macro focus, and Drive mode) So, if you believe the flash should be available but you are unable to turn it on using the Flash button on the sub-command dial, check to see if one of the settings mentioned above has been set.

For now, let's suppose that you have set the camera to Program mode, in which the X10 allows you to choose any of the various flash settings, that you have popped up the flash unit, and that no other settings are interfering with your ability to choose a flash mode. Now, you have to decide whether to choose Auto Flash, Forced Flash, or Slow Synchro. (I'll ignore the red-eye versions, which operate in the same ways as their non-red-eye counterparts except for the red-eye removal aspect.)

Auto Flash is a good mode to use when you don't have time to analyze the scene and decide whether flash should be used. With the Auto Flash setting, you are leaving that decision up to the camera's programming, which will take into account the position and brightness of the subject to determine whether to fire the flash, and, if so, how much intensity to use. This mode is likely to be useful when you are at a party or other informal event taking snapshots, or when you are trying to grab action shots of children at play indoors. When the camera is set to Auto Flash, no flash icon is placed on the screen, but you can tell if the flash will fire under the current lighting conditions, because the camera will display a lightning bolt icon briefly when you press the shutter button halfway down to evaluate exposure and focus.

Let's consider the other possibilities. Why would you use the Forced Flash setting (sometimes called Fill Flash), in which the flash fires with every shot, when you could select Auto Flash and let the camera decide whether flash is needed? One case is when there is enough backlighting that the camera's exposure controls could be fooled into thinking the flash isn't needed. If, in your judgment, the subject will be too dark for that reason, you may want to force the flash to fire. Another such situation could be an outdoor portrait for which you need fill-in flash to highlight your subject's face adequately and remove unflattering shadows. You also might want to try at least one shot with the flash in an outdoor setting in order to see what effect the flash has on the white balance. It may be that the White Balance setting will not compensate properly for the shady setting, and you will get better results for the colors in your image if you use flash. (If you want to compare a shot with flash to the same shot without flash, you also may want to use the Natural & Flash setting in the Scene Position mode, which is designed specifically for making that comparison.)

How about the Slow Synchro setting? With this setting, which, as noted above, is available only when the camera chooses the shutter speed, the camera uses a slower shutter speed than it ordinarily would for a given flash shot. Normally, when the X10's built-in flash fires, the camera uses a fast shutter speed, because the flash provides enough light to expose the image quickly. (The X10 can sync with its flash at shutter speeds as fast as 1/1000 second. At faster shutter speeds, the flash's duration may not be sufficient to illuminate the scene.) If you use the Slow Synchro setting, the camera will attempt to take the picture with a considerably slower shutter speed, so that the ambient (natural) lighting will have time to register on the image.

In other words, if you're in a fairly dark environment and fire the flash normally, the flash will likely light up the foreground subject (such as a person) quite well, but, because the exposure time is short, the background may be too dark, or even black. If you use the Slow Synchro setting, the slower shutter speed allows the surrounding scene to be visible also. For example, the two photographs on the next page were taken at the same time and in the same conditions, in Aperture Priority mode at f/2.2. The first one was taken with the flash set to Forced Flash; the camera chose a shutter speed of 1/30 second. The one on the right was taken in Slow Synchro flash mode, and the camera chose a shutter speed of 1/8 second, long enough to allow the ambient lighting from the room behind the glass door to show up much more clearly than in the first image.

CHAPTER 9: OTHER TOPICS

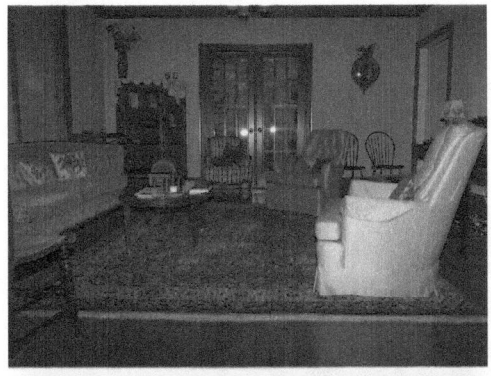

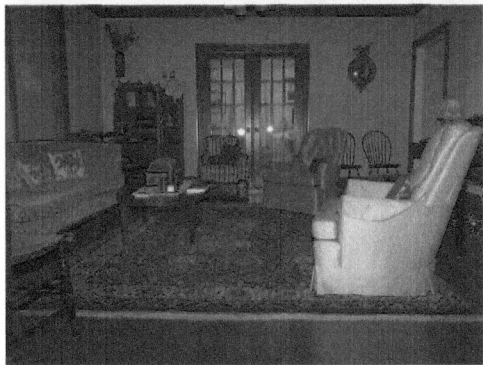

Of course, you don't have to use the Slow Synchro setting to ensure that the background is properly illuminated. You can, instead, use the Forced Flash mode, and just select a slow shutter speed yourself, as long as the camera is set to Shutter Priority or Manual exposure mode. With Slow Synchro, though, the camera does the work for you, figuring out how slow to set the shutter speed while still using the flash.

Flash Exposure Compensation

Another flash-related setting to keep in mind is flash exposure compensation, which is available through the Shooting menu, and is called simply Flash on the menu screen. This setting allows you to increase or reduce the intensity of the flash in increments of 1/3 EV, even when the camera is automatically setting the exposure. Just as with normal exposure compensa-

281

tion, when using flash you can adjust this setting if your test shots appear too bright or too dark.

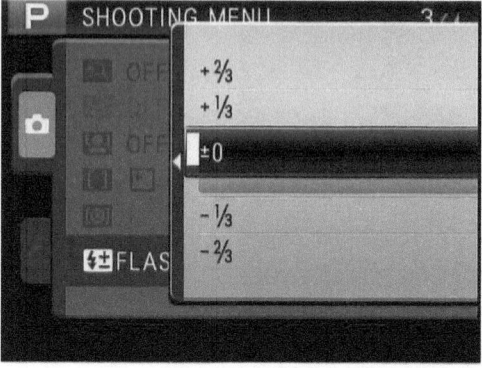

Just go to this menu item and set the value to a positive number to brighten the image or to a negative number to darken it. Just remember to set it back to zero when you no longer need the adjustment, so it does not affect other shots when you don't want it to. Also note that this menu option is available only in the Program, Aperture Priority, and Manual exposure modes, as well as the Resolution Priority and High ISO & Low Noise Priority EXR modes.

Infrared Photography

In a nutshell, infrared photography involves finding a way for the camera to record images that are illuminated by infrared light, which is invisible to the human eye because it occupies a place on the spectrum of light waves that is beyond our ability to see. In some circumstances, cameras, unlike our eyes, can record images using this type of light. The resulting photographs can be quite spectacular, producing scenes in which green foliage appears white and blue skies appear eerily dark.

Shooting infrared pictures in the times before digital photography involved selecting a particular infrared film and the appropriate filter to place on the lens. With the rise of digital imaging, you need to use a camera that is capable of "seeing" infrared light. Many modern cameras include internal filters

CHAPTER 9: OTHER TOPICS

that block infrared light. However, some cameras do not, or block it only partially. (You can do a quick test of any digital camera by aiming it at the light-emitting end of an infrared remote control and taking a photograph while pressing a button on the remote; if the remote's light shows up as bright white, the camera can "see" infrared light at least to some extent.)

The Fujifilm X10 is quite capable of taking infrared photographs. In order to unleash this capability, you need to get a filter that blocks most visible light, but lets infrared light reach the camera's light sensor. (If you don't, the infrared light will be overwhelmed by the visible light, and you'll get an ordinary picture based on visible light.)

As with most experimental endeavors, there are multiple ways to accomplish this. For example, on the internet you will find discussions of how to improvise an infrared filter out of unexposed but developed (*i.e.*, black) photographic film.

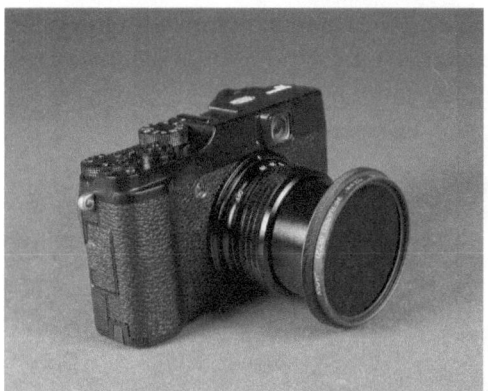

A more certain, if more expensive way to make infrared photographs with the X10 is to purchase an infrared filter and an adapter that lets you attach the filter securely to the camera, as shown here. As discussed in Appendix A, you can obtain an official adapter from Fujifilm that lets you attach any filters with a 52mm thread, or you can obtain similar adapters for less money from other sources.

283

The infrared filter I have seen most often recommended is the Hoya R72, which is what I use. It is a very dark red, and blocks most visible light, letting in mainly infrared rays in the part of the spectrum that tends to yield interesting photographs. You may have to wrap electrical tape around the adapter's open slots to keep unfiltered light from leeching in and ruining the infrared effect.

The next question is to figure out the exposure and color balance. Again, photographers have different approaches, and time spent looking on the internet for discussions of those approaches will be rewarding. For the image shown below, I used the Black & White Film Simulation settings. However, you can also shoot infrared images in color. When doing that, I set a custom white balance, using brightly sunlit green foliage as the base. That is, I call up the camera's white balance setting screen by pressing the WB button, and select the option for setting a custom white balance. To set the custom white balance, I fill the large white rectangle on the camera's screen with the green foliage and press the shutter release button to record the new white balance setting.

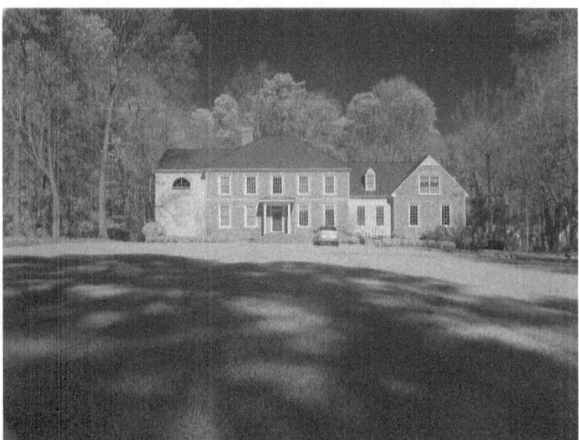

For this exposure, I set the camera on a tripod in Aperture Priority mode and let it select the shutter speed, which was quite long because of the dark filter. The X10 did the rest, exposing the image for 0.5 second at f/2.5, with an ISO setting of 200.

Infrared photography often yields images with leaves and grass that look unnaturally light, and other strange but pleasing effects. This sort of infrared photography often is most successful in the spring or summer, when there is a rich variety of green subjects available outdoors.

Street Photography

One reason many users prize the X10 is because it is great for street photography—that is, for shooting candid pictures in public settings, often without alerting the subjects.

The camera has several features that make it excellent for this type of work: It is compact and unobtrusive in appearance, so it can easily be held casually or hidden in the photographer's hands. Its 28mm equivalent wide-angle lens is excellent for taking in a broad field of view, for times when you shoot from the hip without framing the image carefully. Its f/2.0 maximum aperture lets in plenty of light, and the camera performs very well in low light, with ISO settings as high as 12800 available in some circumstances to let you use fast shutter speeds despite the dim lighting. For those photographers who like to shoot in JPEG format rather than RAW, the X10 offers a rich array of in-camera processing options that are ideal for producing good-looking street photographs, including several monochrome Film Simulation settings and excellent control over highlights, shadows, noise reduction, and sharpening. Also, the very rapid continuous-shooting features of the X10 enable you to fire off a burst of shots, which increases your chance of capturing a high-quality image.

What are the best settings for street shooting with the X10? Well, if you ask that question on one of the online X10 forums, you are likely to get many different responses. I'm going to give some fairly broad guidelines as a starting point. The answer depends in part on your own personal style, such as whether you will talk to your subjects and get their permission before shooting, or will fire away from across the street and hope you are getting a usable image.

Here is one set of guidelines that you can start with and modify as you see fit. To get the gritty "street" look, set image quality to Fine, Film Simulation to Monochrome, Noise Reduction to Low, and Sharpness to Medium Soft. Set Image Size to L 4:3 to use the whole area of the image sensor, giving you options for cropping later. Set ISO to 1600 to give you good image quality while boosting sensitivity enough to stop action with a fast shutter speed. Set the camera to Aperture Priority mode with the aperture at f/5.6 or f/8.0, so you will have a broad depth of field. Leave Dynamic Range set to 100%.

For focus, if you plan on shooting subjects at fairly consistent distances, such as ten feet (three meters), then you might use manual focus with the lens pre-focused at that distance. You can still press the AEL/AFL button to have the camera quickly autofocus on a subject at a different distance if necessary.

You will very likely want to set the camera into Silent Mode by holding down the Display/Back button for a couple of seconds, to keep the camera's beeps, AF Illuminator, and flash from giving you away if you're trying to blend into the environment. Also, you might consider turning the LCD display off by pressing the Display/Back button one or more times to select that option, and turning off the Image Display option in the Setup menu, so the image on the LCD screen does not attract attention to you. You can use the optical viewfinder to compose, or just shoot from the hip.

I generally set my X10 for continuous shooting at its fastest rate (Super High speed), because that type of shooting increases my chances of capturing an interesting position or interaction of people on the street. The downside to that practice is that you then have to wait for the camera to record your multiple shots to the memory card, so you can't shoot again quickly if you see another good opportunity around you.

Also, note that I don't use the "street photography" label too literally; I'm really talking about any candid photography in public places; the image below was taken along a trail in the woods beside a river, when my wife and I happened upon these people and their dog.

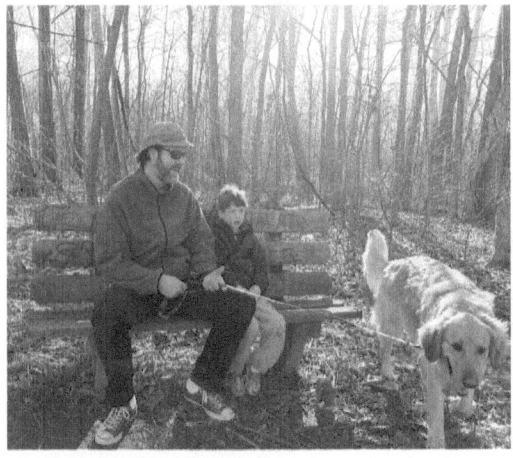

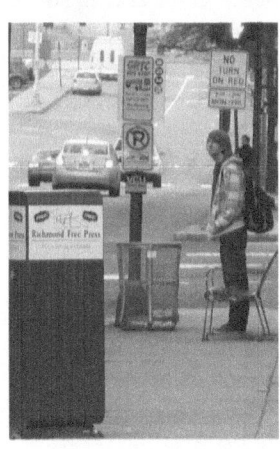

Of course, there are many variations that you can use; the above settings are just suggestions. For example, you might prefer to shoot in color or with RAW quality to give you more options and flexibility for post-processing. The example at left shows the use of color for an actual street scene.

You also might prefer to set the camera to autofocus, rather than relying on the camera's achieving a broad depth of field in manual focus mode. If you use autofocus, you could open up the aperture a bit, and even to f/2.0, for better light-gathering ability and the ability to blur the backgrounds for some shots.

Making 3D Images

There's been a lot of attention paid to three-dimensional (3D) movies and images lately, with the advent of 3D televisions and the renaissance in 3D movies. Some digital cameras have appeared recently that have special features for creating 3D panoramas and other stereoscopic images, including the Sony Bloggie 3D Camera and the Fujifilm Real 3D W3. The X10 has no such built-in capability. But why should its users feel left out of the 3D wave? It's not that hard to create 3D images using just the X10 (well, okay, or just about any other camera, for that matter). Anyway, for you experimental types, here is one way to get into 3D with the X10.

First, you need to take two pictures of the same scene from different positions, separated by a short distance. What I did for the image on the next page was to set up two tripods next to each other at the same height, about 8 inches (20 cm) apart, with the subject about 3 feet (1 m) distant. Then I took two pictures of the three figurines, first one from the left tripod, then one from the right. The camera needs to be facing straight ahead each time, not angled in toward the subject. I took the images in RAW format, but then converted them to JPEG in Photoshop without doing any manipulation of the exposure or white balance, and saved the images as JPEG files.

Next, I used a Windows program called Stereo Photo Maker, which can be downloaded free at http://stereo.jpn.org/eng/stphmkr. From the program's File menu I selected Open Left/Right images. I opened my two JPEG images with this command, which lets you load multiple images at once. Then, I went to the Stereo menu and, with both images appearing on the screen, I selected Color Anaglyph, and, on the sub-menu that appeared, Dubois (red/cyan). The program produced the single image shown on the next page, which looks blurry, with red and blue lines characteristic of 3D images you may have seen in comic books or other printed materials. (If you're using a Macintosh, there are other programs available, though

I haven't used them. One possibility is Anabuilder, at http://anabuilder.free.fr. You also can use Photoshop, but you'll need to experiment a bit, or find instructions on the web.)

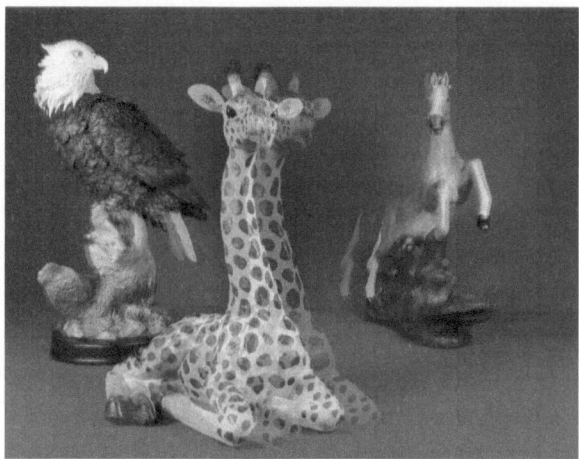

That's all there is to it! If you follow these steps, the resulting image should be ready for viewing either on screen or on paper, using old-fashioned red/blue 3D glasses. (The red side goes over the left eye.) If it doesn't pop out as a 3D image when viewed through the glasses, go to the Adjustment menu and try various options, including Auto Alignment, Easy Adjustment, and others, until it looks good. (I used both of those commands in creating the image shown above.)

Digiscoping and Astrophotography

Digiscoping is the practice of attaching a digital camera to a spotting scope in order to get clear shots of remote objects, generally birds and other wildlife. Astrophotography involves photographing the stars, planets, and other celestial objects using a camera connected to (or aiming through) a telescope.

I can't say that using the Fujifilm X10 is the best possible way to engage in either of these activities; if you want to take close-ups of wild animals and birds, you might do better with a DSLR using a long telephoto lens, and for astrophotography you undoubtedly could do better with a special camera or imaging device that is designed for long exposures through a telescope. However, this book is about the X10, and my goal here is to give you some suggestions about useful and enjoyable ways to use this camera, not to find the best possible methods for long-distance photography. That's not to say that the X10 is a bad camera for these types of photography; it does have some features that equip it nicely for taking pictures through a scope, including light weight, a fairly large sensor, a high-quality f/2.0 lens, manual exposure, manual focus, RAW quality, a self-timer, and a cable release connection.

One of the less-helpful features of the X10 when it comes to astrophotography, however, is that it has a permanently attached lens. You cannot remove the lens and attach the camera's body directly to a telescope or spotting scope as you can with a DSLR. So, you have to use the lens of the X10 in conjunction with the eyepiece and main lens or mirror of the scope. There are many different types of scope and several different ways to align the scope with the X10's lens. I will not discuss all of the various methods; I will talk mainly about the one combination I have recent experience with, and hope that it gives you enough general guidance to explore the area further if you want to pursue it.

I used a Meade ETX-90/AT telescope, pictured on the next page with the X10 connected to its eyepiece. This telescope has a diameter of 90mm (3.5 inches), an effective focal length of 1250mm, and a focal ratio of f/13.8. It is of the Maksutov-Cassegrain design, which uses both mirror and lens to focus light into a relatively small tube (compared to the tube of a comparable reflector or refractor).

CHAPTER 9: OTHER TOPICS

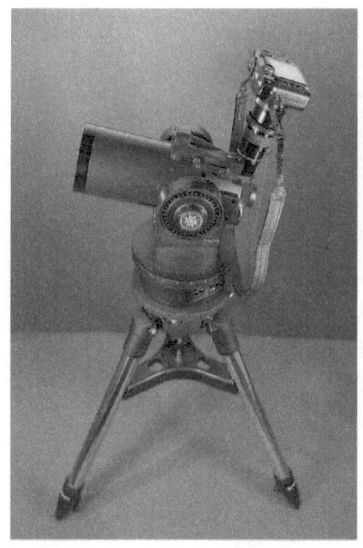

The challenge in using a camera like the X10 to take photos through this telescope is to find a way to get the image that the eye can see through the scope's 1.25-inch (32mm) diameter eyepiece into the camera's lens. There are various types of adapter available to accomplish this. The simplest way is to handhold the camera with its lens as close as possible to the scope's eyepiece and snap pictures until you get a usable image. Of course, this technique will not work with an exposure of any length, because you cannot get a sharp image when you handhold the camera for longer than about 1/30 second. Another way is to use a "universal adapter," which is a kind of clamp that attaches the camera to the eyepiece. I have found that sort of adapter to be bulky, and had problems aligning the camera's lens with the telescope's eyepiece, because that sort of adapter does not create a direct connection between the two.

A much better approach, and the one I used, is to obtain adapter rings that let you connect the camera directly to the telescope's eyepiece, providing a firm and continuous connection. For this system, you need the camera's filter adapter, which comes with the Fujifilm lens hood, model number LH-X10, or the equivalent, as well as adapter rings that let you connect the filter adapter's 52mm ring to the telescope's eyepiece. You can get the proper adapter rings by purchasing the 52mm Digi-Kit, part number DKSR52T, from the online site telescopeadapters.com. That is the setup that is shown above in the picture of the X10 connected to the telescope. The various connecting rings are shown in the images on the next page, along with the telescope's eyepiece.

PHOTOGRAPHER'S GUIDE TO THE FUJIFILM X10

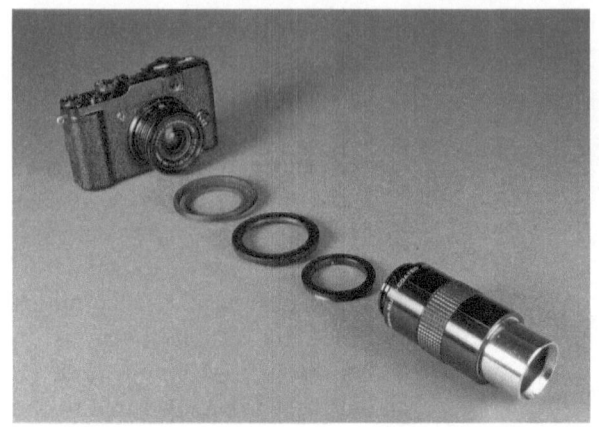

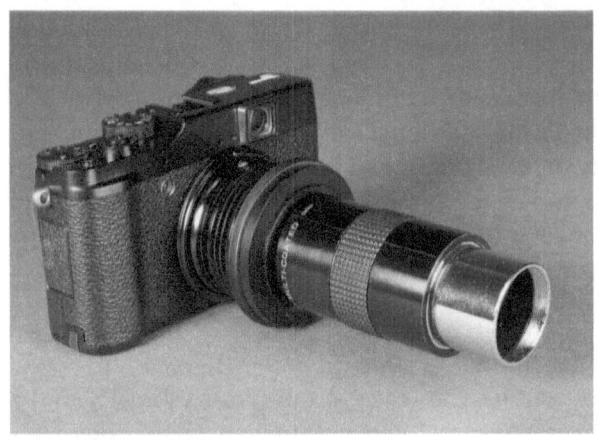

I took the image shown below with the X10 connected to a 40mm eyepiece on the telescope using the adapter rings.

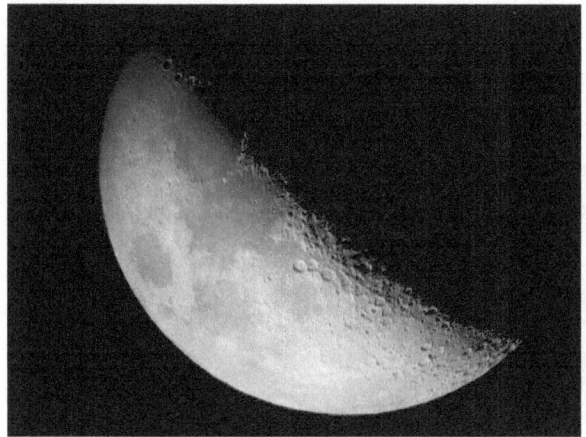

The camera was set to Manual exposure mode; through experimentation I arrived at an exposure of 1/80 second at f/4.5, with the ISO set to 320. The hardest part of the process was to get the image of the moon in focus. My approach was to use manual focus mode on the camera, setting the focus point at infinity, and then to adjust the telescope's focusing control until the image appeared sharp on the camera's LCD display. I also had to adjust the camera's focus, though, and I found it hard to get it adjusted because the enlarged image disappeared whenever I took my hand off of the sub-command dial to adjust the focus on the telescope. It took me many attempts to get the fairly sharp image shown here.

I used the self-timer, set to 2 seconds, to minimize camera shake as the exposure was taken. I set the image quality to RAW to give some extra latitude in case the exposure seemed incorrect. As you can see, the X10 did a pretty good job of capturing the half-moon. Because of the large sensor and relatively high resolution of the X10, this image can be enlarged to a fair degree without deteriorating.

You can also use this setup for digiscoping. I don't currently have a spotting scope, but I did try out the X10 for terrestrial photography through the Meade telescope. I couldn't locate any birds or other animals, so I took a photograph of the stop sign shown here, which was quite far from the camera.

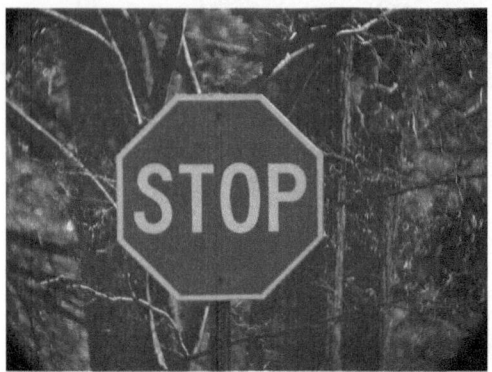

Based on my experience in taking this photo, it appears that the X10 would perform nicely if connected to a traditional spotting scope. For comparison, I'm including below a shot taken from the same location with the camera using only its own lens, zoomed in to its maximum optical zoom range.

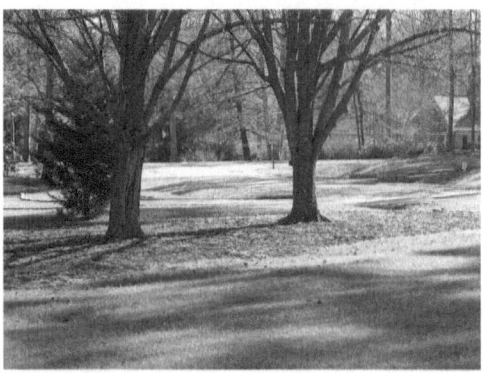

Connecting to a Television Set

The X10 is quite capable when it comes to playing back its still images and videos on an external television set. To do this, you need to purchase an optional audio-video (AV) cable or an HDMI cable to connect the camera to the TV. Fujifilm sells

CHAPTER 9: OTHER TOPICS

an AV cable, model number AV-C1, or you can find a generic cable from other sources; it has to have a micro-USB connector at the camera end and RCA (composite) audio and video connectors at the TV end.

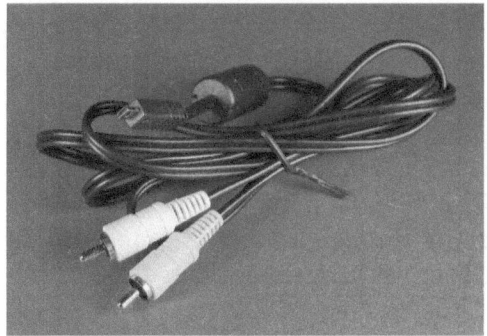

If you are connecting the X10 to an HDTV, you need an optional HDMI cable. Fujifilm apparently does not offer such a cable, but you can use any generic one, as long as the camera end has a mini-HDMI (type C) male connector, and the HDTV end has a standard HDMI male connector.

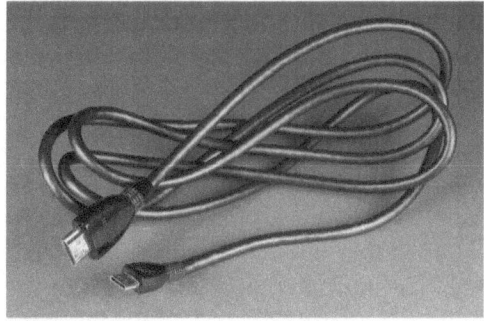

Once the connections are set and the TV is turned on with the correct input selected, turn on the camera in playback mode, and you can play back any images or videos you have recorded.

When you have connected the X10 to a TV, the camera operates very much the same as it does on its own. Of course, depending on the size of the TV set, you will likely get a much larger image, possibly better quality (on an HD set), and cer-

295

tainly better sound. You cannot control the volume of your movies using the camera, though; you have to use the TV's volume control once the camera is connected to the TV. (You can bring the volume control up on the screen using the camera's controls, but that volume control will have no effect.)

Finally, when the camera is connected to a standard TV set with the AV cable, you can see the live view from the camera on the set when the camera is in shooting mode. So, if you want, you can use the TV as a monitor for your shooting session. However, this function does not work when the camera is connected to an HDTV through the HDMI connection. In that case, all you can do is play back images stored in the camera's memory or on the SD card.

The "Orbs" Problem

Finally, I need to talk about an issue that has attracted a great deal of attention in the online forums—the problem of the "orbs" or "white discs" seen in some images taken with the X10. I won't go into great detail; if you want to read lengthy discussions of the situation, go to an X10 forum such as those at dpreview.com or fujix-forum.com and search for the word "orbs"; you will find a mind-boggling number of posts about this topic.

Here is the basic situation, greatly simplified. When you take a still picture with the X10 that has a bright light source in the scene, there is a chance that an unnaturally large, hard-edged white disc or "orb" (or multiple ones) will appear in the image, giving the whole scene an unnatural and unpleasant appearance. There have been various theories put forth as to why this happens, and even whether it happens with all X10 cameras, or just certain cameras. As I write this, Fujifilm has issued a firmware upgrade, to version 1.03, that was supposed to address the "orbs" problem, but it apparently did not help in any significant way. On March 12, 2012, the company announced that it would address the issue by replacing the sensors of cameras with this problem. The replacement program

CHAPTER 9: OTHER TOPICS

was not set to begin until May 2012, after the publication date of this book, so I do not know how effective the replacement of the sensor will be.

In my experience, the orbs have not caused much of a problem; of the one or two thousand images I have taken as of now,

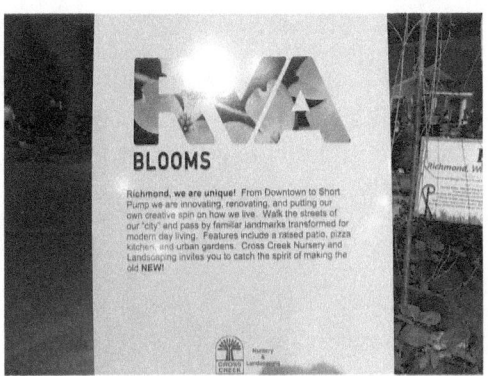

I have had only one image in which I noticed this issue. In that image, shown above, there were some bright lights in the large exhibition hall where I was taking photographs, and the orbs made their appearance for the first time with my X10. Other users, however, have found this issue to be much more significant and troublesome.

If you should find that orbs are showing up and causing problems in your images, there are some options. According to the experts at dpreview.com, who have done fairly extensive testing on this issue, you can decrease the effects of the orbs by increasing the X10's ISO sensitivity to 800 or higher or raising the Dynamic Range setting to 400% or higher. Also, as I noted, there is some indication that particular cameras have worse problems than others, so you might be able to find a fix from Fujifilm. My recommendation is to check your camera for this problem and, if it proves to be bothersome, have the sensor replaced by Fujifilm.

APPENDIX A: Accessories

When people buy a new camera, especially a fairly expensive model like the X10, they often ask what accessories they should buy to go with it. I will hit the highlights, sticking mostly with discussing items I have personal experience with.

Cases

There are endless types of camera cases on the market. I like to keep a camera in a bag that has room for extra batteries, battery charger, connecting cables, the user's manual, flash, and other items. For the X10, I also got the official Fujifilm-branded black leather case that holds just the camera.

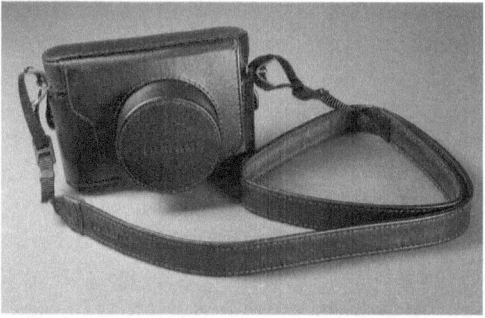

I give this case high marks. It's made from good leather, fits the camera nicely, closes firmly with a magnetic fastener, and comes with an attractive leather strap. To be honest, though, the best features are the classic good looks and solid leather feel of the case. It doesn't let you carry any extra items. On the negative side, it cannot hold the X10 with the filter adapter and lens hood attached.

APPENDIX A: ACCESSORIES

When I'm going on a trip specifically oriented to photography, I use a larger case so I can carry along some other items I may need on the trip.

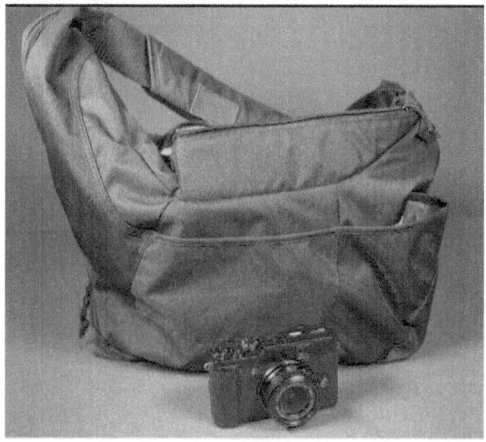

I have often enjoyed photo day trips using the Lowepro Passport Sling bag, shown above, which hangs on my shoulder comfortably and has several compartments that easily accommodate the X10, an extra battery, an external flash unit, the lens adapter and filters, and still has plenty of room for items such as trail mix, bottled water, and a guide book for the day's hike.

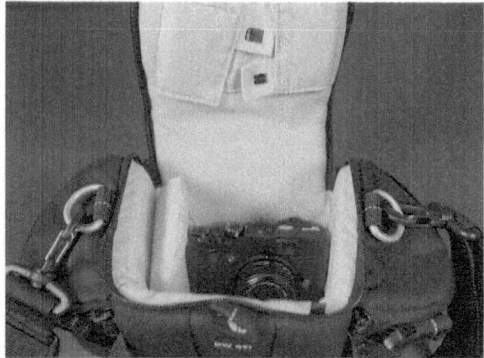

I have also had good success with a waist pack made by Kata, shown above, model number DW-491, which is smaller than the Passport Sling but still has room for the camera, some accessories, and a couple of small water bottles.

I also have used the SnapR 20, a combination strap and soft case made by Blackrapid (www.blackrapid.com). With this system, a short strap is screwed into the X10's tripod socket and the other end of the strap is attached by a loop to the shoulder strap. That strap is attached to the case, which hangs down at waist level. The camera rests inside the bag until you need it. When a photo opportunity arises, you can pull the camera out of the case, and it rides smoothly up and down the shoulder strap by the loop attached to the tripod socket.

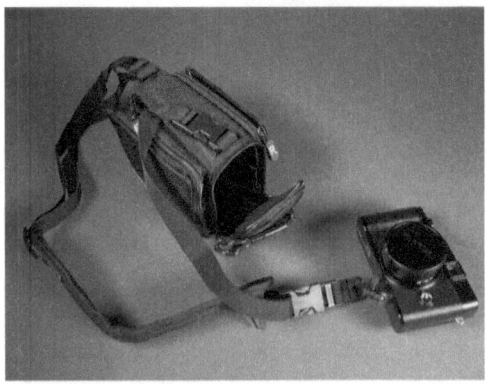

I have found this system secure and comfortable. The case has two outer pockets that zip closed; I was easily able to store two batteries in one and a filter in the other. One drawback is that it is a tight squeeze to fit the X10 in the case with its lens cap on and with the tripod screw attached. There is a larger version of this system, the SnapR 35, that can accommodate the X10 with room to spare, which I prefer, because I don't like to have to tug at the camera to get it out of the case.

I also have tried the Rezo 60, a small case by Lowepro that fits the X10 very nicely. This case, shown on the next page, is a soft, fiber case with a main zippered compartment as well as a smaller compartment that can hold an extra battery or a filter. It comes with a strap and a large, sturdy belt loop, so it is versatile and quite capable of holding the camera safely. If you are looking for a case that is not much bigger than the camera but keeps it quite secure, I recommend the Rezo 60 quite strongly.

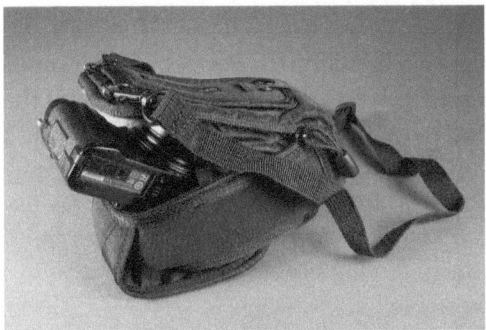

Finally, I have received recommendations from others about several other cases for the X10, including the Manfrotto MB SCP-6BB NANO VI Camera Pouch, the Domke F-9 canvas bag, the National Geographic A1212 Vertical Pouch, and small cases by Crumpler such as the Pleasure Dome model.

Batteries and Chargers

Here's one item you should purchase either when you get the camera or right after. I use the camera heavily, and it runs through batteries quickly. You can't use disposable batteries, so if you're taking pictures and the battery dies, you're out of luck unless you have a spare battery or two. The model number of the official Fujifilm battery is NP-50. You can get a genuine Fujifilm battery for about $21.00 as I write this, and you can get replacement batteries of various brands for lesser amounts, such as one from Maximal Power for about $6.00. I have used the Maximal Power battery extensively with no problems.

Add-on Filters and Lenses

According to the Fujifilm Owner's Manual at page 109, it is not possible to attach a filter directly to the X10's lens, even though the lens has threads where a filter might be screwed on. There has been considerable discussion in the Fujifilm Talk forum at dpreview.com about the possibility of screwing a filter of about

40mm diameter directly on the lens. One user recommended a 40mm Marumi filter, purchased from 2filter.com. Others found 40mm filters on eBay that fit right on the lens.

If you don't use that approach, Fujifilm sells a lens hood, model LH-X10, which comes with an adapter that screws onto the lens and lets you attach any filter or other accessory with a 52mm thread. You can find a similar adapter for less money at lensmateonline.com. The image below shows the less-expensive lens adapter attached to the lens, with the lens hood nearby, ready to be attached. This system works well.

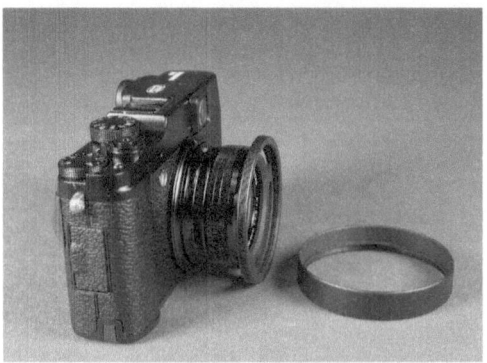

Being able to attach 52mm filters enhances the usefulness of the camera greatly. You can use infrared filters, UV (ultraviolet) filters, polarizers, or any of a wide range of close-up lenses. You also can attach an ND (neutral density) filter, which reduces the amount of light reaching the sensor, giving you the ability to use slower shutter speeds even in bright outdoor light, so you can, for example, slow down the rush of a waterfall to achieve a smooth, silky appearance for the flow of water.

External Flash Units

Whether to buy an external flash unit is very much a question of how you will use the X10. For everyday images that are not taken at long distances, the built-in flash should suffice. It works automatically with the camera's exposure controls to expose the images well. It is limited by its low power, though.

APPENDIX A: ACCESSORIES

If you need to take photos of groups of people in large spaces, or otherwise need additional power or features, there are some other options for flash. One unit designated to work with the X10 is the Fujifilm EF-20, shown below, a small unit that fits very well with the camera in terms of looks and function.

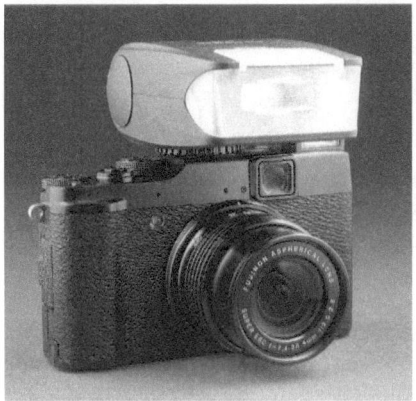

The EF-20 fits into the camera's hot shoe and has a head that can tilt up for bounce flash, along with a built-in diffuser that is useful for wide-angle shots. Fujifilm also makes a larger flash that is compatible with the X10, model EF-42, shown below.

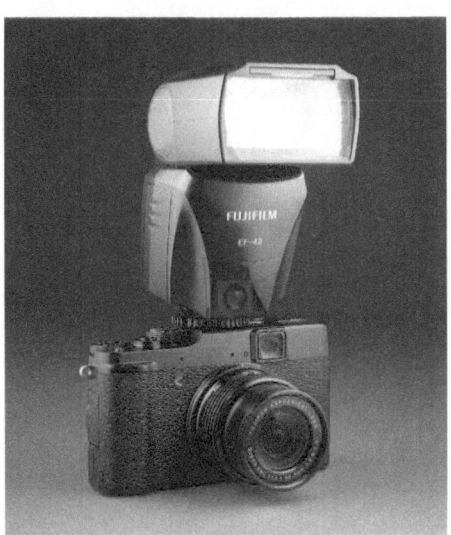

This is a powerful and capable unit, which features a head that not only tilts up and down but also swivels from side to side, and which also has a built-in diffuser. However, the EF-42 is rather overwhelming in size and weight when attached to the hot shoe of the X10 camera.

If you are going to be shooting indoors in a home studio, you may want to consider setting up one or more external flash units with separate optical slave triggers. With those systems, an external flash is attached to the hot shoe on the optical slave device, and aimed at your subject (or, as in the image shown here, positioned to fire into a flash umbrella, which diffuses the flash out toward your subject).

When you press the shutter on the X10, its built-in flash triggers the slave, which fires the external flash. I tried this system using the Fujifilm EF-42 flash unit with the SYK-3, an inexpensive optical slave unit sold by Cowboystudio through Amazon.com. The flash umbrella is attached to an ordinary light stand using an FU SOB Umbrella Mount Bracket, sold by JJC Photography Equipment Company. The image below shows this setup; the small optical slave unit sits just below the flash; the umbrella is partly visible at the right.

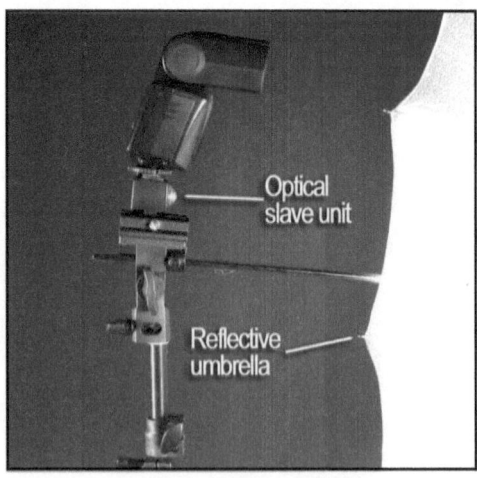

One advantage of using a generic optical slave unit is that you can use many different types and brands of flash unit, provided the unit is compatible with the optical slave. Not all flash units are compatible, so you may want to check with Cowboystudio before deciding what flash to use. Of course, if you have the EF-42, that unit is a good choice for this purpose as well as for use in the camera's hot shoe.

I also experimented with a radio trigger to set off an external flash unit. In this setup, the small transmitter is attached to the X10's flash shoe, and the External Flash option is turned on in the Shooting menu. The receiver is placed on a light stand, with the external flash, in this case the Fujifilm EF-20, attached to the receiver's flash shoe. After making sure both units were set to the same channel, I took some photos with the X10, and the external flash fired each time I pressed the shutter button. (You don't have to pop up the built-in flash for this setup to work.) I set the flash to its Manual mode and the camera to Manual exposure mode, and found the correct exposure by trial and error. The images below show the receiver on the left and the trigger on the right. The receiver and trigger are a set, model no. NPT-04, from Cowboystudio.

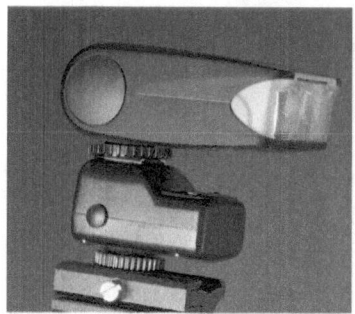
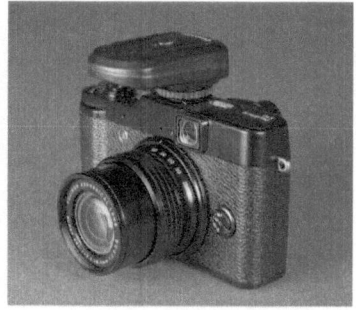

Finally, another option is to use a studio-type flash unit that is connected to the X10 using a traditional PC sync cord. Of course, the X10 does not have a PC sync socket, but you can use a hot shoe adapter that slides into the camera's flash shoe and provides one or two PC sockets on its sides.

I used this system with the AlienBees ABR800 Ringflash unit, pictured here, and the setup worked very nicely. I plugged the sync cord from the flash unit into a hot shoe adapter on the camera, and set the External Flash item on the Shooting menu to On. I then did some test shots to determine the correct exposure with the camera in Manual exposure mode. Once the exposure was set, everything was in place, and the setup worked as expected.

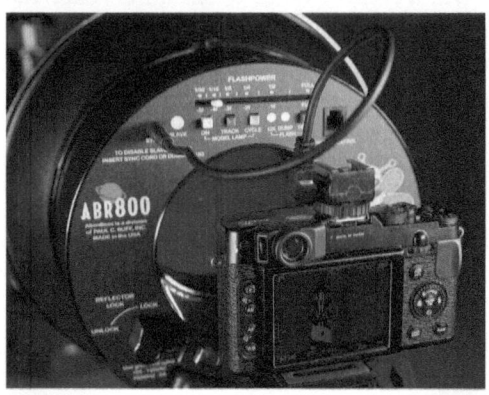

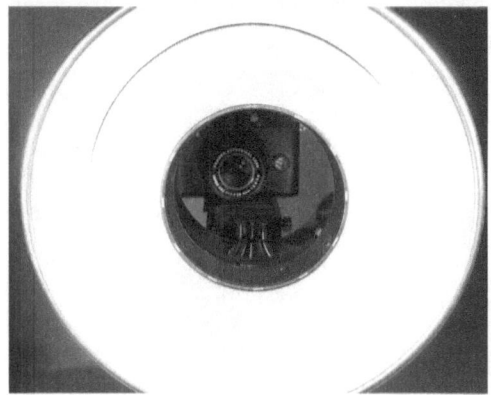

AC Adapter

There may be times when you would like to plug your X10 into a wall outlet for continuous power, such as when you are recording a series of videos or presenting a long slide show with the camera connected to an HDTV set. Fujifilm does offer the equipment to let you do this, though it is quite hard to locate

APPENDIX A: ACCESSORIES

in the United States, at least as of this writing.

You need two separate components: first, the AC adapter that plugs into the electrical outlet, Fujifilm model no. AC-5VX.

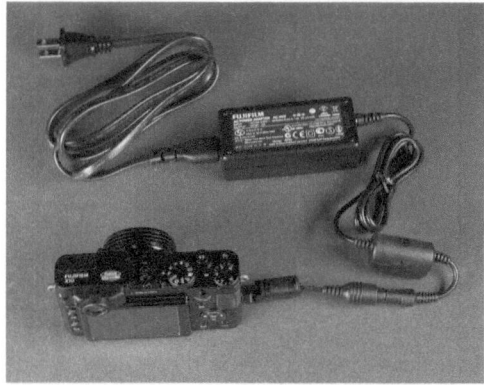

That device includes a power brick with a cord going to the power outlet and a thinner cord with a small, round plug. That plug fits into a separate component, model number CP-50, which is a coupler, shaped just like the camera's NP-50 battery.

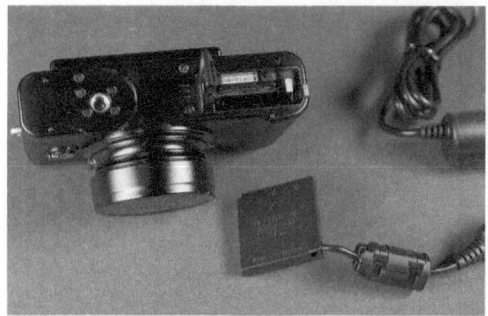

That coupler, shown above with the adapter's plug inserted, fits into the X10's battery compartment. The power cable extends out of the compartment, fitting into a small channel that you have to uncover by pulling out a gray plastic plug, as shown on the next page.

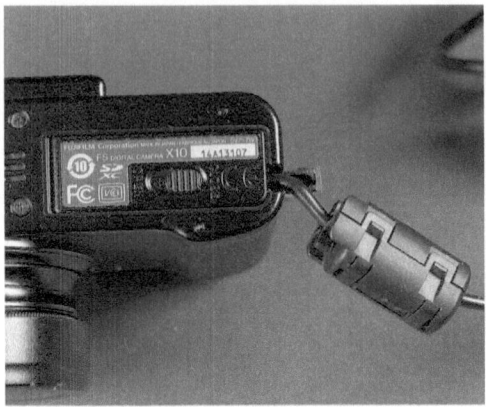

Other Add-ons

Finally, there are a few other items you should consider as accessories for your X10, depending on your needs. The first item shown here is an old-fashioned cable release—the same type that was used on cameras in the days of film and mechanical shutters.

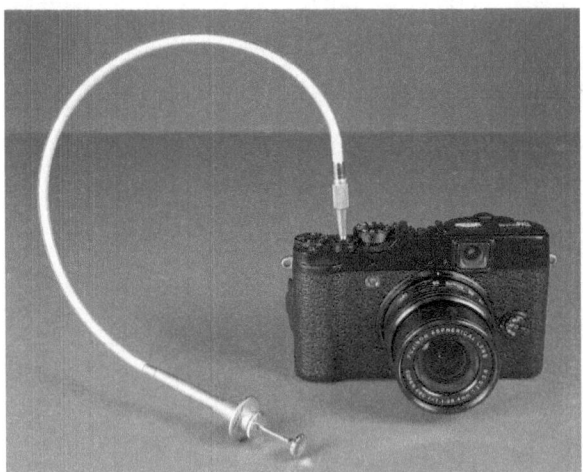

One of the nice design features of the X10 is that it accepts this traditional piece of equipment. The cable release lets you trigger the shutter without pressing your finger on the shutter button, which can cause blur through camera shake. It's nice to be able to use a reliable piece of equipment that doesn't need batteries or any electronic circuitry. You might want to get a cable release that lets you lock it by twisting a screw or with some other mechanism, so you can press the plunger, then lock the release down. That way, you can start a long exposure and not have to keep holding down the release with your hand.

The next two items to be discussed are both shown installed on the camera in the image below. The unusual-looking device that is inserted into the hot shoe is called the Thumbs Up.

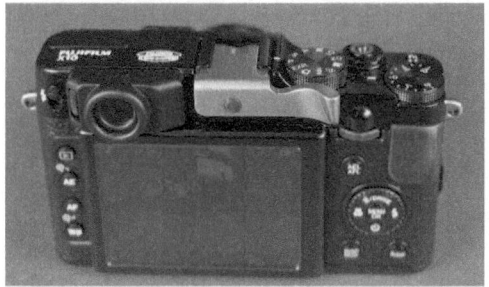

It is a custom-crafted item, originally designed for Leica and other camera models, that gives you a place to rest your thumb. The idea is that, when you press your thumb against the curved handle, you achieve a more comfortable and steady grip, and can therefore handhold the camera without much camera shake. It is costly at over $100.00, but some photographers find that it provides enough additional security in their grip that it is well worthwhile. I bought mine from Popflash Photo (popflash.com). You can find more details at matchtechnical.com, the web site of the manufacturer.

The other item shown in the image above is a soft release—a small button that screws into the shutter release button and gives you a smoother, softer surface to press when releasing the shutter. You can find many different styles and sizes of these releases. Some people like to dress up their camera with a colorful one; I chose the basic black model, shown from a different angle in the image on the next page.

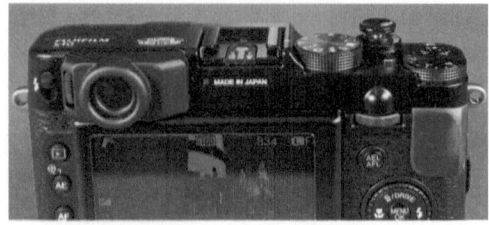

I bought mine from Popflash Photo, but soft releases are available from many sources.

Finally, several useful items are available from lensmateonline.com, including the filter adapter, an automatic lens cap, and an add-on to make the Menu/OK button easier to press. The automatic lens cap is shown below, both open and closed. I have found that it works well, and is a good solution for anyone who may feel nervous about possibly misplacing the original lens cap. The company also offers a lens cap with a tether cord.

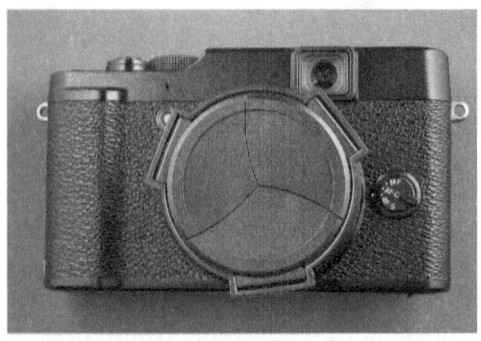

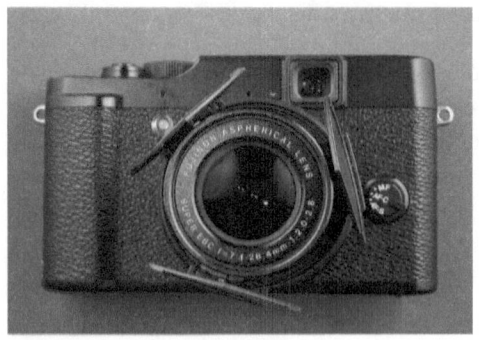

APPENDIX B: Quick Tips

In this section, I'm going to include some tips and facts that might be useful as reminders or as new suggestions. My goal here is to provide small chunks of information that might help you in certain situations, or that might not be obvious to everyone. I have tried to put down bits of information that you might not remember from day to day, especially if you don't use the X10 constantly.

Leave the camera set up to let you shoot quickly. Whenever you turn the camera off, you might want to get into the habit of leaving the controls set so you can pick the camera up and start shooting quickly. For example, you might turn the mode dial to EXR and set the EXR menu to EXR Auto. Similarly, you could leave the Advanced menu set for Panorama shooting (or whatever type of shooting you're most likely to need in a hurry). And, you may want to leave the SP menu set for Portrait shots, so you can turn the mode dial to SP and immediately snap a portrait when the opportunity arises.

Use continuous shooting. The X10 has excellent continuous-shooting capabilities, which can help you catch images ordinary cameras might not. I recommend you consider turning continuous shooting on as a matter of routine, unless you are running out of storage space or battery power, or have a particular reason not to. In the days of film, burst shooting was expensive and inconvenient, because you had to keep changing film, and you had to pay for film and processing. With digital cameras like the X10, you have more options. Even with stationary portraits, you may get the perfect fleeting expression on your subject's face with the fourth or fifth shot. So, press the Drive mode button (up direction button), scroll down to the second option, burst shooting, and choose a speed from Super High to Low. Of course, you should still take care in your composition and other aspects of shooting; don't look on the burst of shots as a way to improve the quality of the images, but as giving you a few more views to choose from for a given scene, especially if any sort of motion is involved.

Take advantage of the Custom Set feature. Use this menu option that lets you store your most important groups of settings to the C1 and C2 slots on the mode dial. For example, right now I have the C1 slot set up for my latest settings for street photography: Shooting Mode = Program; Film Simulation = B&W; ISO = 1600; White Balance = Fine; Sharpness = Medium Soft; Noise Reduction = Low; Drive Mode = Super High continuous shooting. All other saved settings are at their defaults. When I am going out to shoot, I can just turn the mode dial to C1 and all of those settings are ready to use.

Try this other set of custom settings. I could give you long lists of other custom settings to try, or I could even recommend one set as the "best" settings to use. I don't think that makes much sense, because different photographers will prefer different settings, and various subjects will dictate the use of different approaches as well. But people often ask what settings to use, so here is one more set that has been found by some photographers to yield excellent results overall: Dynamic Range = 100; Film Simulation = Astia; Color = Medium High; Sharpness = Hard; Highlight Tone = Medium Soft; Shadow Tone = Medium Hard; Noise Reduction = Standard; other settings at defaults or your choice depending on conditions.

Use the Playback button to turn the camera on. If you turn on the camera's power by pressing and holding the Playback button, then you don't have to remove the lens cap. You can review your images on the LCD display, enlarge them, convert RAW images to JPEGS, and perform any other playback functions. When you are done reviewing images, you can enter shooting mode by removing the lens cap and twisting the lens to the On position, or you can turn the camera back off by holding down the Playback button again.

Use macro shooting for subjects other than nature. Many photographers create great images using the macro capabilities of the X10, shooting insects, flowers, and other natural items. But, with its Super Macro focusing down to 0.3 inch (1 cm), its wide-angle lens, and its terrific low-light performance, the X10 can serve you in many other ways with its macro shooting. If you need a quick copy of a shopping list, memo, driving directions, or cancelled check, you can set the X10's focus mode to Macro or Super Macro, boost the ISO to 800 or so, and snap a quick image of the item. You also can use the Text setting in Scene Position mode. When you get to your destination, you can display the image on the camera's LCD and enlarge it using the AE/Zoom-in button, then scroll around in the document with the direction buttons. The X10 becomes a portable copy machine, if you want it to.

Watch the battery power icon. Keep an eye on the icon that shows how much battery power is left. As long as all three segments of the icon are displayed in white, the power supply is sufficient; but as soon as one segment goes dark, there is not much time left; you should change (or charge) the battery as soon as possible.

Explore the X10's creative potential. The X10 is a sophisticated camera with advanced features for exploring experimental photographic techniques. Here are a few suggestions: Use Manual exposure mode with its shutter speeds as long as 30 seconds to take night-time shots with trails of lights from automobiles, storefronts, and other sources. Use shutter speeds as fast as 1/4000 second to freeze moving motorcycles, airplane propellers, and other speedy subjects in mid-motion. Try "camera tossing," in which you toss the camera in the air, set to a multi-second shutter speed, to capture trails of light and color as the camera spins around. (But be sure to catch it on the way down! You may want to toss it over a cushion or mattress.) Use long exposures (on a tripod) to turn night into day. Try light-painting, for which you keep the shutter open for an extended period in a dark environment, and then "paint" the scene with a flashlight, laser pointer, or other forms of illumination, tracing successive bands of light on the image.

Adjust the camera's color settings. The X10 has several settings for color-related adjustments: White Balance, the Film Simulation settings, and the Color setting on the Shooting menu. Try different settings until you find color combinations that convey what you would like to express with your images. You can achieve unusual effects by purposely setting a custom White Balance while aiming at a colored surface, rather than a white or gray one, and you can also adjust the white balance along the red-cyan and blue-yellow axes using the White Balance Shift item on the Shooting menu.

Take advantage of the RAW format. If you haven't previously used a camera that shoots RAW files, get to know the benefits of this capability and use them to improve your images. Install and use the RAW conversion software that comes with the X10, or use other software, such as Adobe Camera Raw or Lightroom, to "develop" the RAW images. Learn how to fix problems with white balance, exposure, and other settings after the fact, using the flexibility of RAW shooting. You also can use the camera's very capable built-in feature for RAW Conversion through the Playback menu.

Diffuse your flash. If you find the built-in flash produces light that's too harsh for macro or other shots, some users have reported success with using translucent plastic pieces from milk jugs, other food containers, or broken ping-pong balls as homemade flash diffusers. Just hold the plastic up between the flash and the subject. Another approach you can try when using fill-flash outdoors is to use the Flash setting on the Shooting menu to reduce the intensity of the flash by up to 2/3 EV.

Use the self-timer to avoid camera shake and with continuous shooting. The X10 has a self-timer that is easy to use; just select it with the down direction button and choose 2 seconds or 10 seconds for the delay period. This feature is not just for group portraits; you can use it whenever you'll be using a slow shutter speed and you need to avoid camera shake. It can be useful when you're doing macro photography, digiscoping, or astrophotography, also. And don't forget that you can set the self-timer in conjunction with the Best Frame Capture feature, which can increase your chances of getting more great images.

Set zone focusing. If you're doing street photography or are in any other situation where you will need to shoot quickly and want to set the camera on manual focus for a specific zone or general distance, here's one way to do so. Set the focus switch to AF-S, then aim at a subject that is approximately the distance you want to be able to focus on quickly. Once focus has been confirmed, use the focus switch on the front of the camera to select manual focus. Now you have locked in the manual focus at your chosen distance, and you're ready to shoot any subject at that distance without the need to re-focus.

Select flash mode and macro focusing quickly. When you press the Macro focus button (left direction button) or the Flash mode button (right direction button), a small menu pops up to let you make your choice, but the menu disappears very quickly. The quickest way to use these menus is to keep pressing the initial button. That is, to select flash mode, press the Flash button once, then quickly press it as many more times as needed to get to your chosen flash mode; then just release it. For macro focus, press the Macro button 2 or 3 times quickly to change to or from Macro or Super Macro focus.

Use manual focus in conjunction with the AEL/AFL button. When you're faced with a challenging focus situation in which the camera may not be able to autofocus quickly, turn on manual focus with the focus switch, but press the AEL/AFL button (above and to the left of the sub-command dial) to make the camera autofocus if it can. Fine-tune the focus by turning the sub-command dial.

Pay attention to the depth-of-field scale. Remember that there is a focus scale available at the bottom of the display. It is always present for manual focusing on the Standard display, but you have to turn it on using the Display Custom Setting item on the Shooting menu if you want it to show up for autofocus. It will display only when the Custom display screen is in use. Besides the blue distance scale and the red indicator for the focus point, the scale contains a white region that expands and contracts to indicate the depth of field—that is, how much of the scene will be in sharp focus. You can use this scale to help you decide if you can shoot without refocusing when doing street photography, for example. It's not precise, but can give a general idea.

APPENDIX C: Resources for Further Information

Photography Books

A visit to any large general bookstore or a search on Amazon.com will reveal the vast assortment of books about digital photography that is currently available. Rather than trying to compile a long bibliography, I will list a few books that I consulted while writing this guide and that can give you further technical advice.

J. Canfield, *Camera RAW 101* (Amphoto Books, 2009).

C. George, *Mastering Digital Flash Photography* (Lark Books, 2008)

J. Gulbins & R. Gulbins, *Photographic Multishot Techniques* (Rocky Nook, 2009).

C. Harnischmacher, *Closeup Shooting* (Rocky Nook, 2007)

J. Paduano, *The Art of Infrared Photography* (4th ed., Amherst Media, 1998)

S. Seip, *Digital Astrophotography* (Rocky Nook, 2008).

Web Sites

Since web sites come and go and change their addresses, it's impossible to compile a list of sites that discuss the X10 that will be accurate far into the future. One way to find the latest sites is to use a good search engine such as Google or Bing and type in "Fujifilm X10." I just did so in Google and got more than 2 million results.

Another approach is to go to Amazon.com, search for the camera's product page, and read the users' reviews, though you have to be careful to weed out the reviews by people who are disgruntled for reasons that don't have anything to do with the camera itself. You can also visit a reputable dealer's site, such as that of B&H Photo Video, and read the users' reviews of the camera there. I will include below a list of some of the sites or links I have found useful, with the caveat that some of them may not be accessible by the time you read this.

Digital Photography Review

http://forums.dpreview.com/forums/forum.asp?forum=1012

This is the current web address for the "FujiFilm Talk" forum within the dpreview.com site, where the X10 is discussed in great detail. Dpreview.com is one of the most established and authoritative sites for reviews, discussion forums, technical information, and other resources concerning digital cameras.

Reviews of and Articles About the X10

The links below lead to reviews of the X10 by organizations and individuals at various sites. In fact, there are so many reviews of this camera available that I gave up trying to list them all. The ones listed below seem quite thorough and useful.

http://www.photographyblog.com/reviews/fujifilm_finepix_x10_review/

http://reviews.cnet.co.uk/compact-digital-cameras/fujifilm-x10-review-50006420/

http://www.luminous-landscape.com/reviews/fuji_x10_first_impressions.shtml

http://www.pcmag.com/article2/0,2817,2399338,00.asp

http://www.stevehuffphoto.com/2011/11/08/the-fuji-x10-digital-camera-review-a-look-at-the-baby-brother-of-the-x100/

http://www.digital-photography-school.com/fujifilm-x10-review

http://www.dcresource.com/reviews/fuji/x10-review

http://www.imaging-resource.com/PRODS/X10/X10A.HTM

http://www.kenrockwell.com/fuji/x10.htm

http://www.boxedlight.com/x10/index.htm

http://www.fujixseries.com

The Official Fujifilm Site

The Fujifilm company provides resources on its web site, including the downloadable version of the user's manual for the X10, firmware upgrades, and other technical information.

http://www.fujifilm.com/products/digital_cameras/x/fujifilm_x10/

The following link leads to a press release issued by Fujifilm on March 12, 2012, concerning its plans to replace the sensors on X10 cameras that exhibit the problem of "white discs," also known as "orbs," discussed in Chapter 9.

http://www.dpreview.com/news/2012/03/12/Fujifil-X10-X-S1-white-disc-cause-and-fixes

Fujiguys Videos on YouTube

Fujifilm has produced a series of highly informative videos that appear on YouTube, featuring two Fujifilm employees known as the Fujiguys, who provide tips about using the X10, answer questions from users of the camera, and demonstrate the camera's features, using their inside knowledge of its workings. The link below leads to one of their detailed videos with frequently asked questions; from there, you can find links to other videos in the series.

http://www.youtube.com/watch?v=cj25re-1UpM

Flickr Discussion Group

This site hosts a discussion forum about the X10; there also are photos taken by the camera posted in other parts of the site.

http://www.flickr.com/groups/1773207@N23/discuss/

Infrared Photography

This site provides helpful general information about infrared photography with digital cameras.

http://www.wrotniak.net/photo/infrared/

Lensmate Online Store

This is the site for Lensmate, which is a provider of some excellent accessories for the X10 and other advanced compact cameras. The web address for the X10 page is:

http://www.lensmateonline.com/store/fujifilm_finepix_x10.php

White Knight Press

Finally, at my own site I have already posted some videos and other examples illustrating the functions of the X10. I will be posting other examples and updates on the site as time goes on.

http://www.whiteknightpress.com

Index

A

AC adapter 306
Adobe RGB color space 255
Advanced Anti Blur setting 89, 90, 121
Advanced mode 83
AE/AF-Lock Button menu option 160, 249
AE/AF-Lock Mode menu option 160, 248
AEL/AFL button
  controlling behavior of 248
  controlling function of 249
  in general 160
  using for autofocus in manual focus mode 138, 161, 276, 315
  using to lock exposure or focus 160
  using to lock focus in AF-C mode 140
AE/Zoom-in button 190, 241
  using to select metering method 150
  using to zoom images in playback mode 151, 193
AF Illuminator menu option 143, 177, 248
AF Illuminator/self-timer lamp 143, 248
AF Mode 125
  not available with AF-C focus 140
  selecting for movie recording 37
AF/Zoom-out button 151, 191, 241
  using in playback mode 193
  using to call up index screens in playback mode 152
  using to shrink images in playback mode 152
  using to vary size and position of focus frame 151
AlienBees ABR800 Ringflash 277, 305
Aperture 64
  restriction on setting f/11 69
Aperture Priority mode 64
  flash modes available 176
  limitations on settings 69
  settings 68
Apple iTunes software 274
Apple QuickTime software 272
Area autofocus mode 125

moving and resizing focus frame 126
Aspect ratio 103
  different ones available with X10 105
Astia setting 113
Astrophotography 289–293
  settings for 293
Audio-video cable 294
Auto Dynamic Range setting 111
Autoexposure bracketing 171
  using for HDR processing 113
Auto Flash mode 32, 34, 278, 279
Autofocus-continuous 140
  limitations on other settings 140
Autofocus for movies 266
Autofocus-single-shot 125, 139
Auto ISO 102
  availability in Manual exposure mode 102
Automatic lens cap 310
Auto mode 29, 45
  focus options available 45
  menu settings available 45
  recommended settings 46
  using 46
Auto Power Off menu option 244
Autorotate Playback menu option 256
Auto White Balance setting 153
  limitations of 156

B

Background Color menu option 257
Battery 301
  charging 18
  Fujifilm NP-50 17
Battery charger
  Fujifilm BC-45W 17
Battery power icon 313
Beach setting 81
Best Frame Capture 169
  limitations 171

using with self-timer 171, 178
  Blurring background 67, 142
  Bokeh 67, 87, 142
  Bracketing 171–173
    compatibility with RAW images 166
  Burst shooting 167

C

  C1 and C2 modes 91
  Cable release 145, 308
  Canon 430EX II flash unit 131
  Cases 298
    Fujifilm leather case 17
  CCD sensor 51
  CMOS sensor 51
  Color setting 115
  Color Space menu option 255
  Color temperature meter 156
  Color Temperature setting for White Balance 155
  Compression of images 109
  Continuous shooting 78, 311
    deleting shots 202
    file names of shots 203
    high-speed bursts 167
    image size limitations 168
    incompatibility with flash 35
    incompatibility with other settings 167
    indicator light 24
    in general 165
    limit on number of shots in burst 169
    playback of shots 40, 164, 200
    rates of speed 168
    uses of 165
    using for street photography 285
    using with self-timer 169
  Controls
    diagram of main controls 24
    front of camera 26
    top of camera 25

Copy menu option 227
Crop menu option 224
Custom display 253
  not available in EXR Auto mode 52, 135
Custom Reset menu option 258
Custom Set menu option 131
Custom setting for White Balance
  how to set 155
  using for creative effects 155
Custom shooting modes 91, 312
  how to set up 91
  saving settings 92

D

Date and time menu option
  setting 26
Deleting images
  using up button 164
Depth of field 64
Depth of field indicator 134, 137, 253, 315
Detailed information screens
  calling up with main command dial 160
Digiscoping 293
Diopter adjustment wheel 149
Direction buttons
  in general 162
  specific uses of 164
Display Aspect menu option 231
Display/Back button 191
  in general 180
  using to turn off LCD display 141
Display Custom Setting menu option 131
Display screens 132
  in playback mode 182, 191
    for videos 184
  restrictions on availability 180
  selecting 180
  Standard 44
DPOF (Digital Print Order Format) 229, 233
Drive mode

INDEX

how to select 164
Drive mode menu 166
Dual IS Mode. *See* IS Mode menu option
Dynamic Range
  setting to highest values 55, 111
Dynamic Range bracketing 174
Dynamic Range setting
  relationship to Image Size setting 108

E

Electronic level 133
Enlarging images in playback mode 40, 196
Erase Face Recognition menu option 229
Erase menu option 215
Exposure bracketing 171
Exposure compensation
  not available in Auto mode 50
  not available in Manual exposure mode 73
  when to use 145
Exposure compensation for movies 269
Exposure compensation scale 146
Exposure for movies 269
EXR Auto mode 29, 44, 52, 90, 125
  basic steps for taking pictures 30
  manual focus not available 52
  menu settings available 45
  recommended settings for 36
  scene detection 53
  settings available in 35
EXR mode 50, 89
  choosing a sub-mode 54
  Dynamic Range Priority 55
  High ISO and Low Noise 55
  Resolution Priority 54
  settings available 52
  using for Dynamic Range processing 113
EXR-Resolution Priority 54
EXR sensor 29, 51
  effect on image size 101, 107
  special functions of 51

325

External Flash menu option 130
External flash unit
  using with Fujifilm X10 camera 130
External flash units 302
Eye-Fi card 23

F

Facebook
  uploading images or videos to 216
Face Detection
  in EXR Auto mode 53
  playback of shots taken with 204
  relationship to Red Eye Removal 222
Face Detection in Movie mode 266
Face Detection menu option 124, 247
Face Recognition 128
Favorites
  marking images as 198
Favorites display screen 183, 191
Fill Flash 76, 279
  using flash exposure compensation with 130
  using for portraits 34
Film Simulation bracketing 173
Film Simulation for movies 269
Film Simulation setting
  in general 113
Filters
  attaching directly to lens 301
  attaching to lens 143, 283
Fine Image Quality setting 109
Fireworks setting 79
Firmware
  updating 185
  version 1.03 upgrade 186
Flash
  built-in unit 33, 35
  diffusing 314
  disabled in some shooting modes 174
  disabled with certain settings 174
  incompatibility with continuous shooting 35, 167

INDEX

optical slave trigger 304
preventing from firing 35
radio trigger 305
studio type 305
turning off 175
use of 32, 33
using in Auto mode 49
Flash button 35, 174
  locking function of 278
Flash exposure compensation 129, 281
Flash menu option 129, 281
Flash mode menu 175
Flash modes 277
  selecting quickly 315
Flash Off mode 278
Flash pop-up switch 35, 174
Flash units
  external 302
Flower setting 82
Focus Check menu option 138, 252
Focus Control Dial menu option 137, 162, 252
Focus distance indicator 134
Focus frame
  changing position and size of 152
  resizing with main command dial 152
Focus point
  zooming in on in playback mode 197
Focus points
  49 crosses on display 151
Focus range 178, 276
Focus scale 253
Focus Scale Units menu option 253
Focus switch 136
  setting macro focus 275
Forced Flash 34, 176, 278, 279
Format menu option 239
  using for internal memory 240
Frame Number menu option 241
Framing guideline 133
Framing Guideline menu option 253

Fujifilm EF-20 flash unit 130
Fujifilm EF-42 flash unit 130
Fujifilm X10 camera
  accessories shipping with 17
Function button 96
  assigning settings to 147
  in general 147
Function Button menu option 187, 245

G

Gray card
  using to set white balance 156
Grid
  on shooting display 254
Guidance Display menu option 257

H

HDMI cable 294
HDR (High Dynamic Range) photography 70, 110, 171
HDTV
  connecting camera to 231
Highlight Tone setting 116
Histogram
  displaying on Custom display screen 134
  explained 192
Histogram display screen 184, 191
Hoya R72 infrared filter 284
HS movie formats 265

I

Image Display menu option 40, 190, 238, 240
Image Quality setting 108
Image Rotate menu option 226, 257
Image Search menu option 208
  By Date 209
  By Face 211
  By Favorites 212
  By Scene 213
  By Type of Data 213

By Upload Mark 214
  Image Size setting 103
    limitations with high ISO settings 101
    RAW files 103
    relationship to Dynamic Range setting 108
    relationship to ISO setting 107
    unavailability in some situations 103
  Image stabilization options 246
  Index screens 193
    displaying in playback mode 152
    significance of gray and green image frames 194
  Indicator lamp 161
  Information screens in playback mode 197
  Infrared photography 282–283
  Intelligent Digital Zoom 119
    advantages of 121
    disadvantages of 121
  Internal memory 20
    copying images to and from memory card 228
    formatting 240
    storage capacity 20
  IS Mode menu option 246
  ISO
    considerations for choosing 100
    how to set 101
    in general 99
    limitations on image size 101
    limitation with RAW images 101
    setting with Fn button or RAW button 102
  ISO bracketing 173

J

JPEG files 109, 251

K

Kelvin scale for color temperature 153

L

Landscape setting 78

Language menu option 237
  setting 28
LCD Brightness menu option 244
LCD display
  adjusting brightness 244
  turning off 181
LCD Off display option 181, 238
Lens
  focal length 141
  maximum aperture 142
Lens adapter 143, 283, 291, 302
Lens assembly 141
Lens barrel 26
Lens cap
  automatic 310
Lens hood 143
Locking control buttons 163, 188, 278

M

Macro focus 77, 178
  incompatibility with some settings 179
  not available for movies 268
Macro focus mode
  selecting quickly 315
Macro photography 275, 313
  using self-timer or cable release 277
Main command dial
  in general 159
  using as push-button 159
  using to zoom on focus point 159
Manual exposure mode 69
  exposure compensation unavailable 73
  exposure scale 72
  flash modes available 176
  restrictions on settings 73
  settings 71
  settings when manual focus is in use 72
  using for HDR images 70
Manual focus

enlarging display for 138, 252
how to set 137
in general 137
macro shots 276
not available with EXR Auto mode 52
overridden in some shooting modes 139
reasons for using 137
zooming in on image taken with 197
Manual focus scale 137
Mark for Upload to menu option 216
Meade ETX-90/AT telescope 290
Megapixels 104
Memory
internal 20
Memory card
how to choose 22
inserting into camera 24
types of 21
Menu/OK button
in general 163
using to lock control buttons 163
using to return focus frame to center 152
Metering method
selecting Multi, Spot, or Average 150
Metz 36 AF-4 flash unit 131
Monochrome setting 113
Movie mode 36
Intelligent Digital Zoom not available in 119
Movie Mode menu option 264
Movies
adjusting volume 42, 272
autofocus options 266
available settings 262, 263
editing 43, 272
exposure compensation 269
exposure control 269
Film Simulation setting 269
high speed recording 265
in slide show 214
limitations on length 261

overview of recording 36
playback 41, 164, 271
playing on portable devices 274
quick guide to recording 261
recording formats 264
settings that carry over from still shooting 263
taking still photos while recording 164, 272
using zoom lens 270
white balance 268
Multi autofocus mode 125
MultiMediaCard
  not usable in X10 22
My Studio software 216

N

Natural & Flash setting 76
  comparing images in playback mode 194
  Intelligent Digital Zoom not available with 119
Natural Light setting 76
Neck strap
  attaching to camera 17
Neutral density filter 302
Night setting 79
Night (Tripod) setting 79, 123
Noise Reduction setting 117
Normal Image Quality setting 109

O

Operation Volume menu option 241
Optical slave unit for flash 304
Orbs problem 186, 296

P

Panasonic DMW-FL220 flash unit 131
Panorama 84, 256
  playback 203
  selecting angle 84
  selecting direction 85
  shooting technique 85

INDEX

tip for getting maximum resolution 87
Parallax 149
Party setting 81
PhotoBook Assist menu option 205
PhotoBooks 205–207
  editing or deleting 208
  selecting images for 211
Photomatix Pro software 112, 113, 172
Photometry 135
  heading for metering method 150
Photoshop Elements software 231
Photoshop software 70, 110, 113, 222, 231
PictBridge printing protocol 232
Playback
  basic operations 40, 190
  continuous images 40, 200
  movies 41, 271
  panorama 203
  reviewing images while in shooting mode 40, 190
Playback button 149, 191, 200, 204
  using to turn camera on and off 149, 312
Playback menu 98, 204
Playback mode 191
  display screens 183
Playback Volume menu option 243
Portrait Enhancer setting 77, 125
Portrait setting 77
Power Management menu option 259
Power saving 244, 259
Printer
  connecting camera to 232
Printing images from camera 231
Print Order menu option 229
Pro Focus setting 87, 256
  limitations of 89
Program mode 56
  shutter speed limitation 58
Program Shift 56, 162
  not available in some situations 57
Pro Low-Light setting 89, 256

333

limitations of 90
Protect menu option 223
  no protection against Format command 239
Provia setting 113

Q

Quick Start Mode menu option 245

R

Radio trigger for flash 305
RAW button 96, 186, 199
  assigning settings to 187, 246
  behavior under firmware version 1.03 187
  locking function of 163, 189
  using in playback mode 219
RAW Conversion menu option 188, 199, 214, 219, 251
  selecting settings 220, 221
RAW files
  different sizes of 103
RAW format 109, 314
  compatibility with bracketing 166
  effect on other settings 251
  inability to upload to Facebook 217
  incompatible with some continuous shooting options 167
  limitation on ISO setting 101
  selecting with Image Search menu item 219
  unavailable in Scene Position mode 74
RAW+JPEG setting 109, 251
RAW menu option 250
Red Eye Removal 81, 256
  and flash modes 175, 279
Red Eye Removal menu option 222, 247
Reset menu option 238
  using to restore default settings 99
Resize menu option 225
Resolution 103
Ring flash
  using for macro photography 277

S

INDEX

Save Original Image menu option 89, 256
Scene Position mode 73
  limitations on settings 74
SD card 21
  recommended speed 22
SDHC card 21
SDXC card 21
  capacity of 22
Sekonic Prodigi color meter 156
Self-timer 314
  and continuous shooting 169, 171, 178
  behavior of lamp 143
  incompatibility with some settings 178
  setting and using 176
Setup menu
  designated by wrench icon 98
  in general 234
Shadow Tone setting 117
Sharpness setting 83, 115
Shooting menu
  in general 96
  navigating 96
  unavailability of some items 97
Shutter Priority mode 58
  flash modes available 176
  how to set 61
  settings when using manual focus 61
  shutter speeds available 59
Shutter release button
  in general 144
Shutter Sound menu option 243
Shutter speed
  chart of fractional equivalents 63
Shutter speed restrictions 62, 69
Shutter speed settings
  colors of numbers on screen 63
Shutter Volume menu option 242
Silent Mode 143, 174, 248
  activating with Display/Back button 35, 185, 238
  disabling flash with 35, 278

335

using for street photography 286
Silent Mode menu option 237
Slide show
  consisting of movies 214
Slide Show menu option 217
  options 218
  selecting images or movies for 218
Slow-motion movies 265
Slow Synchro flash mode 79, 176, 278, 280
SnapR strap 17
Snow setting 80
Soft release accessory 145, 309
Sport setting 79
sRGB color space 255
Stereo Photo Maker software 288
Still Image mode 167
Street photography 285–286
  recommended settings 285
  using Silent Mode with 237
Sub-command dial
  in general 162
  using for manual focus 137, 162
  using to set aperture or shutter speed 162
Sunset setting 80, 81
Super Macro focus 77, 179, 275
Suppressed Flash 278

T

Telescope
  connecting to camera 291
  focusing through 138
Television set
  connecting camera to 294
  using as monitor for camera 296
Text setting 82
Three-dimensional photography 288
Thumbs Up support device 309
Time Difference menu option 236
Time zones
  setting different ones 236

Tracking autofocus mode 125, 127
Two-Frame Display screen 194

U

Underwater setting 81
Up button
  uses of 164
USB cable
  using to connect camera to computer 23
  using to connect camera to printer 232

V

Velvia setting 113
Video System menu option 258
Viewfinder 148
  parallax error when using 149
Virtual horizon 133
Voice Memo 228
  playing 229
Volume
  camera sounds 241
  movie playback 42, 243, 272
  shutter sound 242

W

Waterfall
  photographing with ND filter 302
WB button 115
  non-functional in Auto mode 50
White Balance
  how to set 153
  in general 152
  preset menu options 154
White Balance button 152
White Balance setting for flash 158
White Balance setting for movies 268
White Balance Shift menu option 115, 158
WiFi (wireless) network 23

Y

YouTube
 uploading videos to 216

Z

Zone focusing 315
Zooming for movies 270
Zooming on focus point in playback mode 159
Zoom ring
 using to turn camera on and off 142

www.ingramcontent.com/pod-product-compliance
Lightning Source LLC
Chambersburg PA
CBHW020627220526
45464CB00001B/53